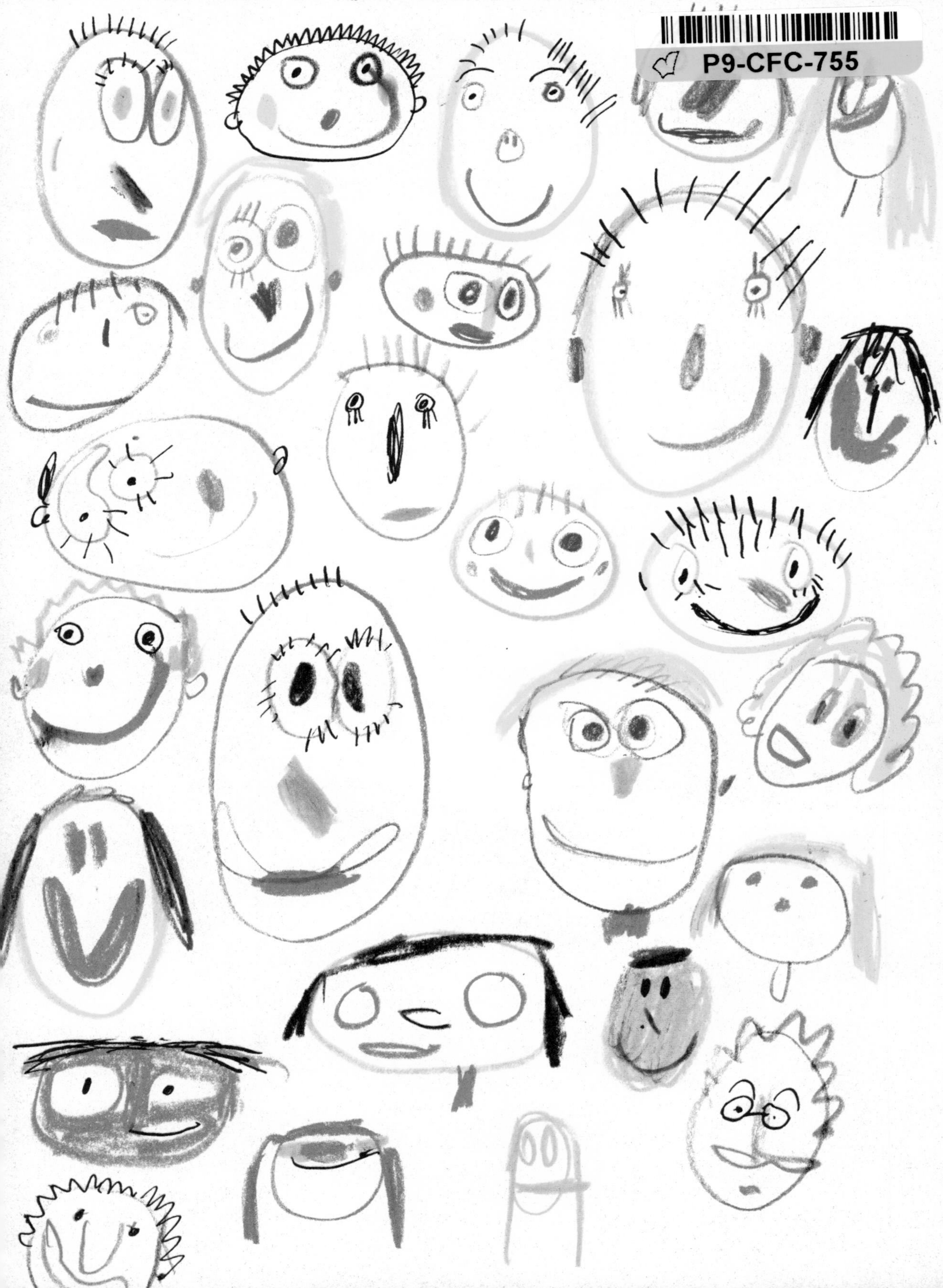

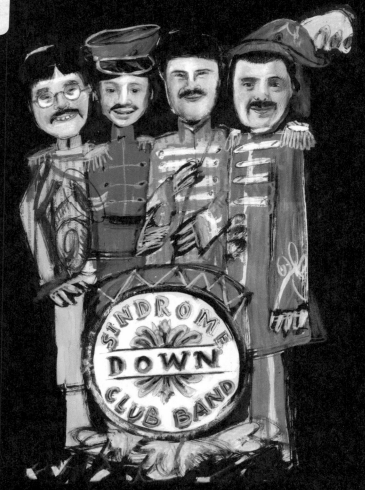

SINDROME
DOWN
CLUB BAND

Translated from the Spanish by Mara Faye Lethem

www.enchantedlion.com

First English-language edition published in 2018 by Enchanted Lion Books,
67 West Street, 317A, Brooklyn, NY 11222

Originally published in Spanish as *Mallko Y Papá* by Editorial Océano, S.L.
Text and illustrations copyright © 2014 by Gusti
Original edition copyright © 2014 by Editorial Océano S.L. Barcelona (Spain)
English-langage translation copyright © 2018 by Mara Faye Lethem
English-language edition copyright © 2018 by Enchanted Lion Books
Editor: Claudia Zoe Bedrick

A CIP record is on file with the Library of Congress

ISBN 9781592702596

Printed in China by RR Donnelley Asia Print Solutions Ltd.

FIRST PRINTING

GUSTI

MALLKO And DAD

MALLKO!!
TIME TO GO

NO!

ENCHANTED LION BOOKS

NEW YORK

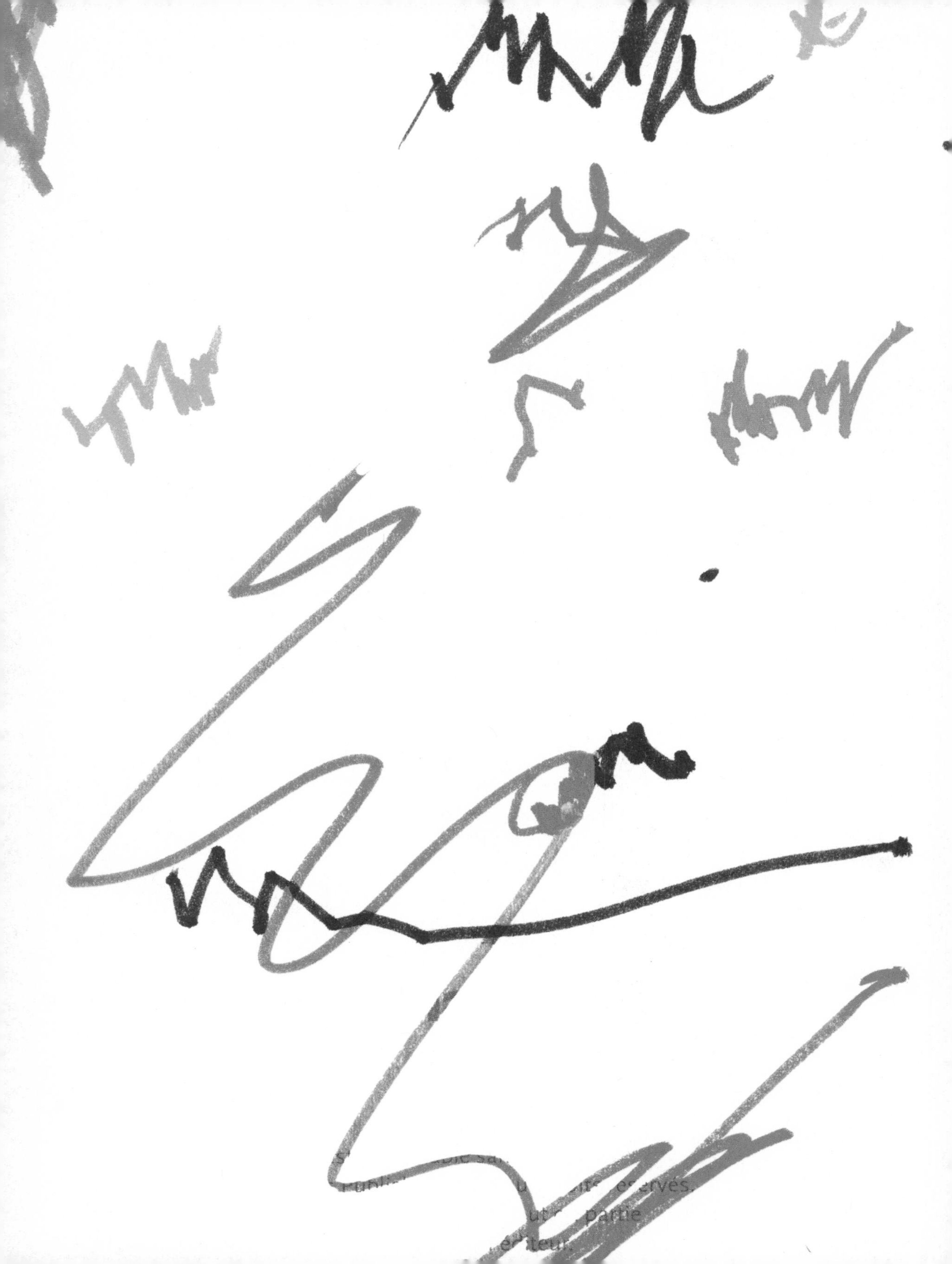

NOM _Gusti_

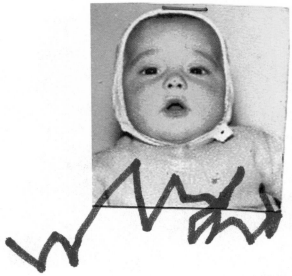

Some years ago, I asked the universe, or great spirit, or whatever you want to call it, for the opportunity to experience "unconditional love." Not some carbon copy, but honest-to-goodness true love.

It seems you have to be careful what you wish for, because you will get it.

When Mallko was born, he laid siege to my castle with all his forces—his entire army.

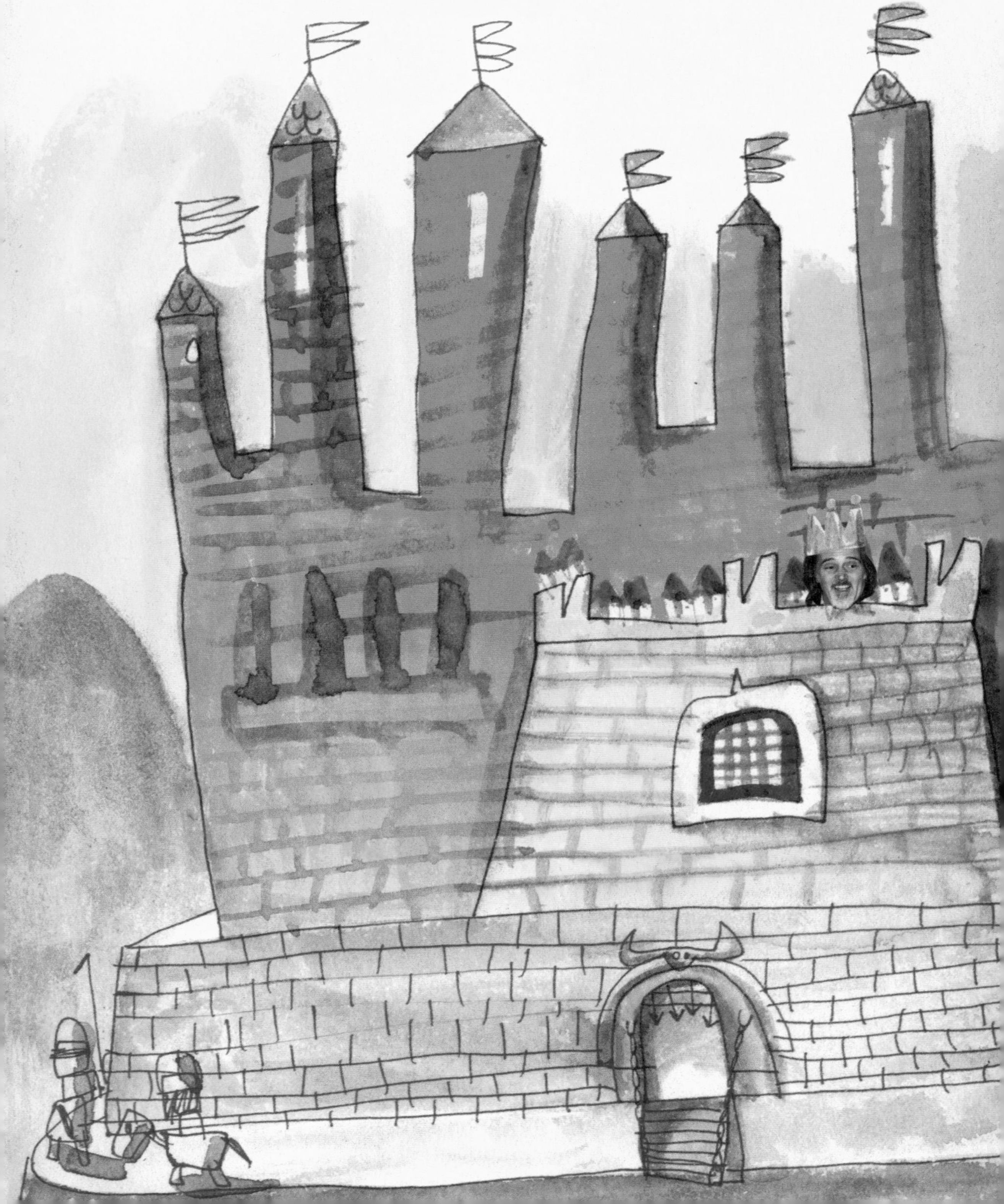

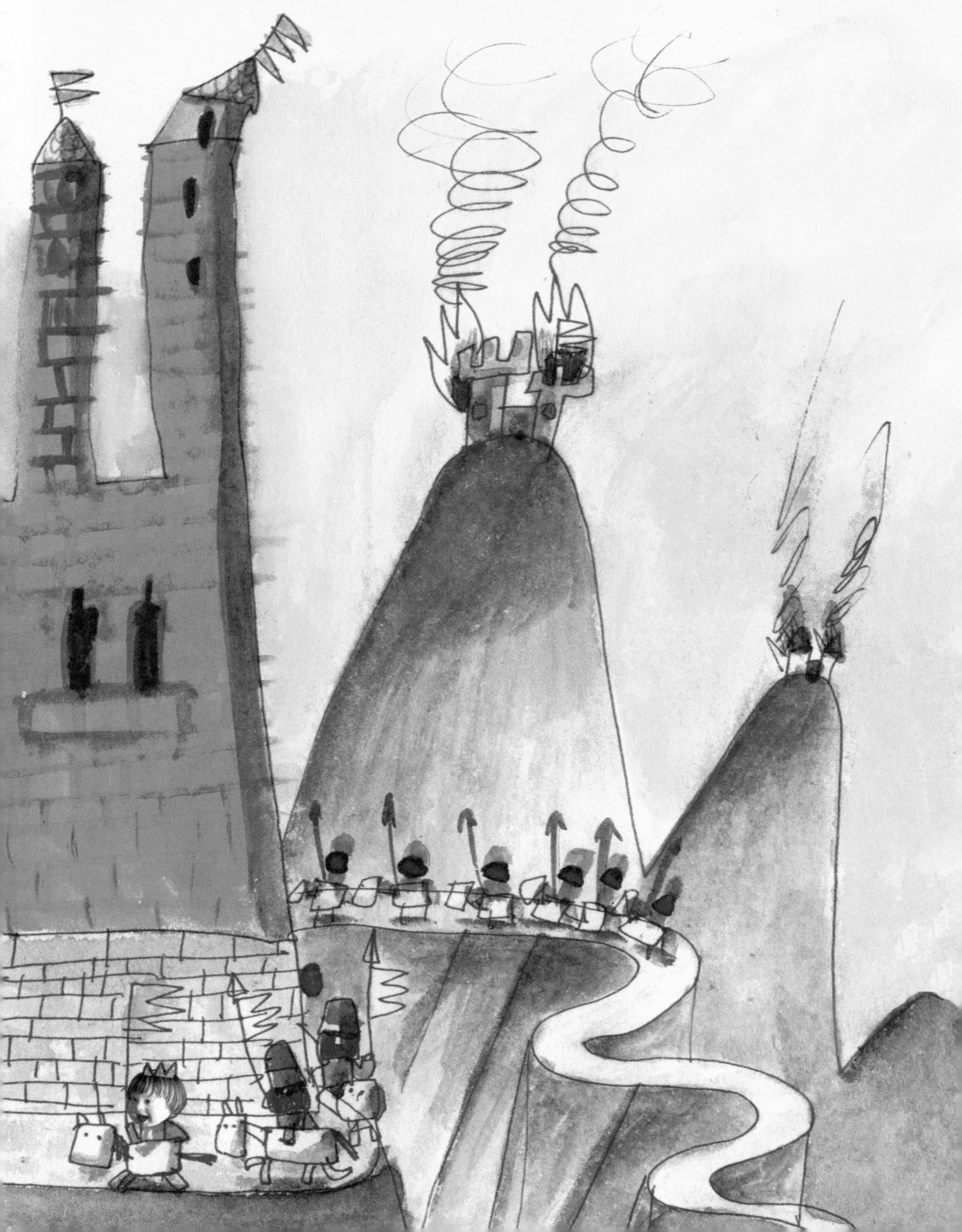

WHY, GOD?

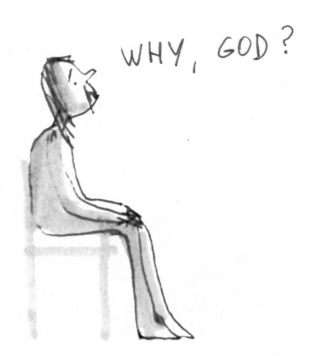

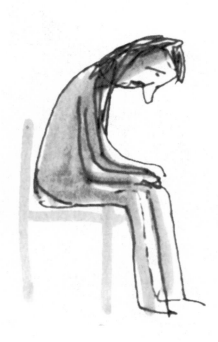

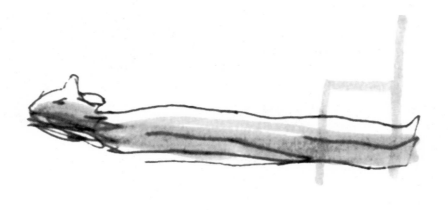

Sometimes having kids
is like making a drawing:
it doesn't come out quite the
way you were imagining it.

With a drawing, you can tear it up and do it over.
    You can erase it.

Or you can retouch it, making it just the way
you want—perfect, even—with Photoshop.

But with a child, an actual child...
Well,
        you can't do that.

That's what happened with me and Mallko:
he wasn't the way I'd been imagining him.

He arrived early, without warning, and...

I did not accept him.

I DID
ACCEP

NOT
T HIM

PAPA OWIE

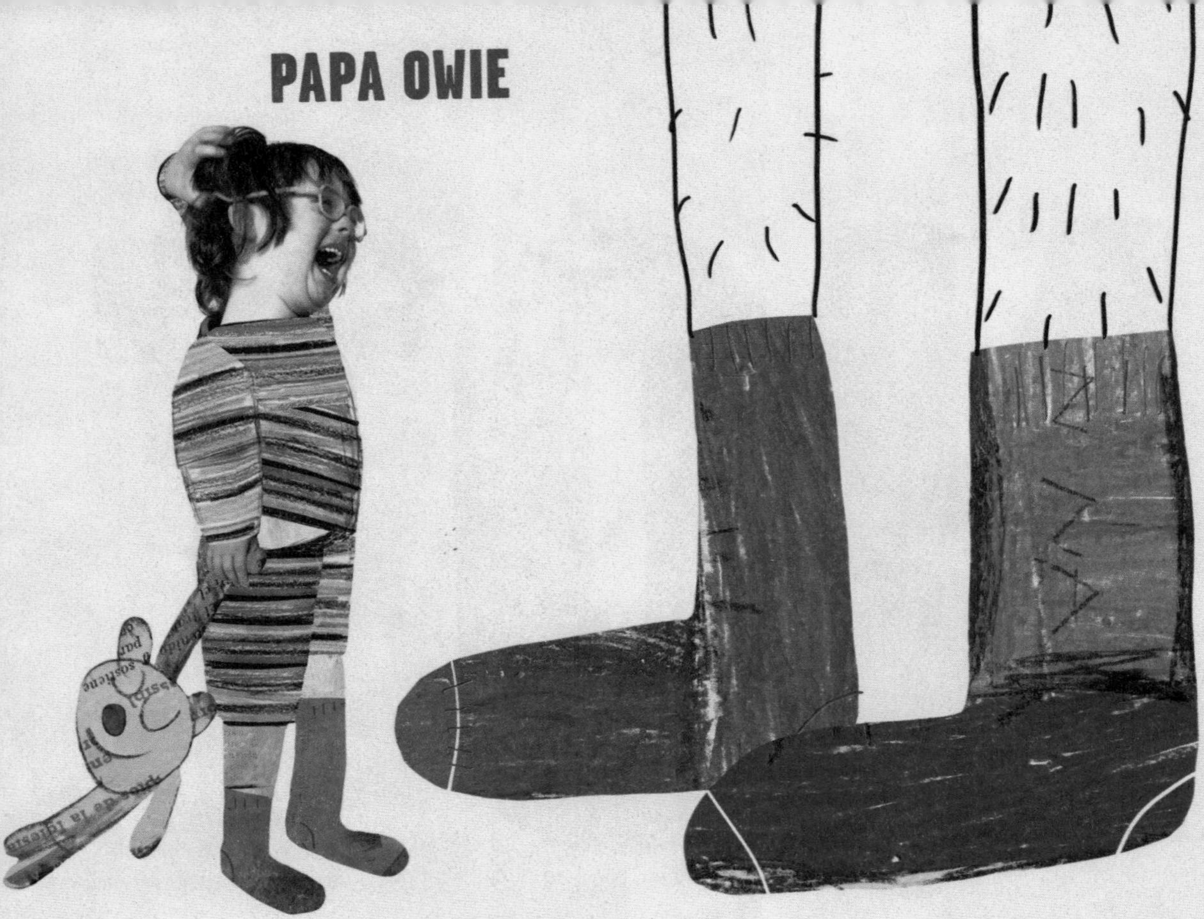

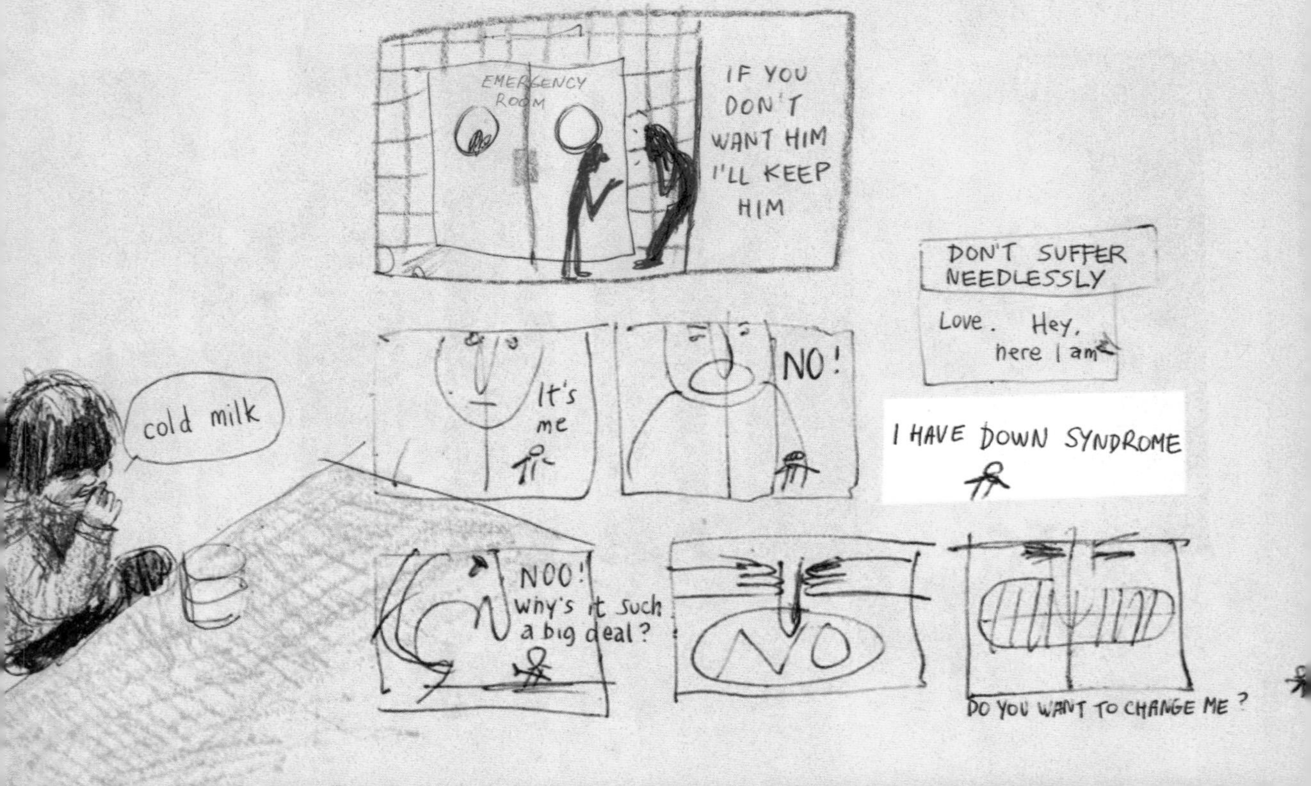
EMERGENCY ROOM
IF YOU DON'T WANT HIM I'LL KEEP HIM
DON'T SUFFER NEEDLESSLY
Love. Hey, here I am
cold milk
It's me
NO!
I HAVE DOWN SYNDROME
NOO! why's it such a big deal?
NO
DO YOU WANT TO CHANGE ME?

The same thing has happened to me with some
of my drawings.
     They showed up and I did not accept them.

It's happened many times:
I've rejected them,
thinking they were no good.

Why wasn't I able to see that Mallko was just fine?

This is what happened to me with Mallko.
I didn't accept him when he was born.
He wasn't the way I'd been imagining him.

Home for
so many
drawings

Studio

Wastepaper
basket

INSIDE YOUR
MOMMY'S WOMB
IT'S DARK
BUT YOU'RE NOT
AFRAID...

God

Open the
door

It's dark

Every drawing is like one of my children.
I accept it as it comes or I don't.

I AM MUSIC

PLAY IS SACRED

How many little drawings
have I not accepted in my life?

Eraser

DON'T GET HURT

LET'S PLAY?

LOVE, HEY, HERE I AM

FEED YOUR HEART

Home for
so many
drawings

Studio

Wastepaper
basket

INSIDE YOUR
MOMMY'S WOMB
IT'S DARK
BUT YOU'RE NOT
AFRAID...

God

Open the
door

It's dark

I AM MUSIC

Every drawing is like one of my children.
I accept it as it comes or I don't.

PLAY IS SACRED

How many little drawings
have I not accepted in my life?

Eraser

LET'S PLAY?

DON'T GET HURT

FEED YOUR HEART

LOVE, HEY, HERE I AM

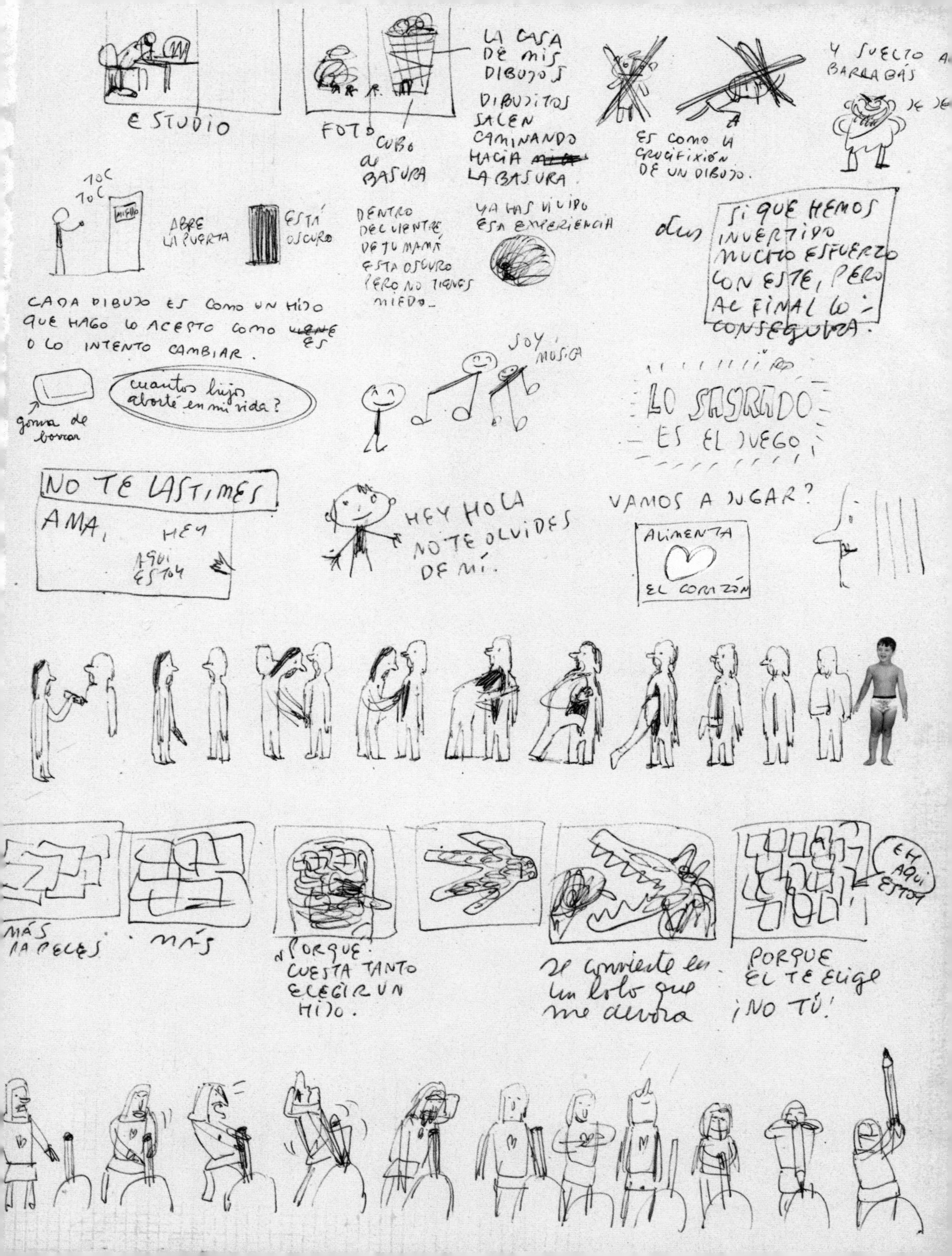
ESTUDIO
FOTO
CUBO DE BASURA
LA CASA DE MIS DIBUJOS
DIBUJITOS SALEN CAMINANDO HACIA LA BASURA.
ES COMO LA CRUCIFIXIÓN DE UN DIBUJO.
Y SUELTO A BARRABÁS
JE JE
TOC TOC
MIEDO
ABRE LA PUERTA
ESTÁ OSCURO
DENTRO DEL VIENTRE DE TU MAMÁ ESTÁ OSCURO PERO NO TIENES MIEDO_
YA HAS VIVIDO ESTA EXPERIENCIA
dios
SÍ QUE HEMOS INVERTIDO MUCHO ESFUERZO CON ESTE, PERO AL FINAL LO CONSEGUIRÁ.
CADA DIBUJO ES COMO UN HIJO QUE HAGO LO ACEPTO COMO ES O LO INTENTO CAMBIAR.
goma de borrar
cuantos hijos aborté en mi vida?
SOY MÚSICA
LO SAGRADO ES EL JUEGO
NO TE LASTIMES
AMA, HEY AQUÍ ESTOY
HEY HOLA NO TE OLVIDES DE MÍ.
VAMOS A JUGAR?
ALIMENTA EL CORAZÓN
MÁS PAPELES
MÁS
¿PORQUE CUESTA TANTO ELEGIR UN HIJO.
EH AQUÍ ESTOY
se convierte en un lobo que me devora
PORQUE ÉL TE ELIGE ¡NO TÚ!

BUT HE'S FINE
THE WAY HE IS

After a while, I realized that
like the drawings I'd tossed out...

Mallko was already complete.

And not only that: I realized he was great.
The greatest.

I realized how lucky I was not to have been able
to tear him up or erase him.

I know that sounds very cruel.
    But it's the truth.

            My truth.

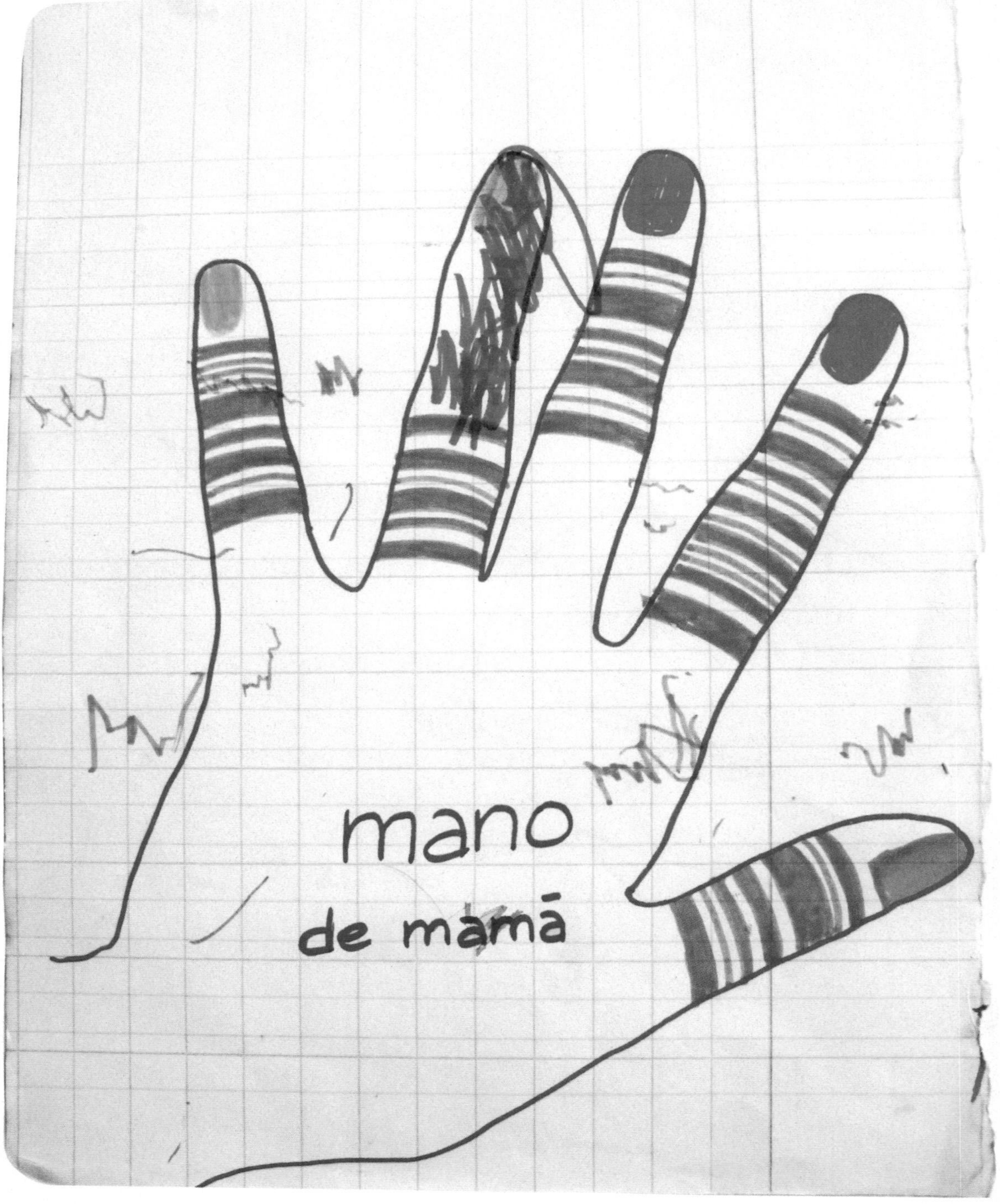
mano
de mamá

Mommy's hand

Anne

Anne never had a problem
accepting Mallko.

That's how moms are and there's a lot we can learn from women.

MOM

When Mallko was born, did you think that anything
was wrong?

When he was born, I saw that he had five little fingers
on each hand, five little toes on each foot, and two eyes,
and I brought him to my breast.

And when you found out he had Down syndrome, what did
you think?

Well, I didn't find out right away. You were the one who
asked me the day after he was born, "why does he have such
squinty eyes?"

"Maybe because he's premature," I said.

The only different thing I noticed was maybe his floppiness.
That made me wonder.

When I made the decision not to have an amniocentesis,
I already knew that there were two possibilities:
that our child would be one way or another way, and that was it.

I felt guilty because you couldn't accept him as he was.
But deep down I knew that he had every right to arrive as he did.
And that it was going to be a learning experience for us.

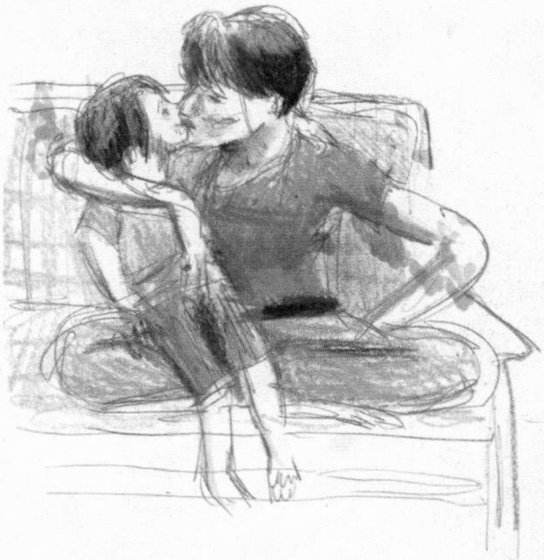

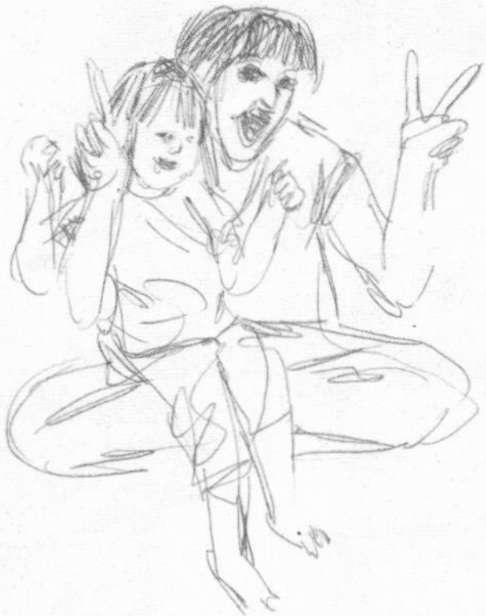

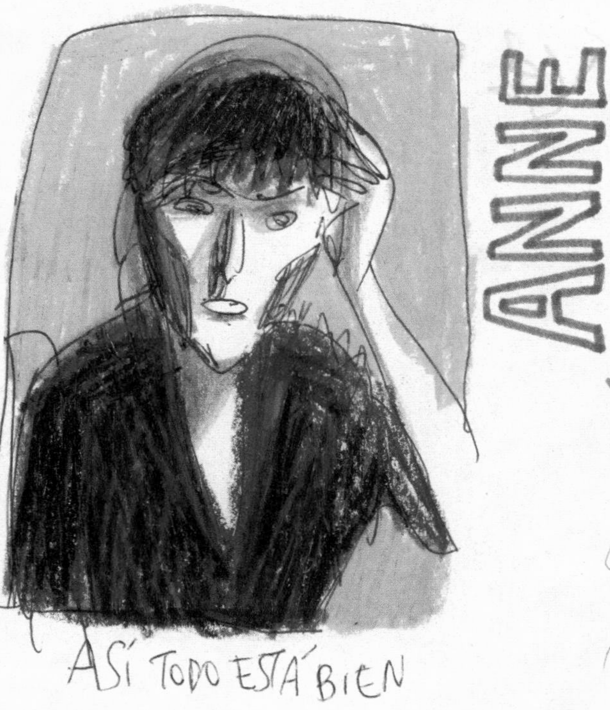
ANNE
ASÍ TODO ESTÁ BIEN

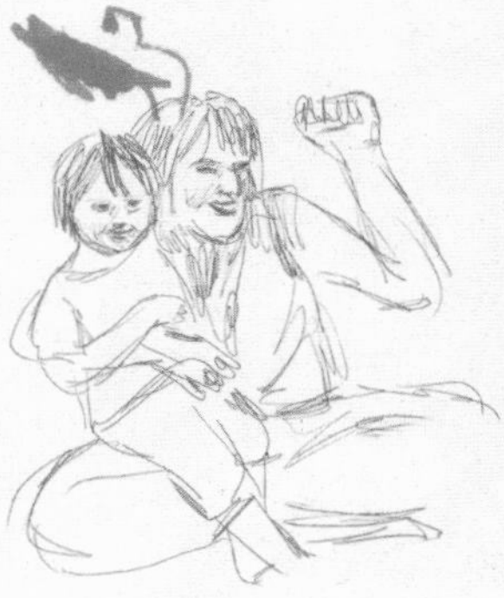

As I breastfed him, the only thing I felt was that he was a defenseless baby and that he would need twice as much love because his father was having trouble understanding.

THEO

13 years old
ALMOST 14

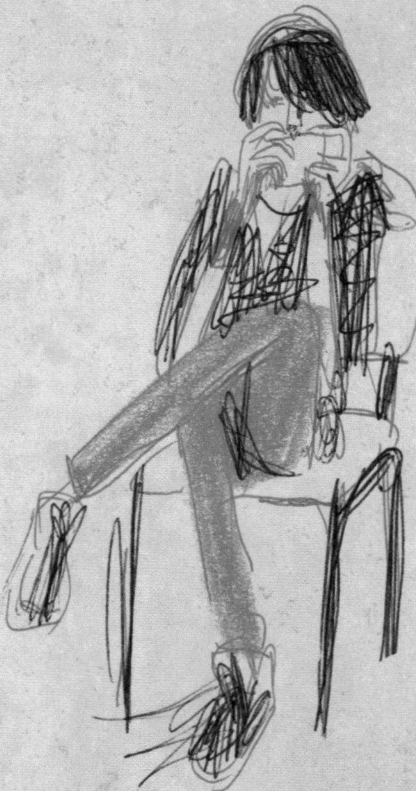

THE LITTLE
ENLIGHTENED
ONE

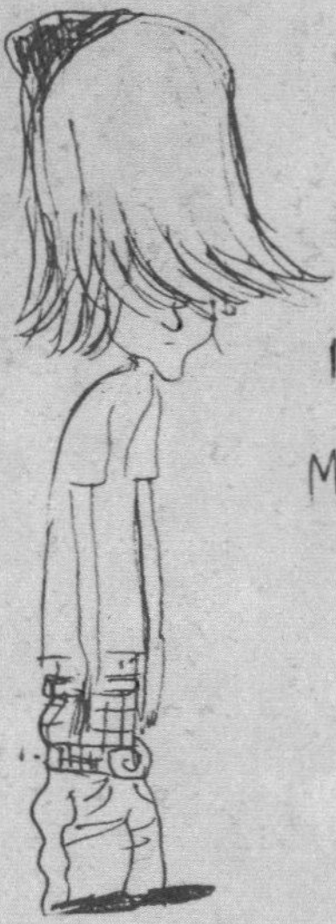

My son
♡
Mon fils

drawing by
Anne

Theo

Theo

What's it like to be an older brother when your little brother has Down syndrome?

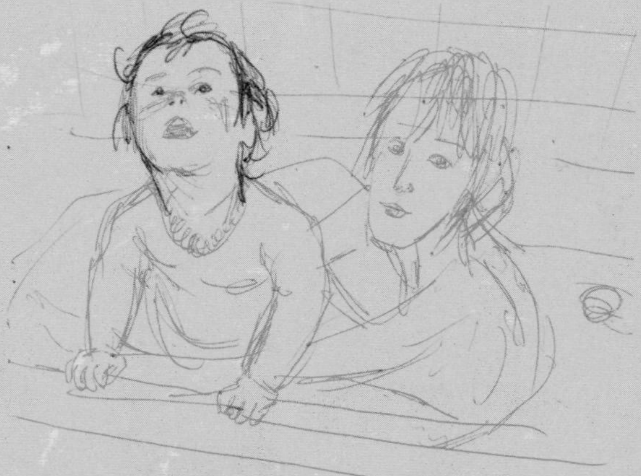

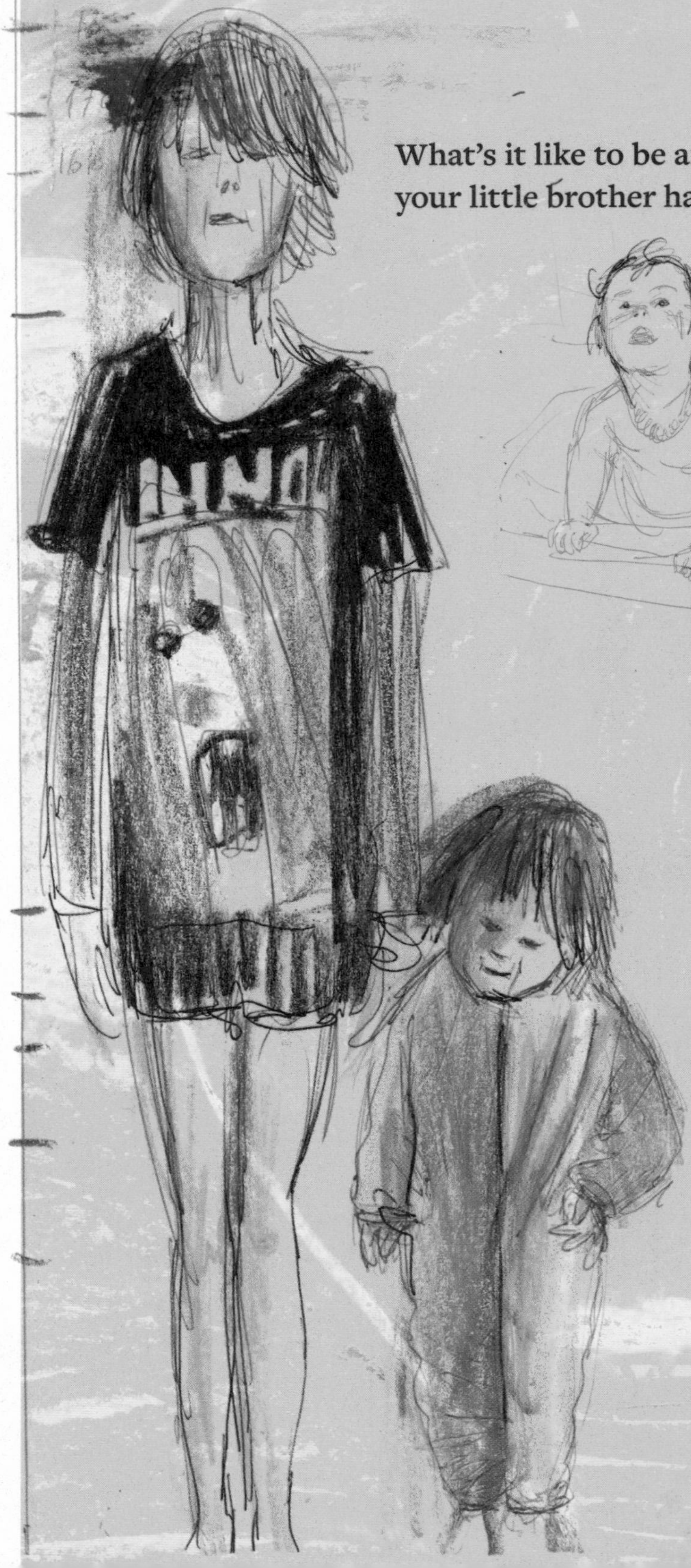

THE RELATIONSHIP BETWEEN BROTHERS

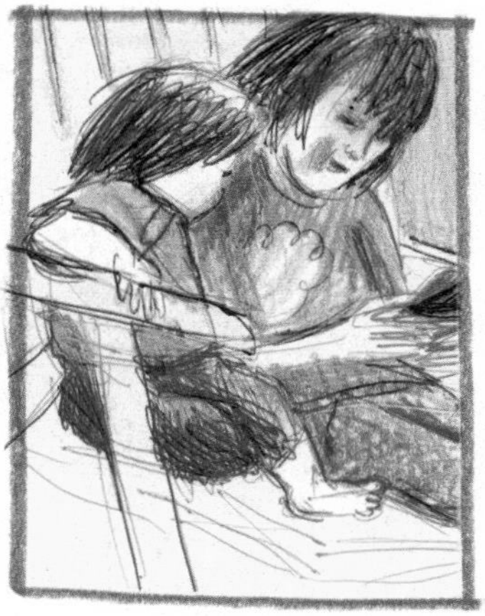

A lot of times as parents we suddenly put most of our energy into the new baby and we forget to pay attention to their sibling. But if we are careful, we can find a balance, so the older one doesn't feel pushed away.

Theo helps us a lot with Mallko. When we're overwhelmed, we can always count on him. This makes him feel like a good person and gives him a sense of responsibility.

De: Gusti <[redacted]>
Asunto: **Hola hermanito**
Fecha: 17 de agosto de 2007 22:15:08 GMT+02:00
Para: luis jacome <[redacted]>

Nothing. Just wanted to tell you not to worry about us.
I realized it's not worth getting bitter over and I gotta keep on keeping on.
I talked with Theo in France and he was telling me about aliens and hulk movies and it made me realize that life goes on and everything's fine. There's just one path not two
And it's the path of love that's just how it is
Hey I love you, xoxo Gusti

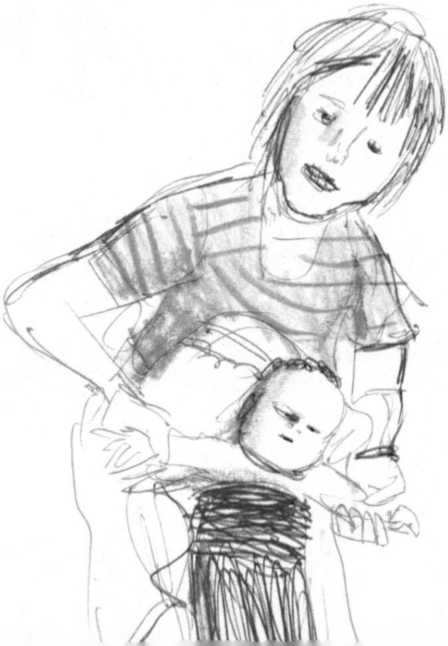

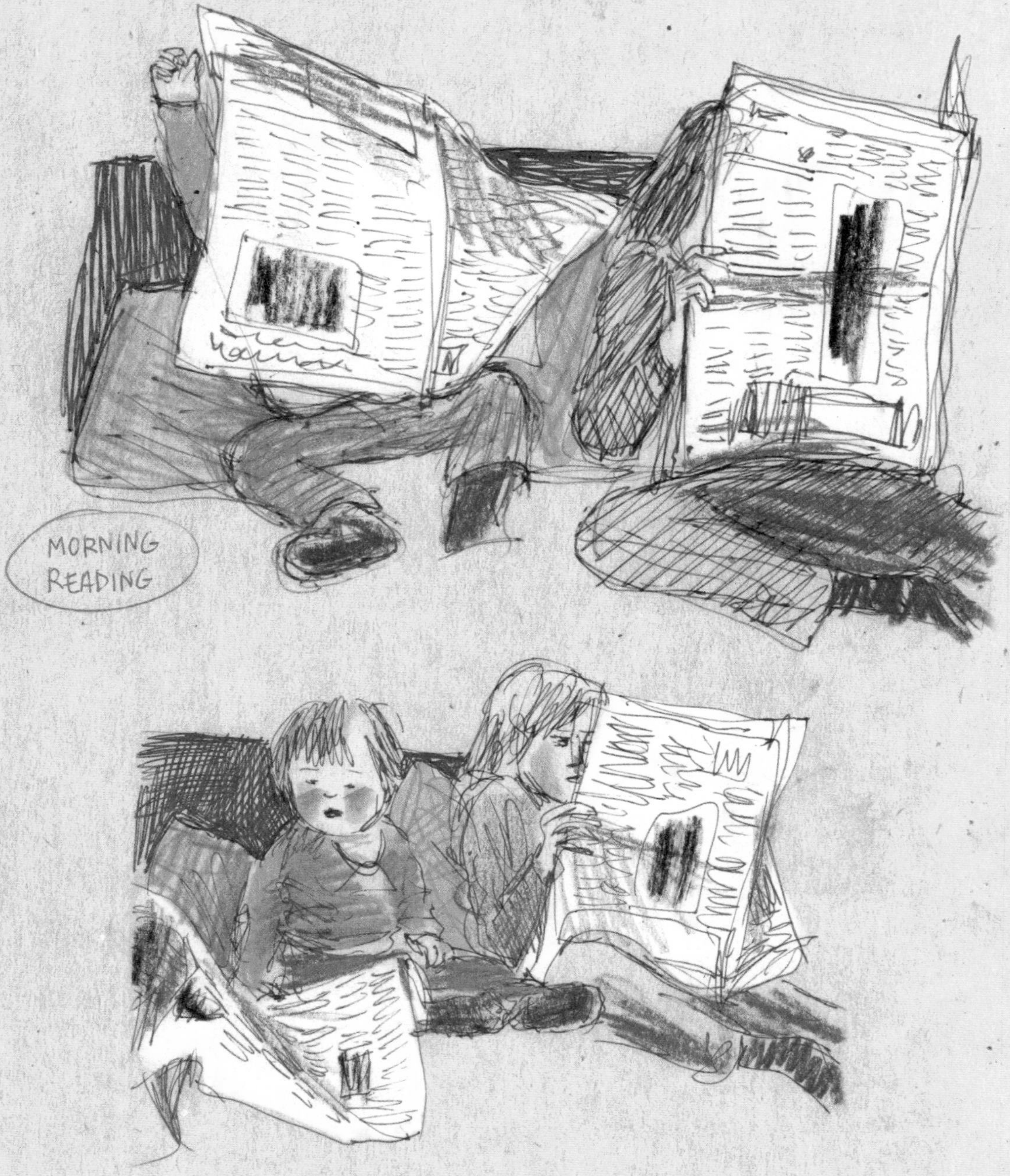
MORNING
READING

FAB. 12-B

HYPNOTIZED

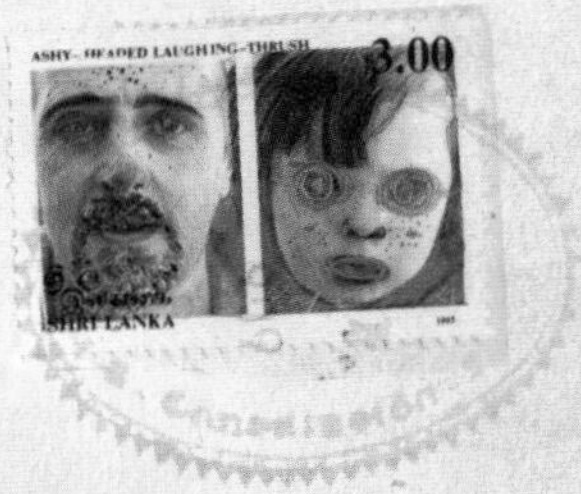
ASHY–HEADED LAUGHING–THRUSH
3.00
SHRI LANKA

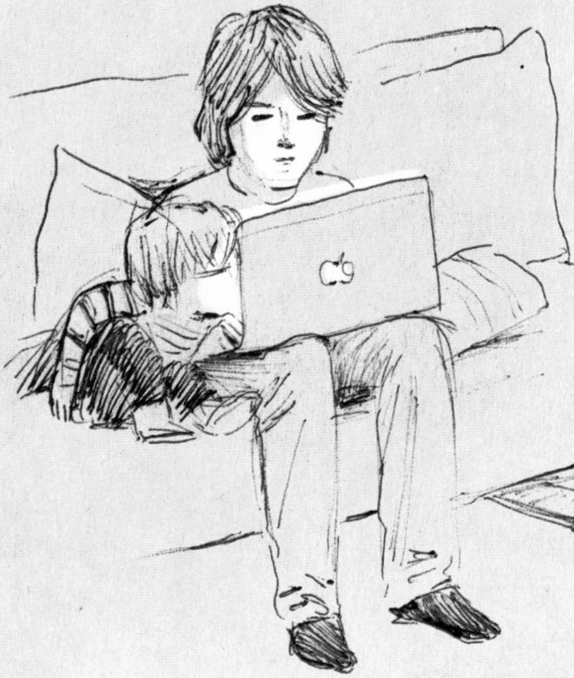

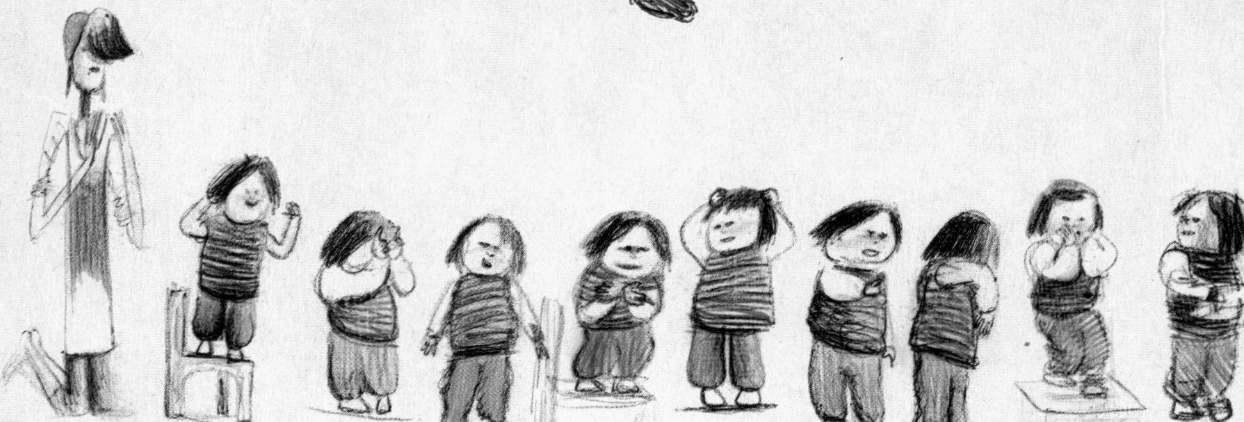

Théo y Mallko interpetando una obra de teatro.

Theo and Mallko acting out a play

"What is Down syndrome?" Theo asked when he was eight.

"It's what Mallkito has," I answered.

"But we're gonna love him just the same." I said it,
but unconvincingly.

So Theo told me: "I don't care if he's green, red, blue, silver,
hairy, or short and fat. He's always going to be my best
little brother."

I looked at Theo and saw an enlightened master.
That was my first lesson after Mallko's birth.

A STORYBOOK

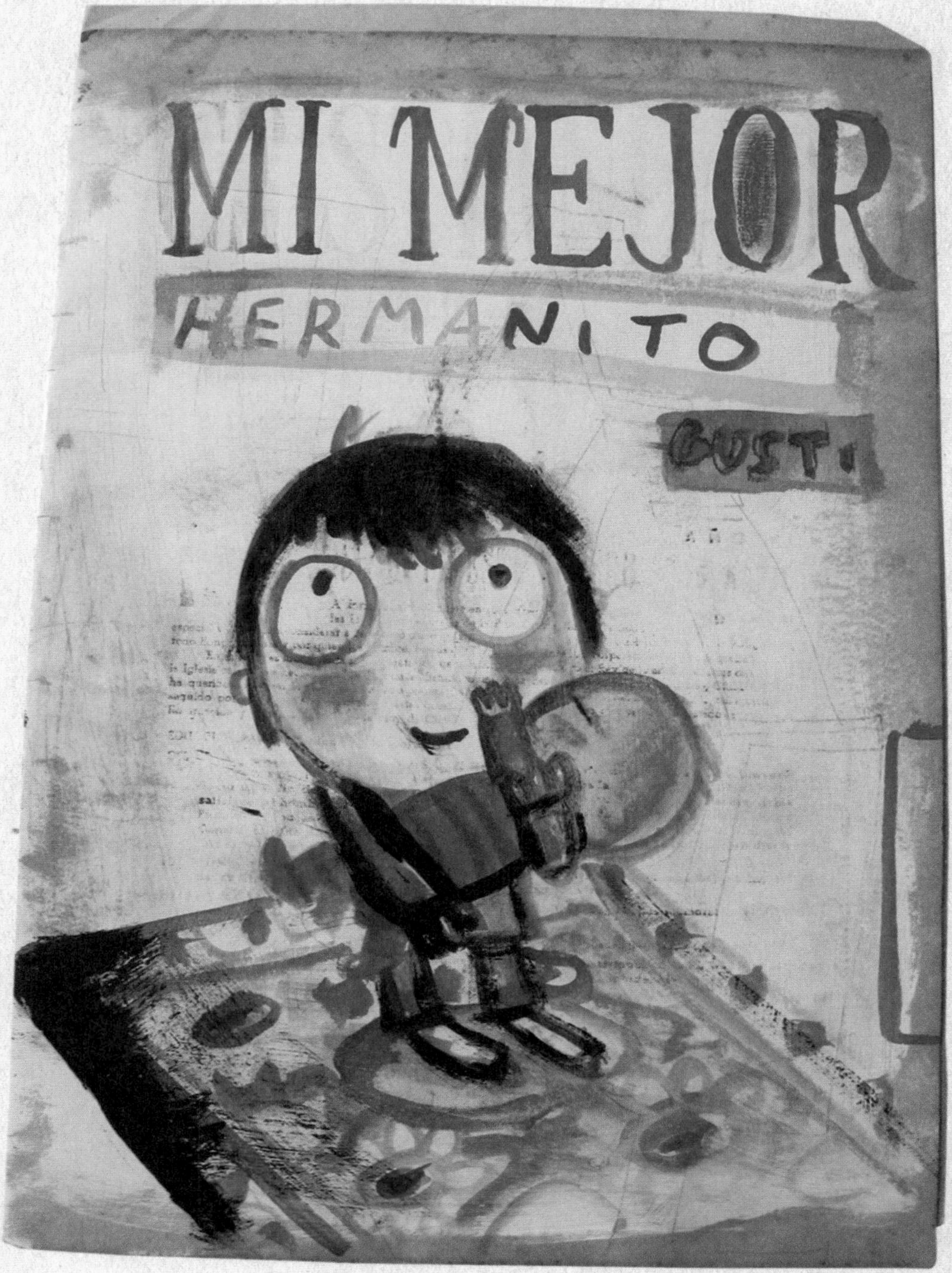
MI MEJOR
HERMANITO
GUSTI

My Best Little Brother

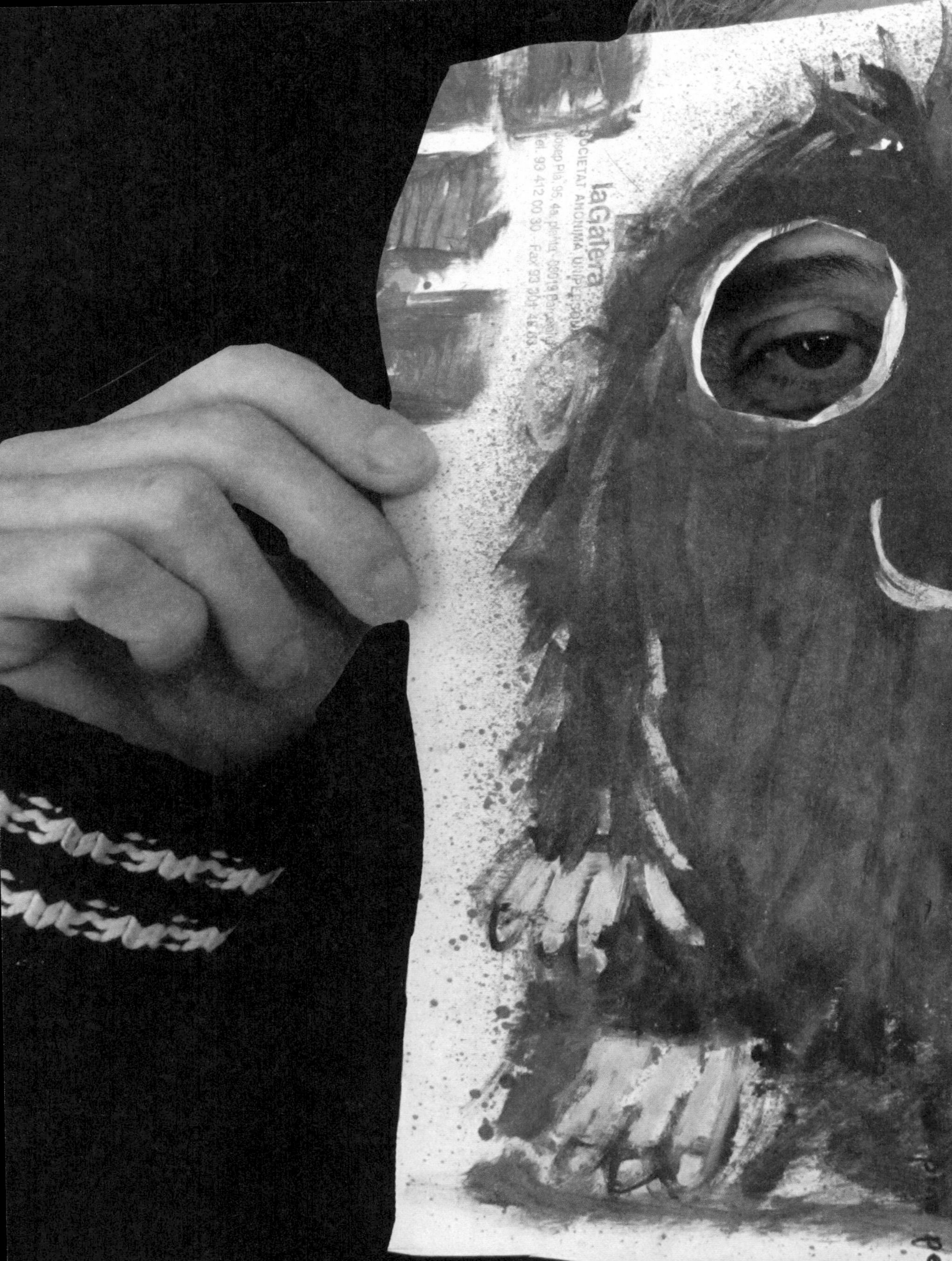
laGalera

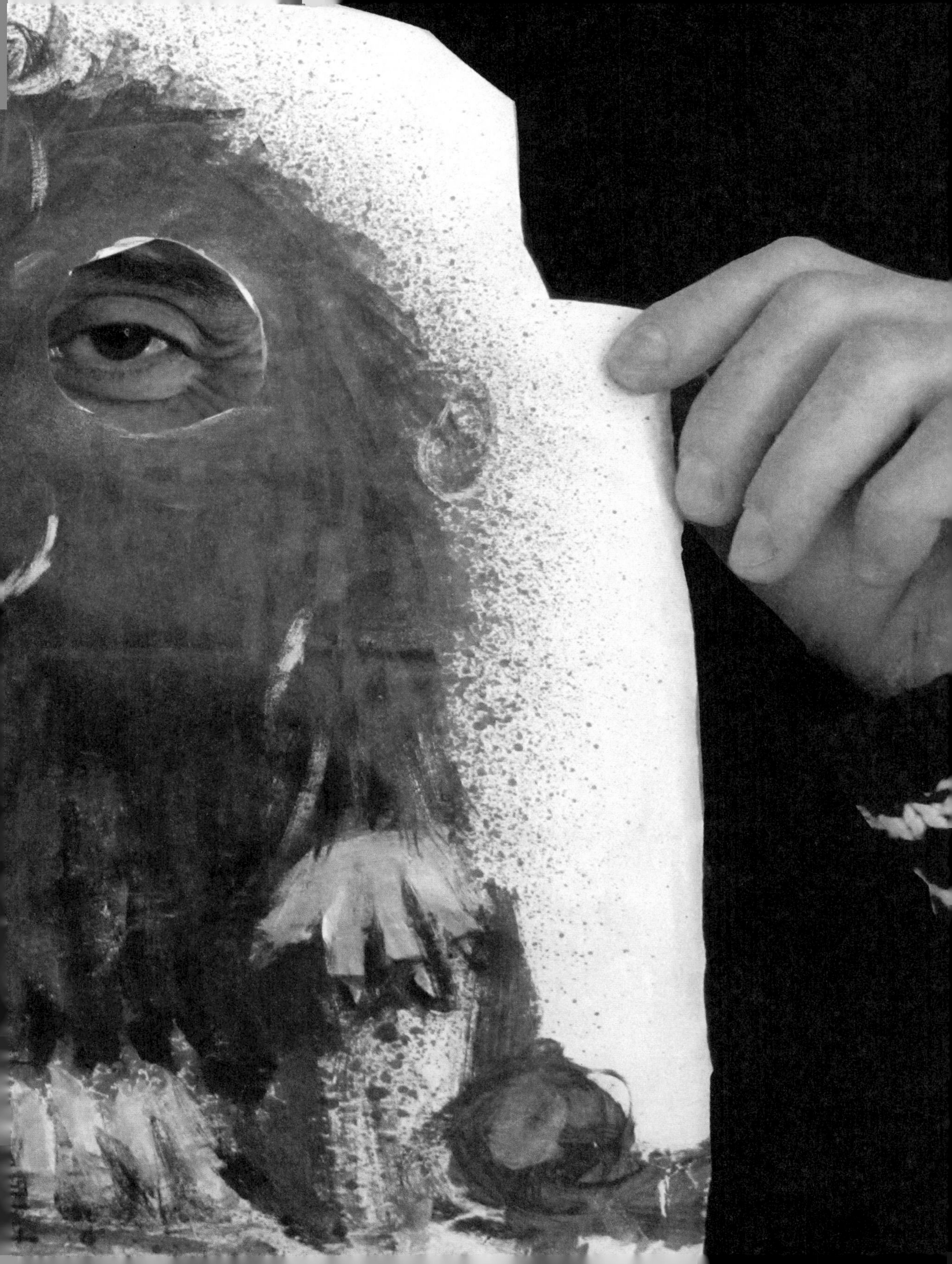

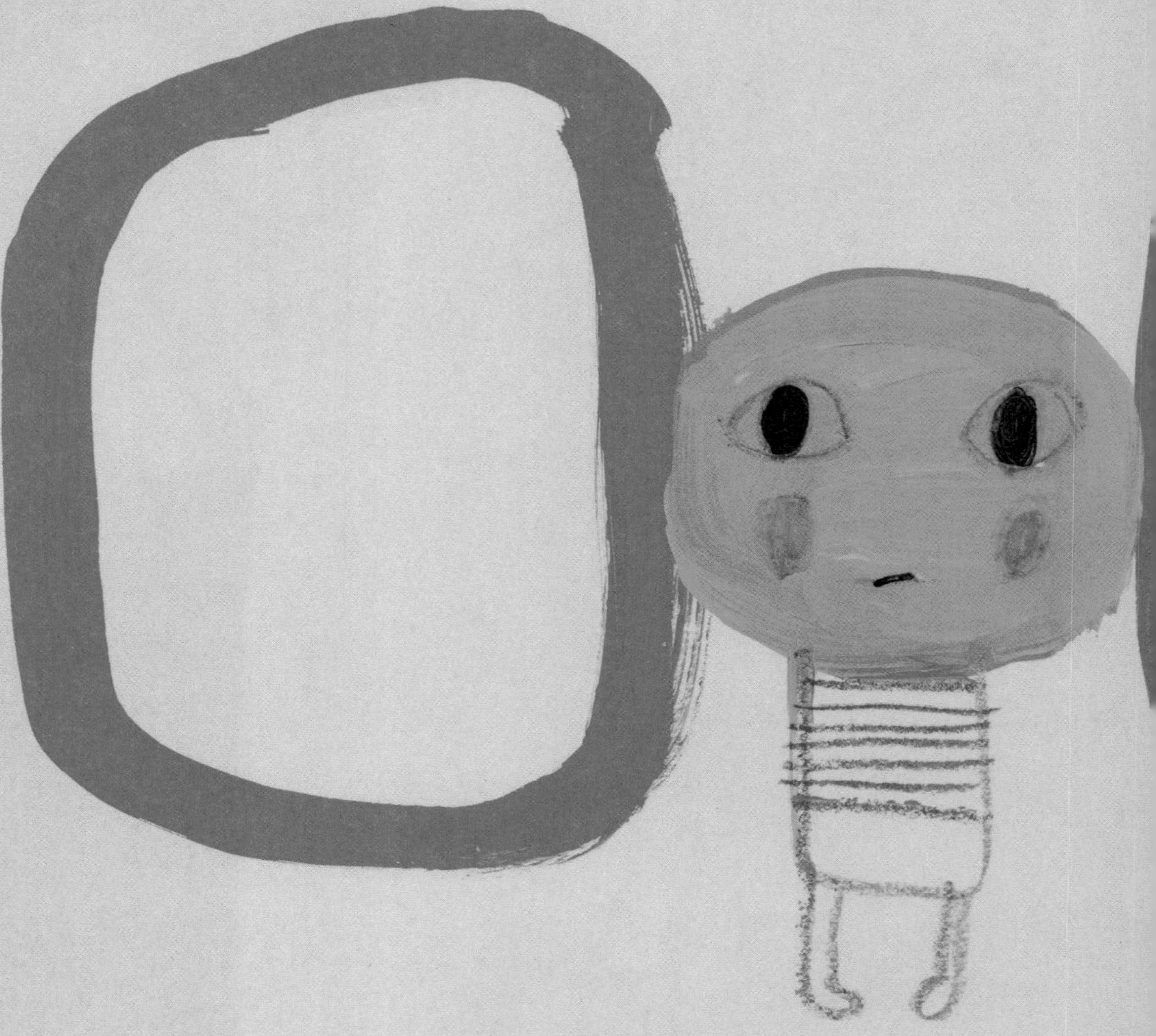

ORCEJAS DE ELEFANTE AFRICANO,

African Elephant Ears

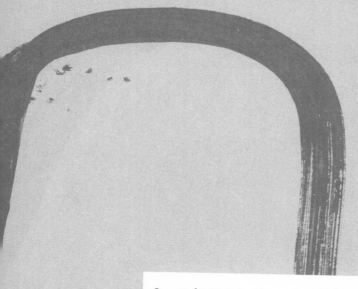

O LARGAS ANTENAS DE HORMIGA.

Long Ant Feelers.

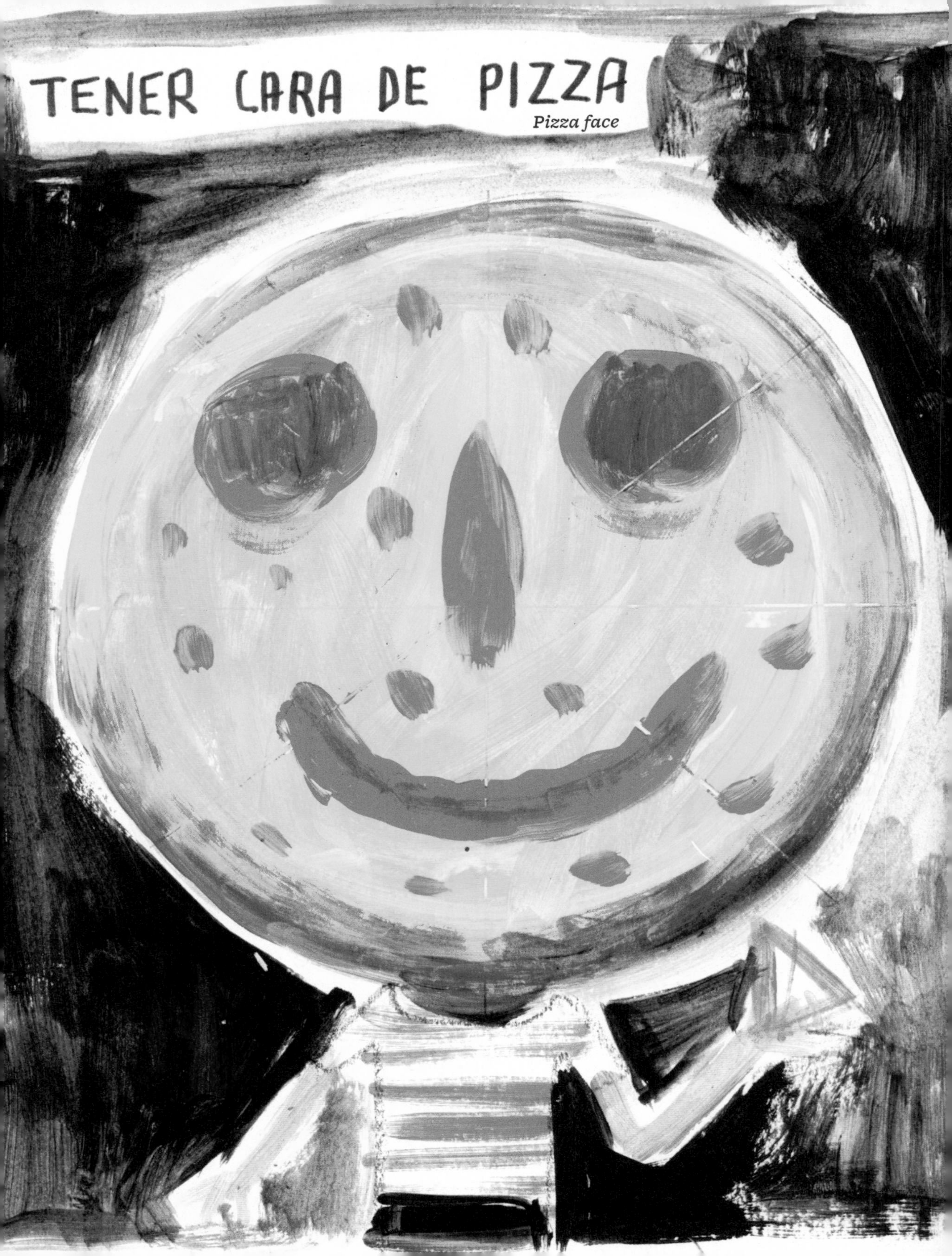
TENER CARA DE PIZZA

Pizza face

QUÉ MÁS DA SI ES ROJO COMO UN TOMATE.

I don't care if he's red as a tomato.

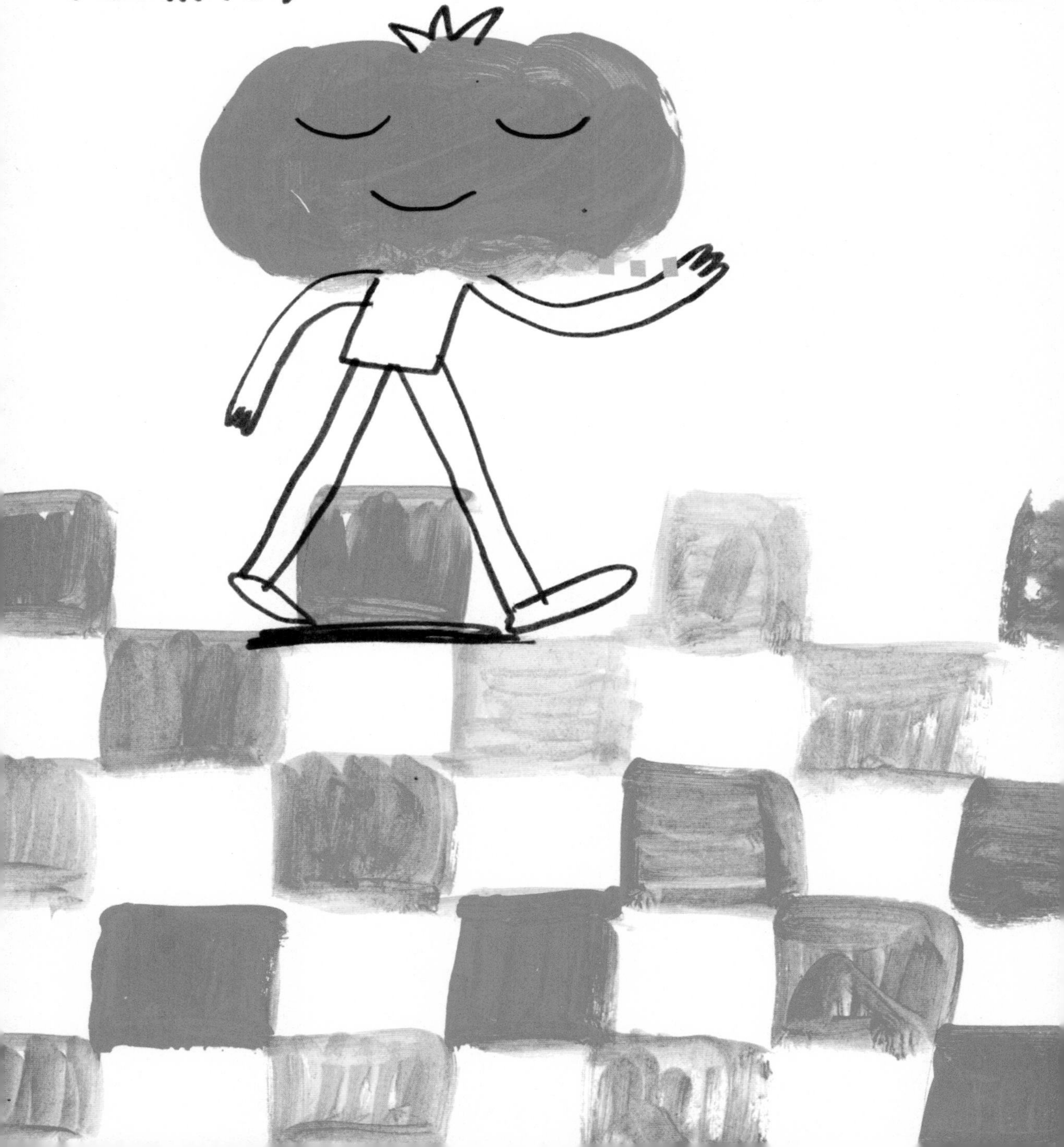

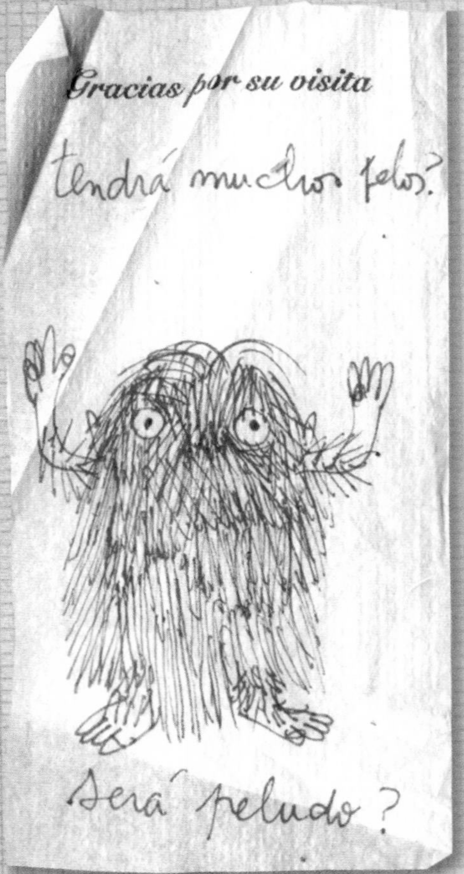
Gracias por su visita
Tendrá muchos pelos?
Será peludo?

Will he have a lot of hair?

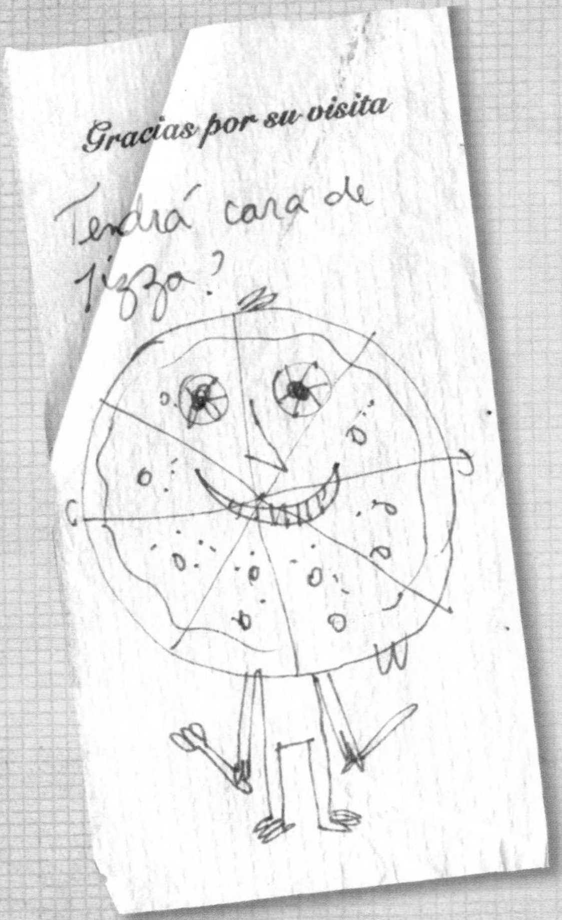
Gracias por su visita
Tendrá cara de pizza?

Will he have a pizza face?

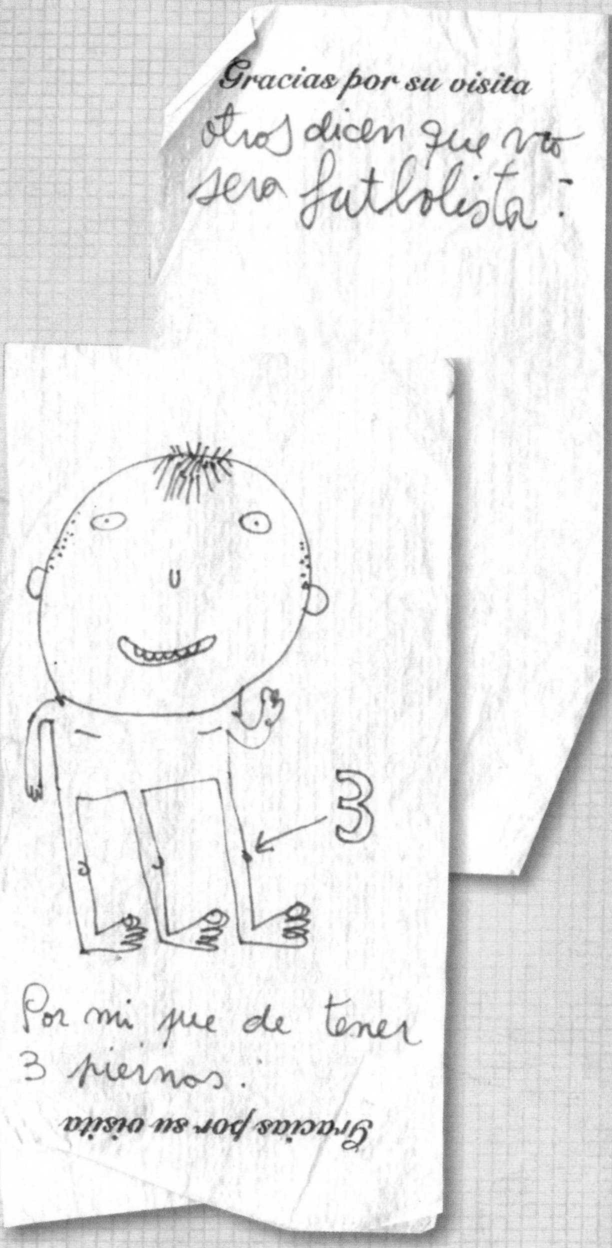
Gracias por su visita
Otros dicen que no sera futbolista:
3
Por mi pue de tener 3 piernas.
Gracias por su visita

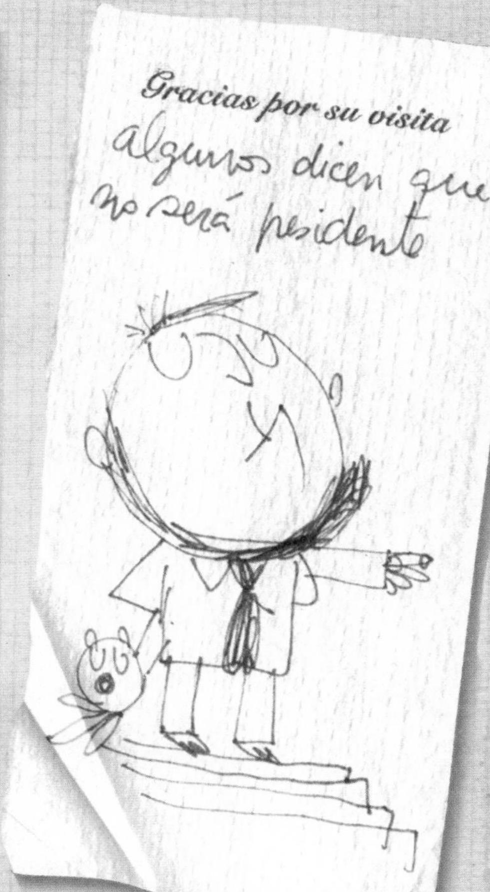
Gracias por su visita
Algunos dicen que no será presidente

Others say that he will never be president.

Some say he'll never be a soccer player.

I don't care if he has three legs.

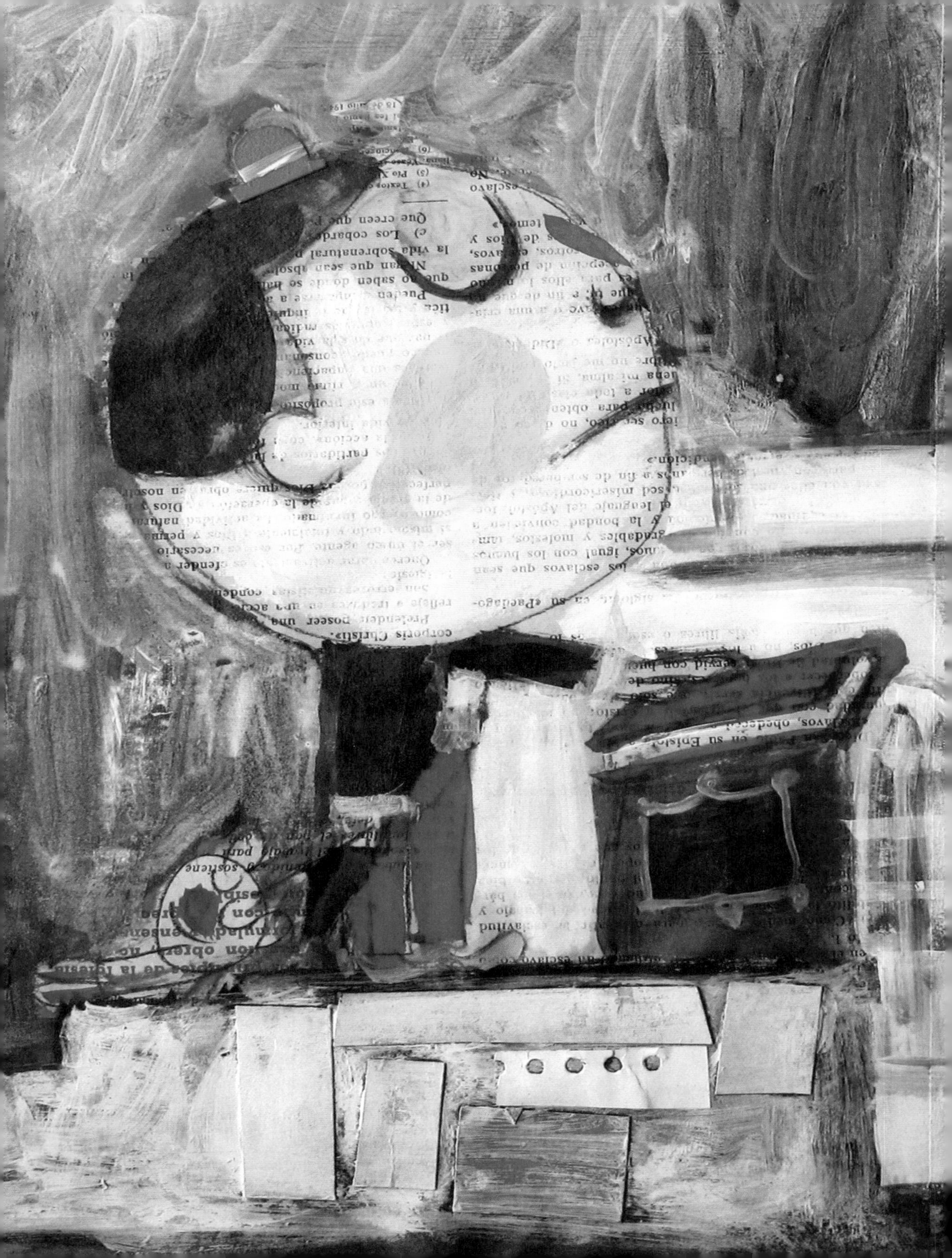

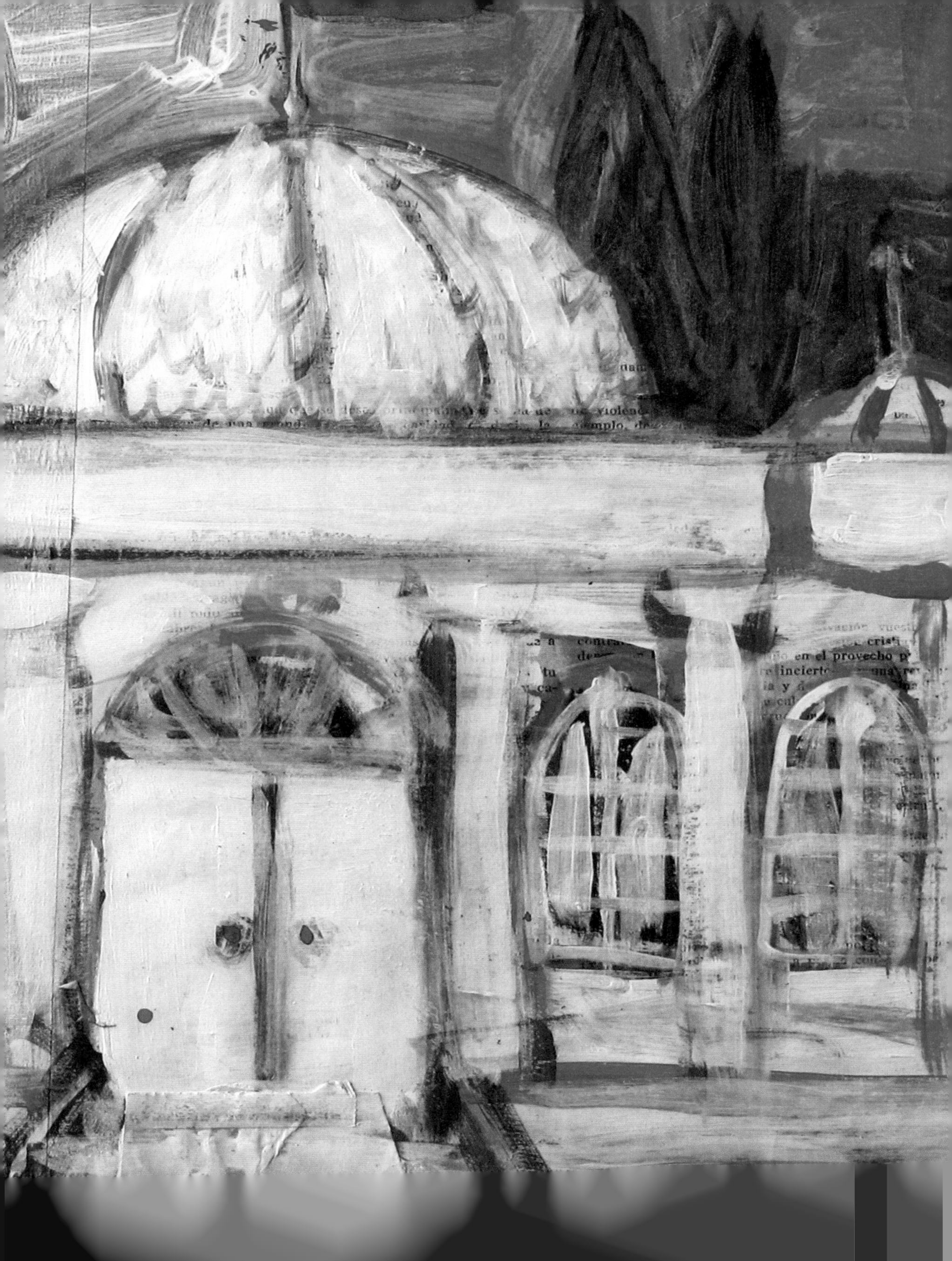

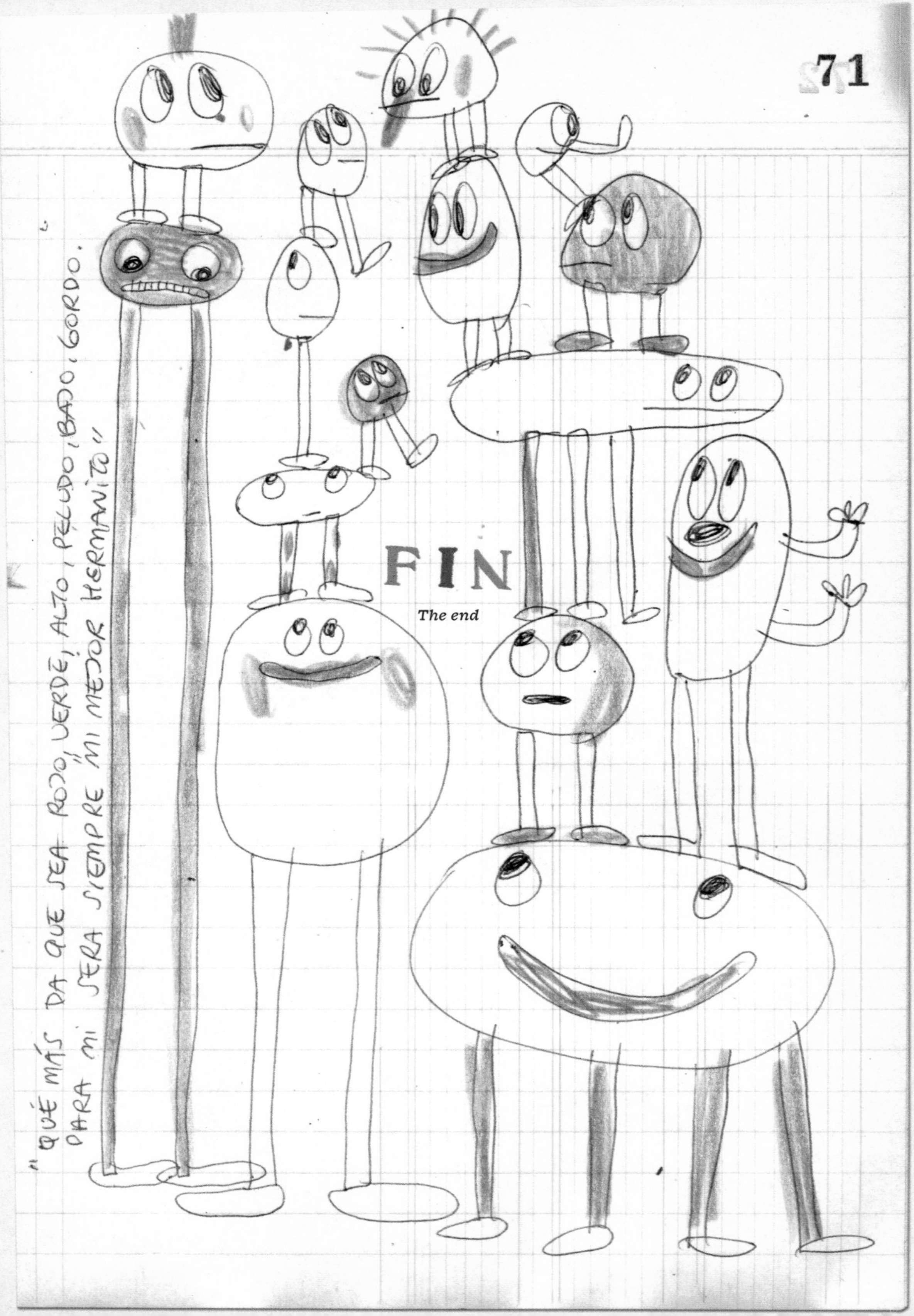
"QUÉ MÁS DA QUE SEA ROJO, UERDE, ALTO, PELUDO, BADO, GORDO.
PARA MI SERÁ SIEMPRE MI MEDOR HERMANITO"

FIN

The end

"I don't care if he's green, red, blue, silver, hairy, or short and fat.
He's always going to be my best little brother."

mi mejor hermanito.

My best little brother

What will my little brother be like?

We'll do tons of things together!

Will he have green eyes? Or purple ones?

If he has grandpa's big fat nose...

        I'll take him to smell wildflowers.

And what if his nose is long and pointy, like a mosquito's?

        Then we'll have chocolate milk together,
        and he can use it as a straw.

Maybe he'll be fat, like a sumo wrestler.

Or he'll be a math whiz and help me understand square roots.

Maybe he'll be all hairy, like our cousin Ismael.

Or he'll have a pizza face,

    or incredible superpowers, and he'll be able to see through walls,

        like a superhero.

Who cares if he's red like a tomato,

yellow like an egg yolk,

green as grass,

or blue like the sky and the sea.

For all I care, he could come from a distant galaxy,

or Jupiter or Mars.

He could have a hundred eyes of different sizes,

twenty arms and four paws,

the ears of an African elephant,

or long ant feelers.

My little brother's been born.

Mom and dad already brought him home.

A cloud hangs over daddy's smile.

Some say he'll never be a soccer player.

Others say that he will never be president.

And that he won't be able to play the piano.

That he'll never be a paratrooper,

or drive a bus.

But I couldn't care less.

He's sweeter than a chocolate cake covered in whipped cream.

He'll always be my best little brother.

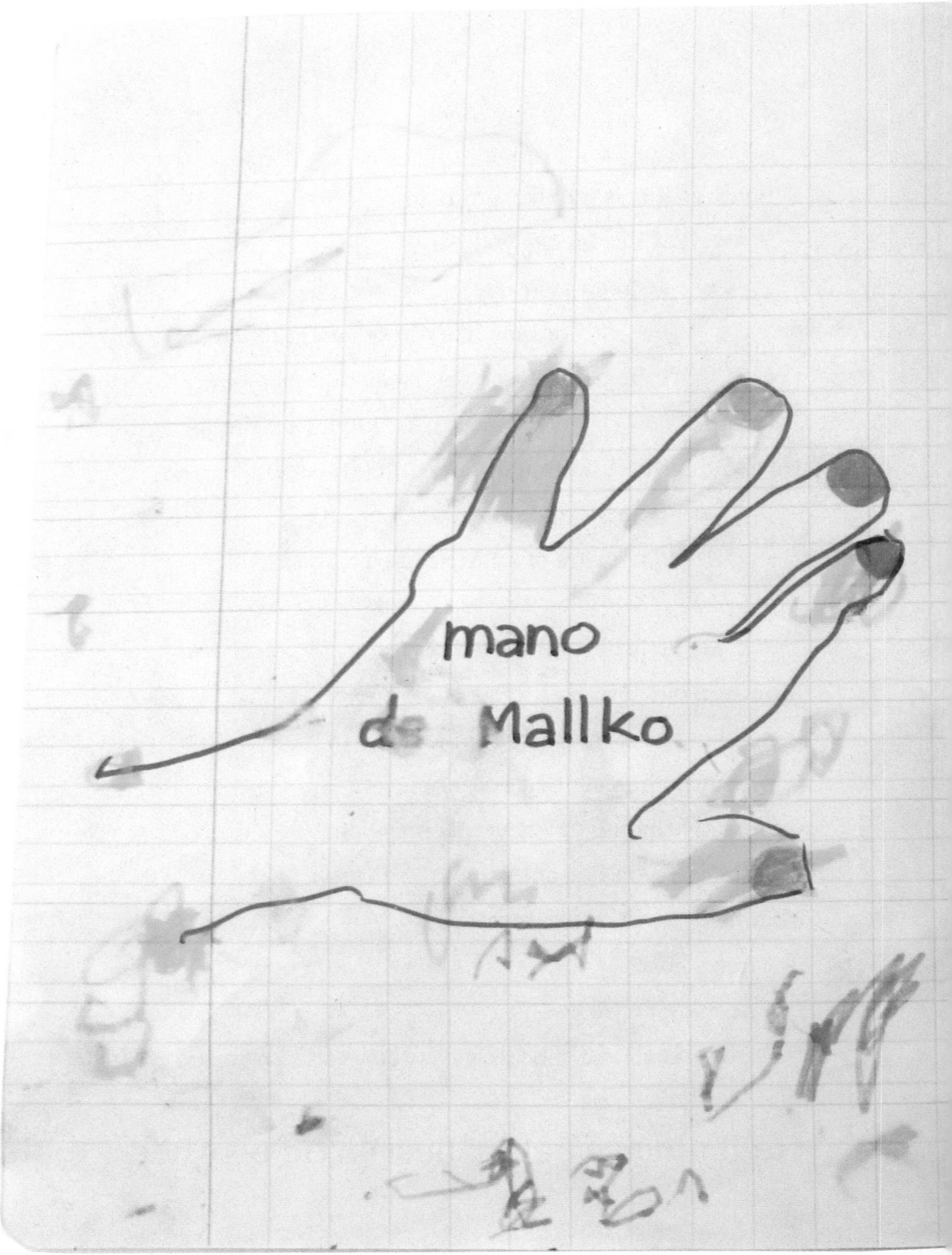
mano
de Mallko

Mallko's hand

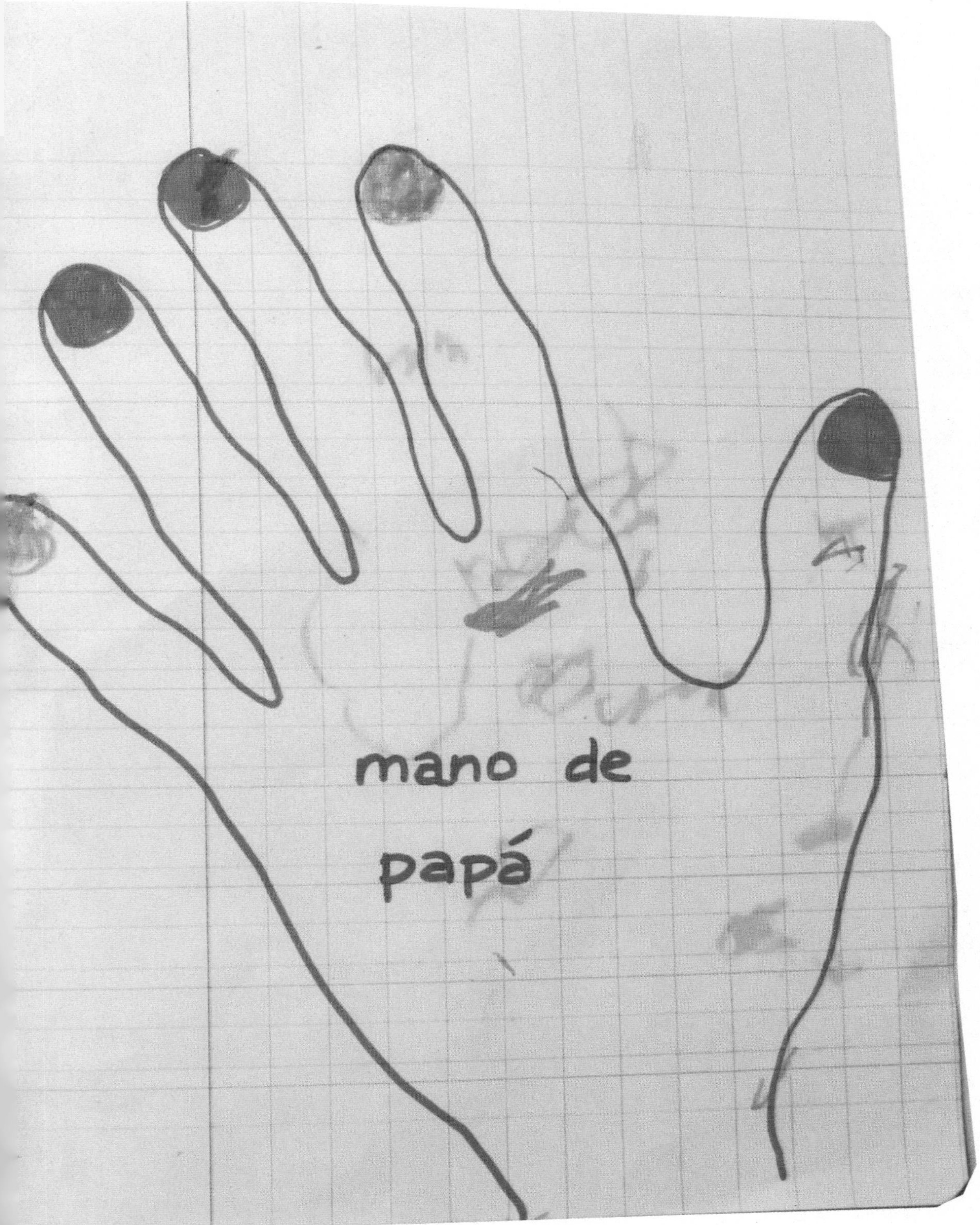
mano de
papá

Daddy's hand

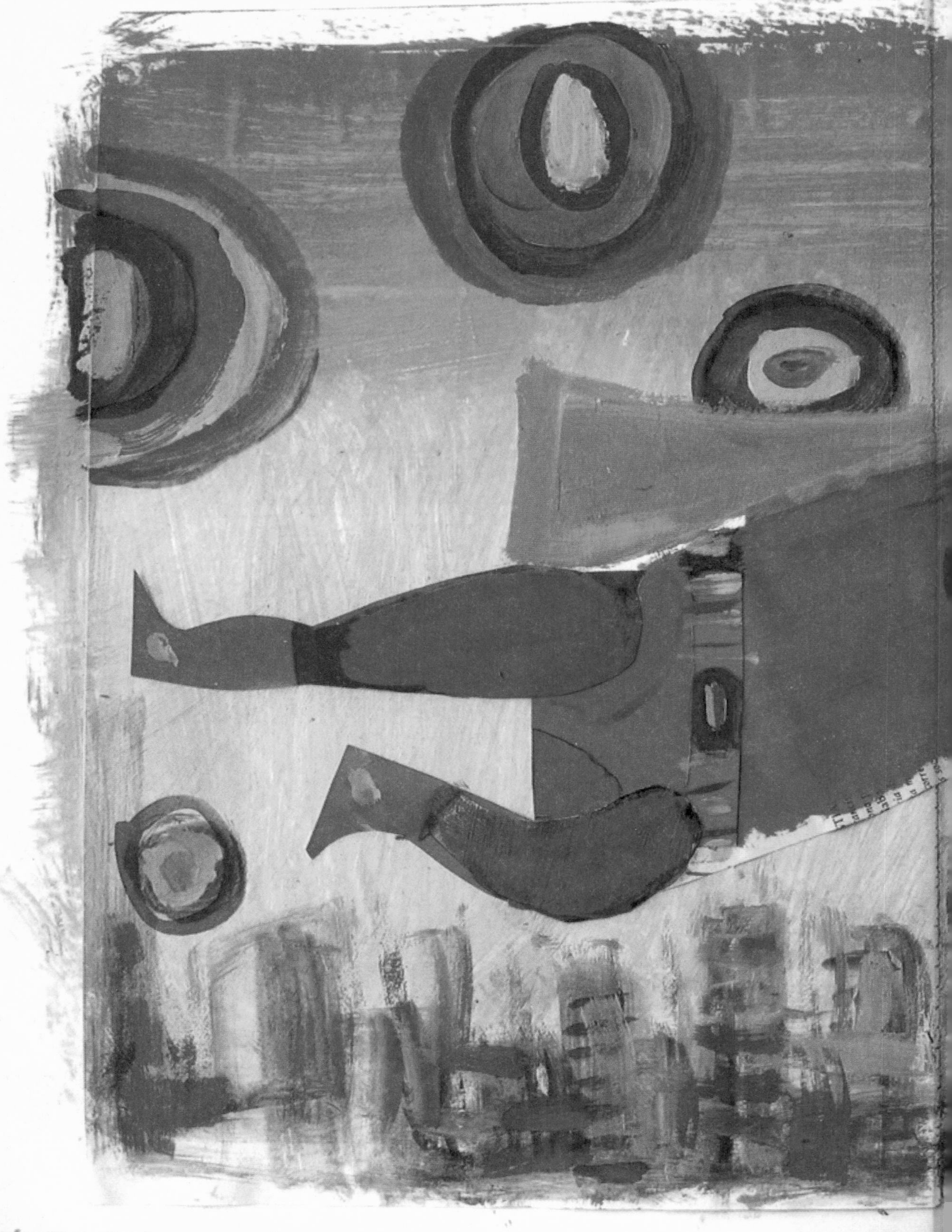

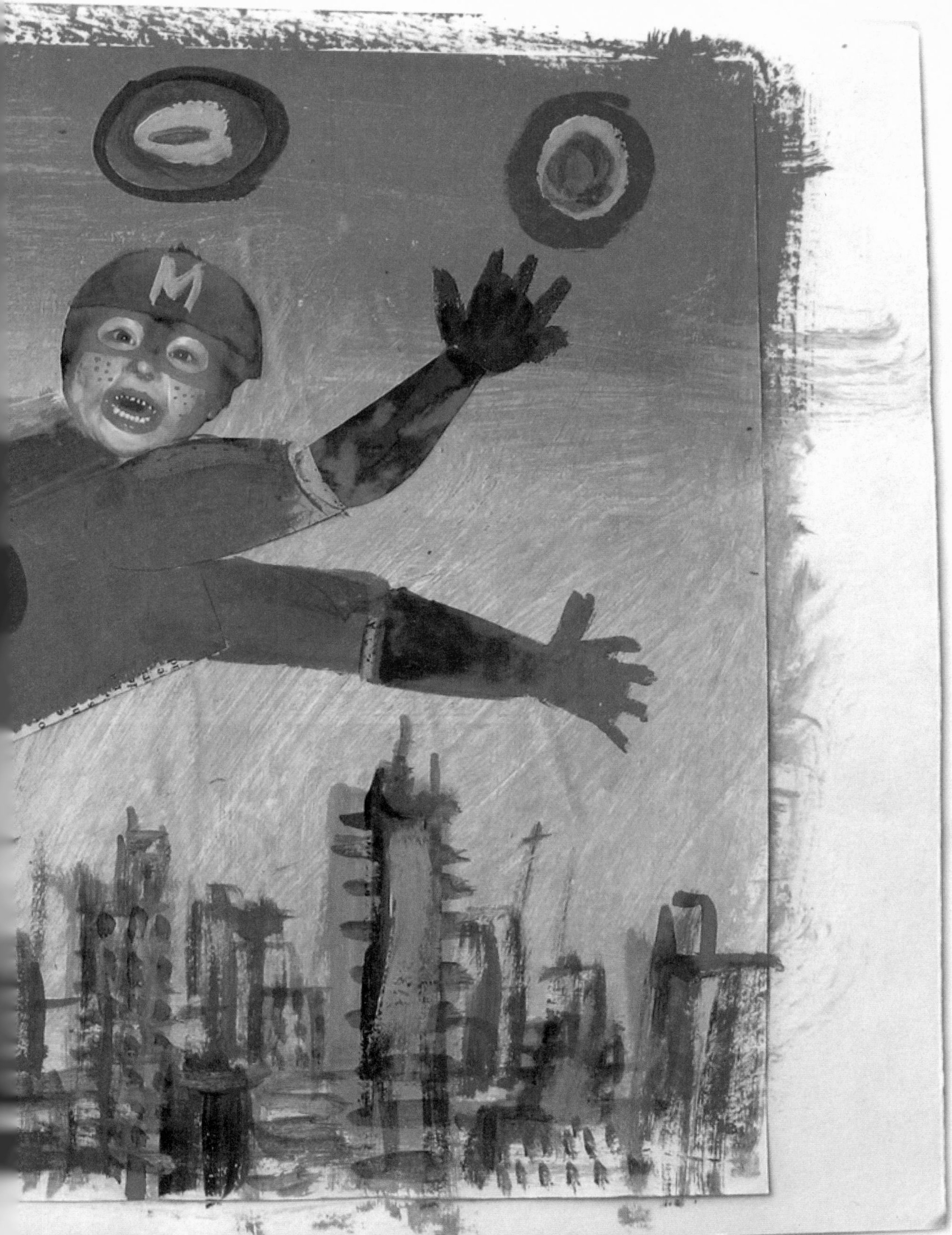

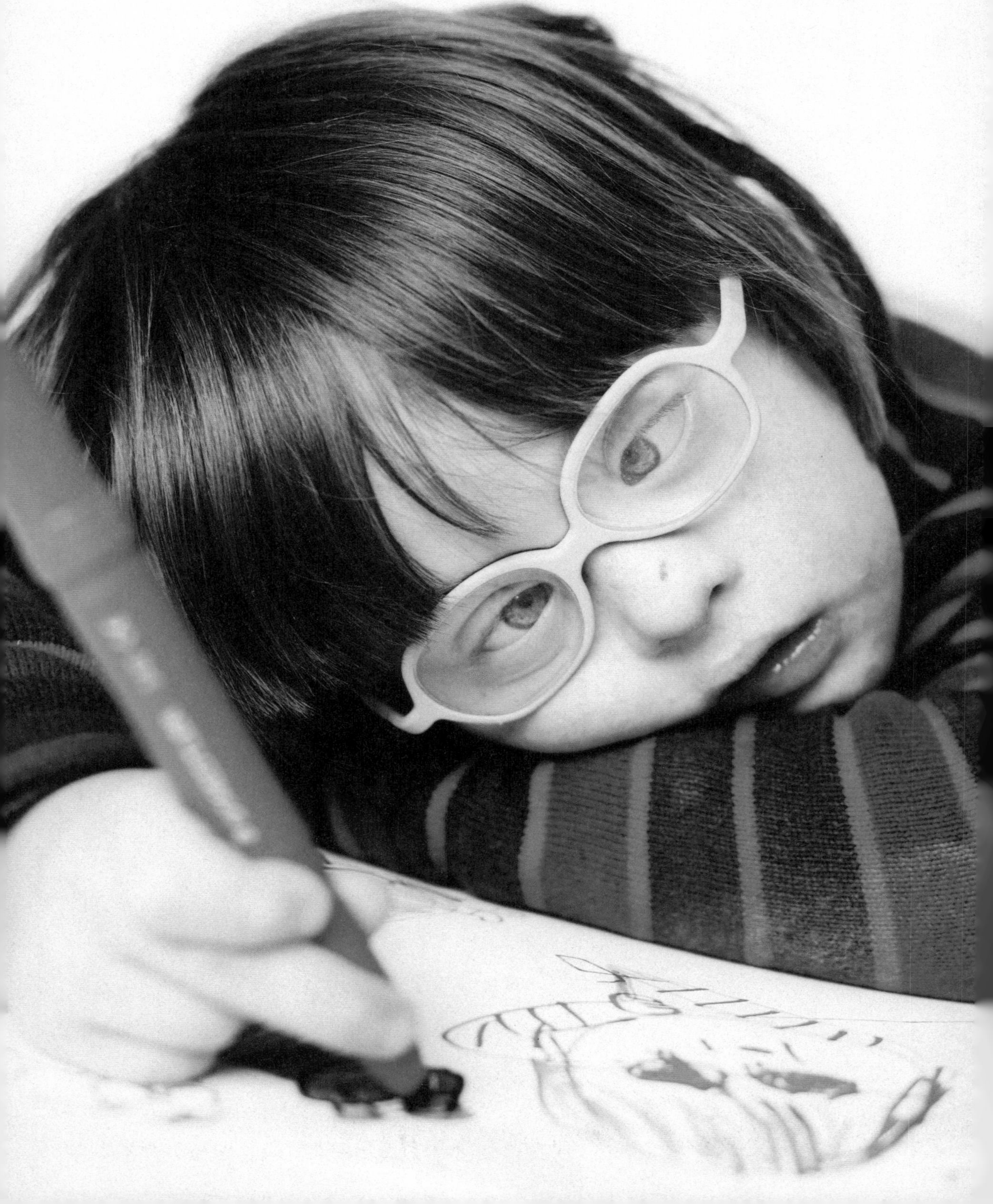

Mallko

SU
UNIVERSO

HIS UNIVERSE

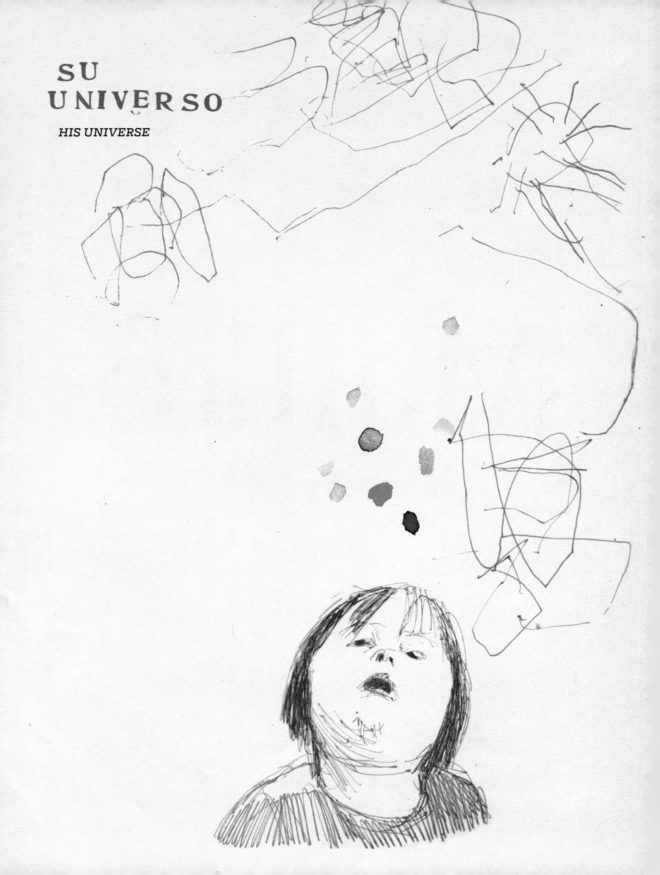

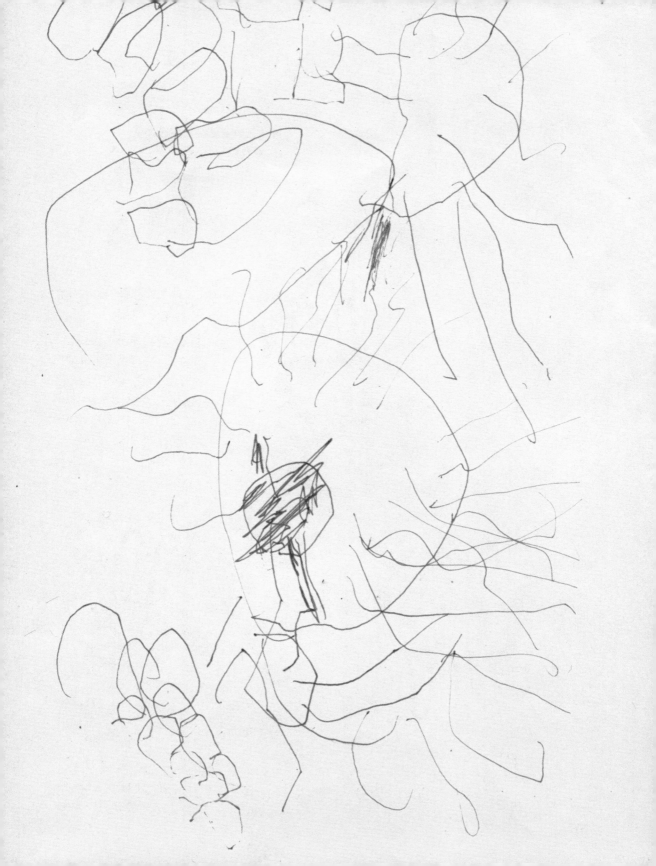

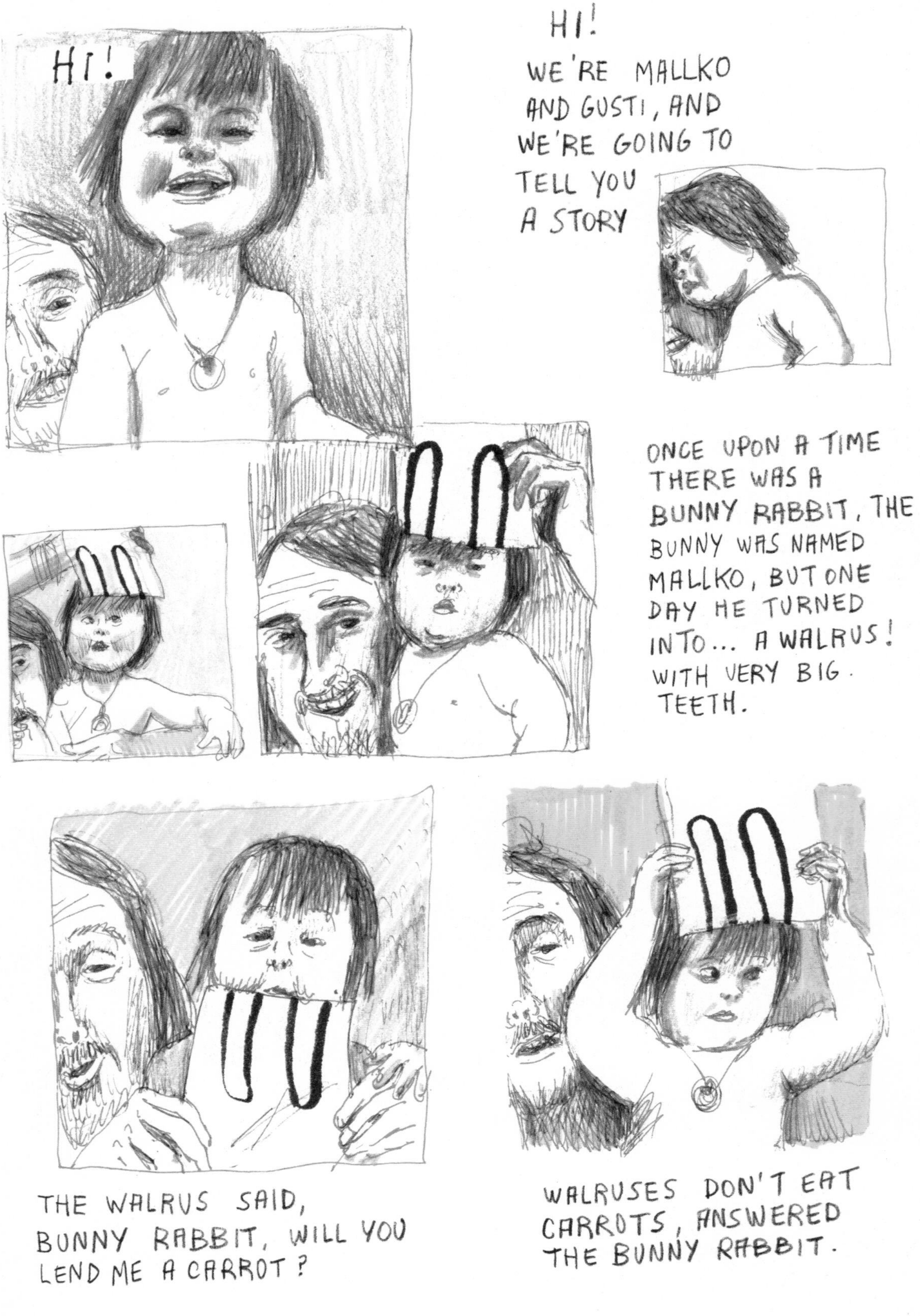
HI!
HI!
WE'RE MALLKO AND GUSTI, AND WE'RE GOING TO TELL YOU A STORY
ONCE UPON A TIME THERE WAS A BUNNY RABBIT, THE BUNNY WAS NAMED MALLKO, BUT ONE DAY HE TURNED INTO... A WALRUS! WITH VERY BIG TEETH.
THE WALRUS SAID, BUNNY RABBIT, WILL YOU LEND ME A CARROT?
WALRUSES DON'T EAT CARROTS, ANSWERED THE BUNNY RABBIT.

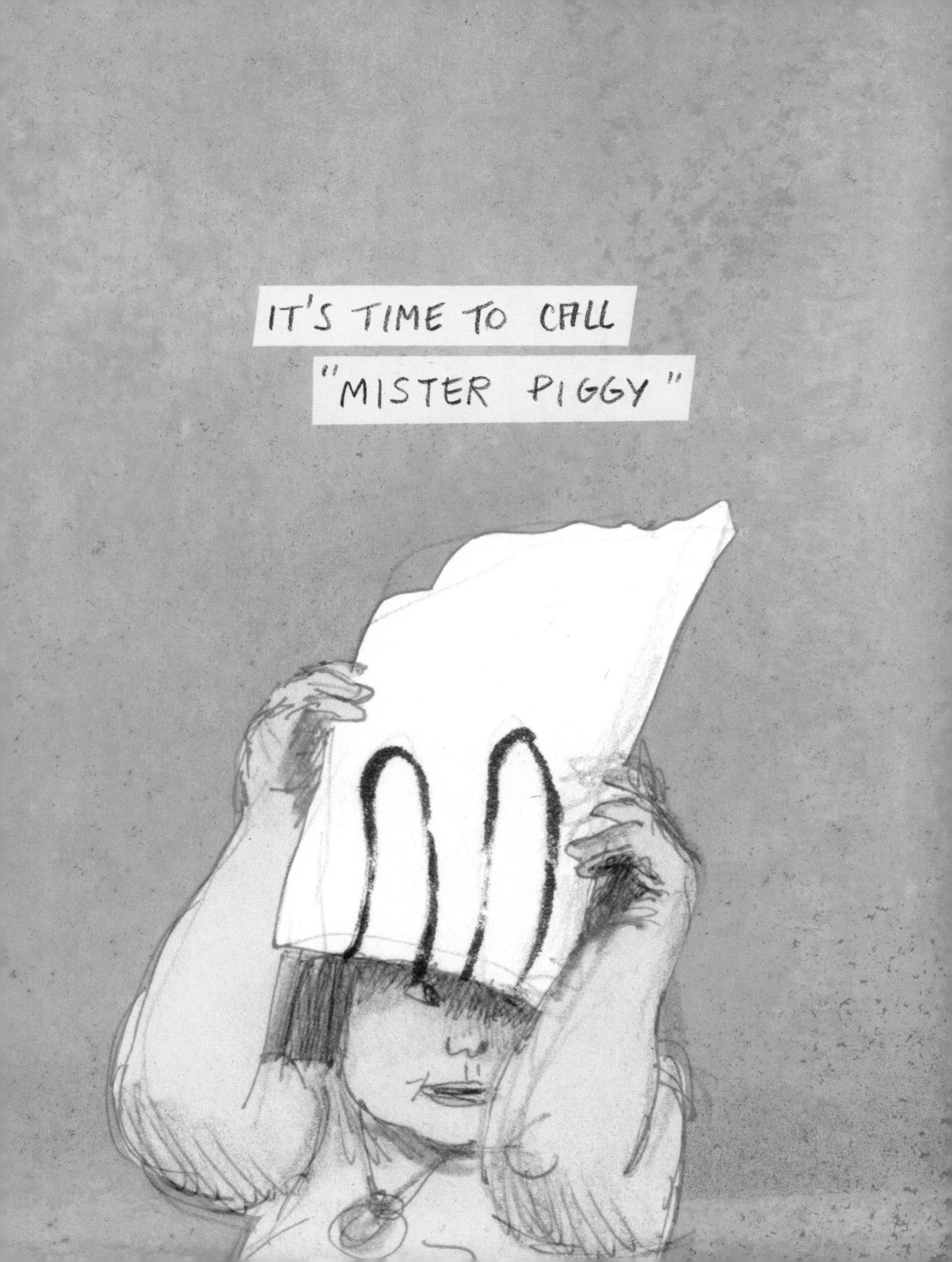
IT'S TIME TO CALL
"MISTER PIGGY"

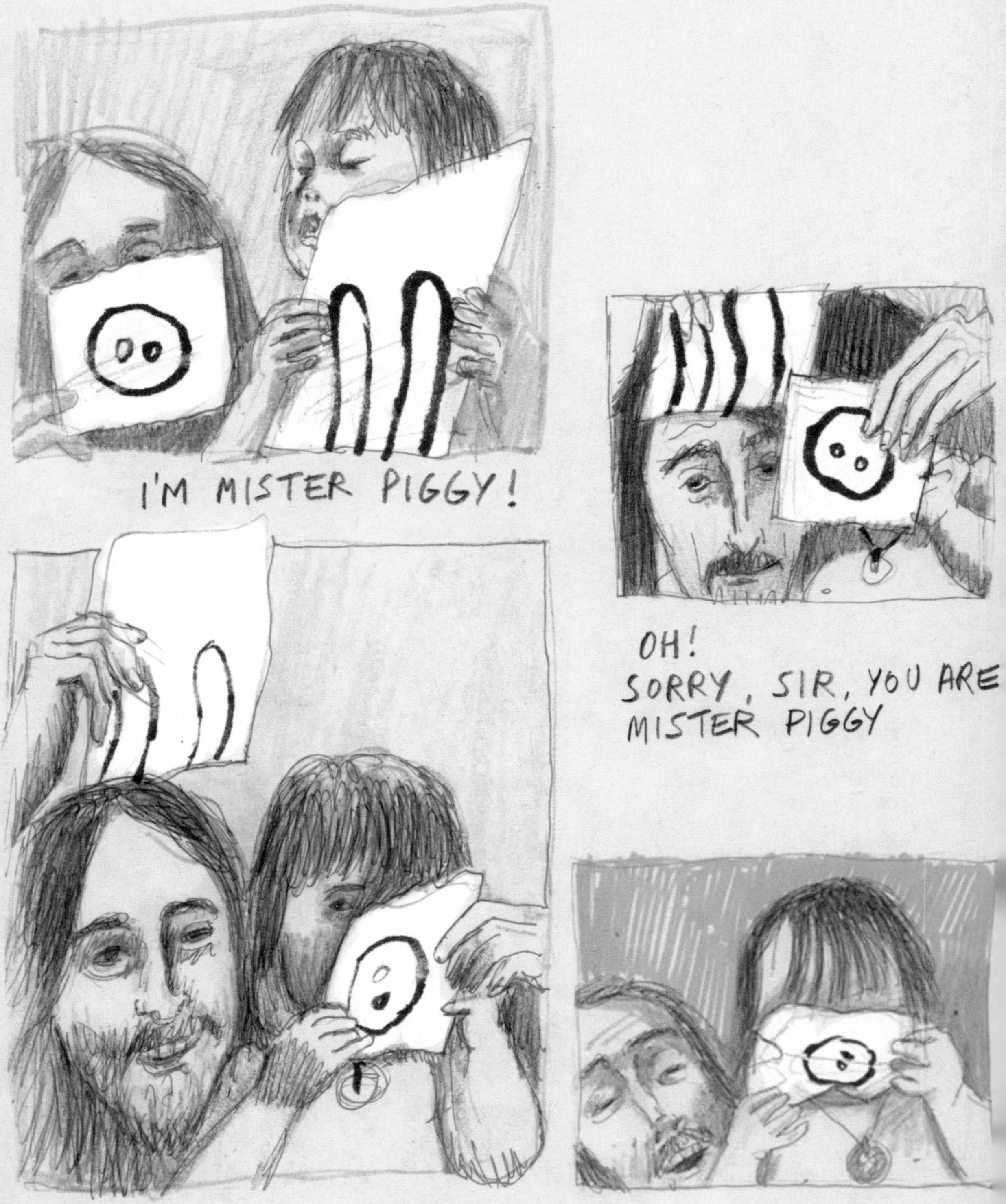
I'M MISTER PIGGY!
OH!
SORRY, SIR, YOU ARE MISTER PIGGY

I'M THE
LITTLE PIGGY!
GRRR GRRR
GRRR

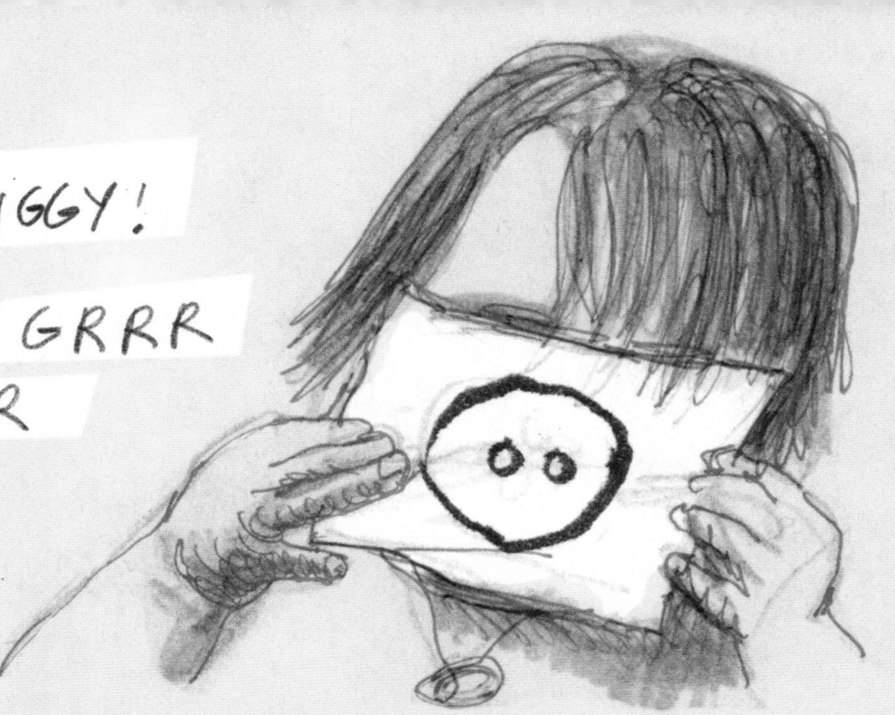

LITTLE PIGGY WAS VERY IMPATIENT,
SO HE CALLED HIS FRIEND LITTLE ANT.

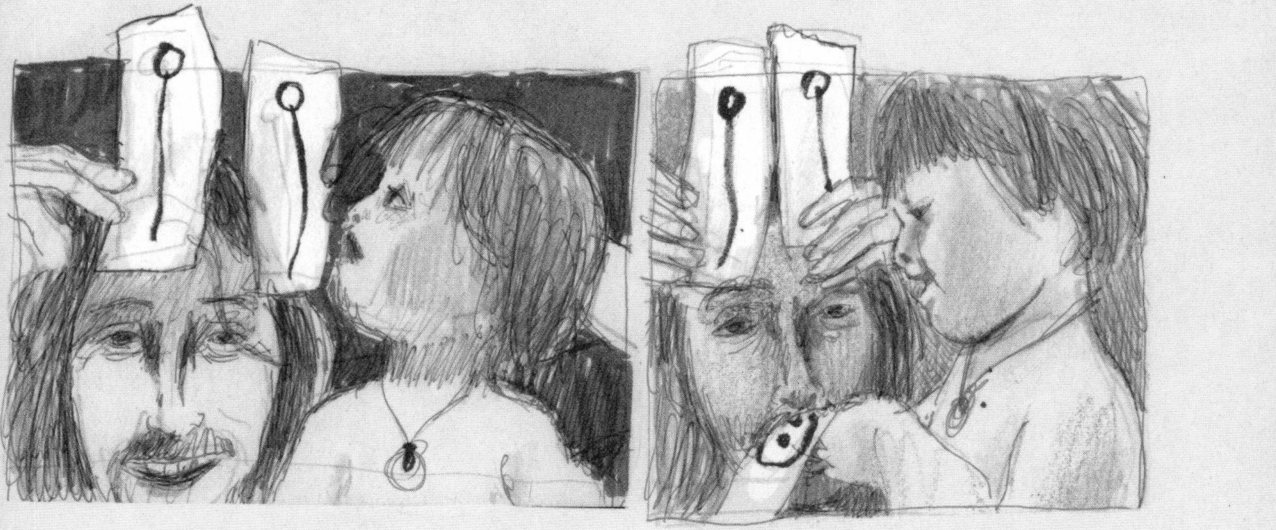

I'M A LITTLE ANT!
I'M A LITTLE ANT!

BE CAREFUL.
MISTER PIGGY!

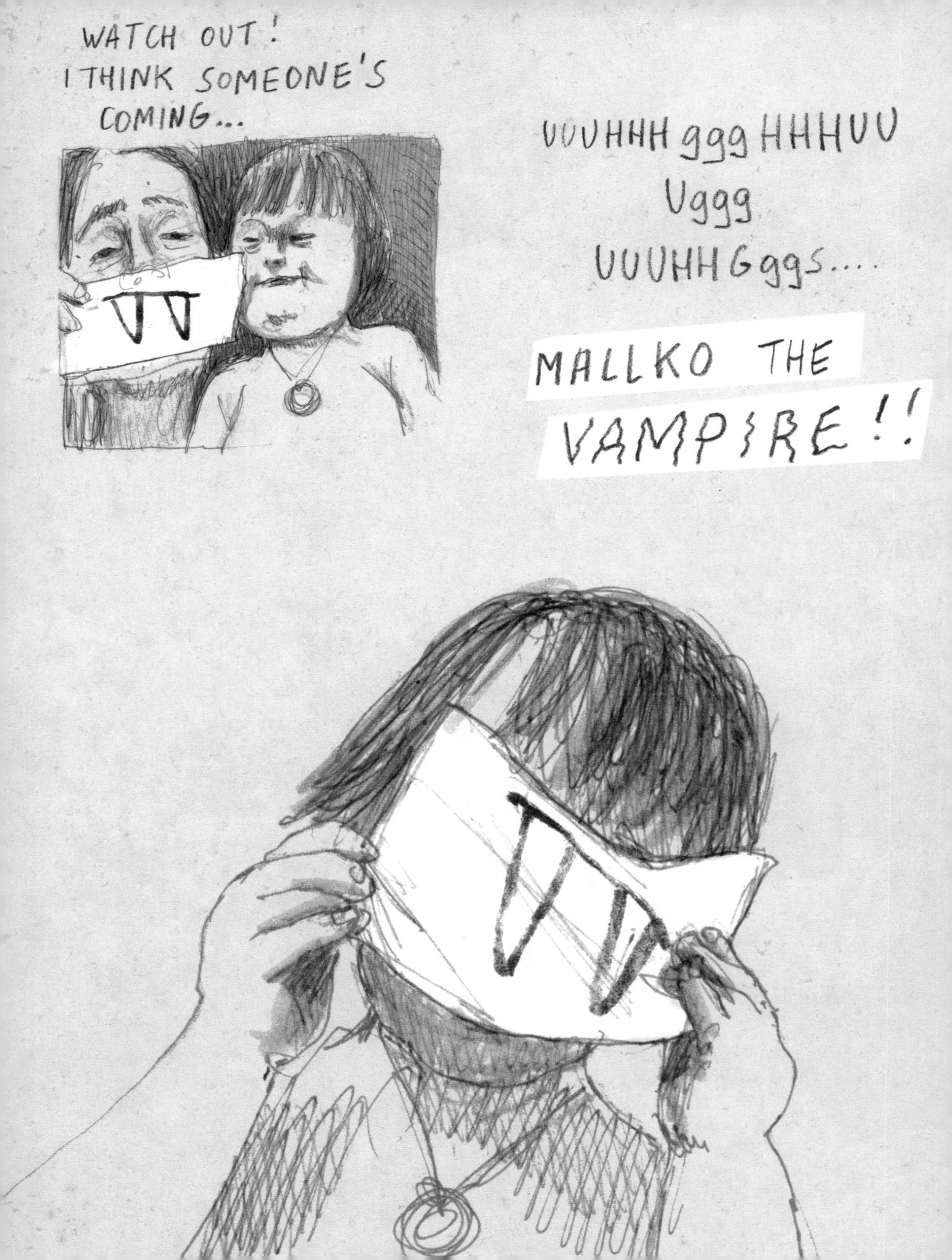
WATCH OUT!
I THINK SOMEONE'S
COMING...
UUUHHH ggg HHHUU
Uggg
UUUHH Gggs....
MALLKO THE
VAMPIRE!!

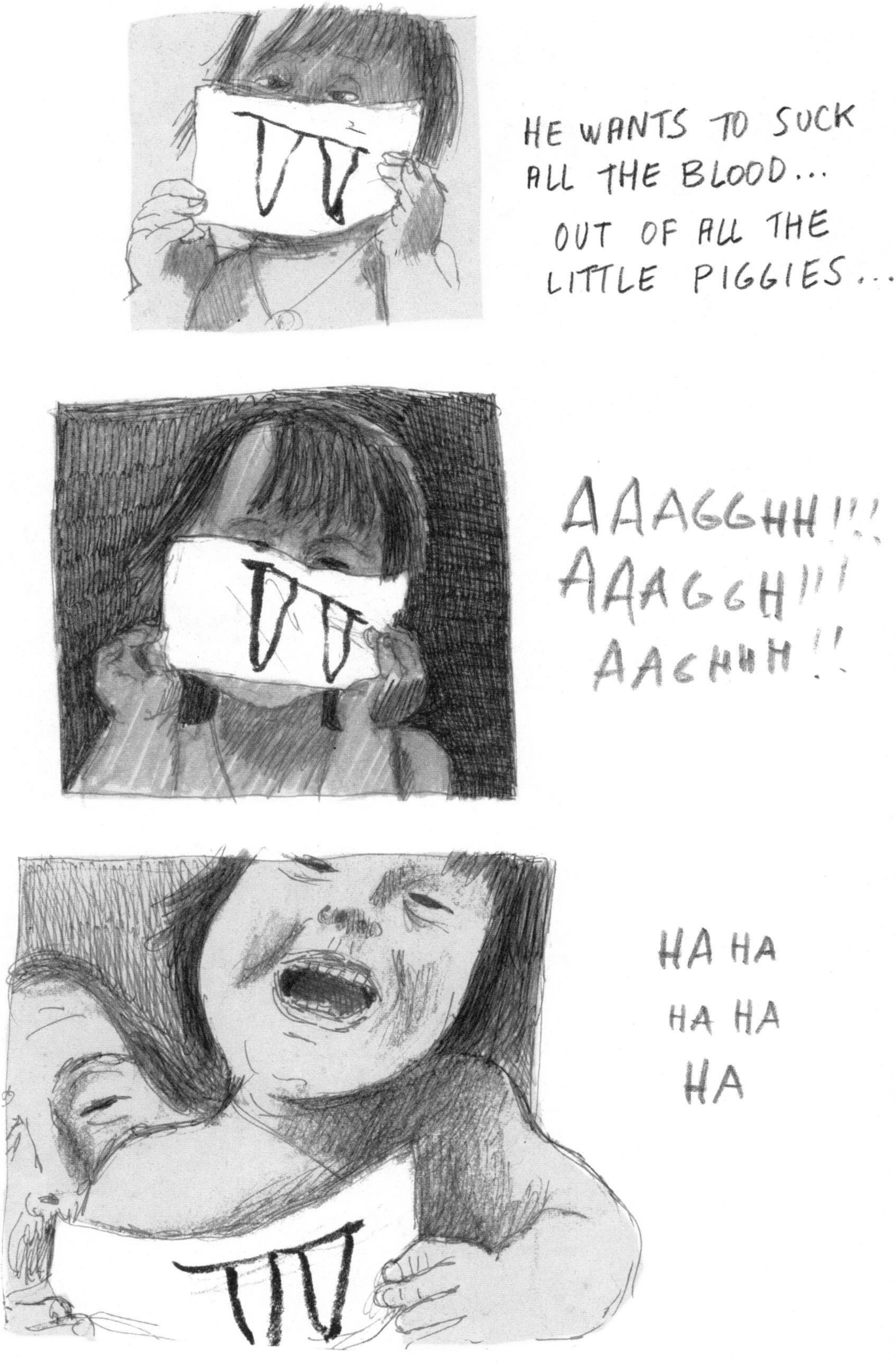
HE WANTS TO SUCK ALL THE BLOOD...
OUT OF ALL THE LITTLE PIGGIES...
AAAGGHH!!! AAAGGH!!! AAGHHH!!
HA HA HA HA HA

MR. VAMPIRE, MR. VAMPIRE
IF YOU WANT TO SUCK
BLOOD I SUGGEST
YOU TRY...
AN ELEPHANT'S !!!

TTTUUUUTTUUUU
GRRR GRRR
TTUUTTUUUTT

AND WHAT DOES AN ELEPHANT SAY ?
BBOOOOWWW WOOWW GGGRRR !!!
GGRRRR !!!
NO! THAT SOUNDS LIKE A LION-DOG!

AND NOW I'M THE VAMPIRE.

AND I'M GONNA EAT THIS
ELEPHANT UP!
YUM, YUM, YUM!

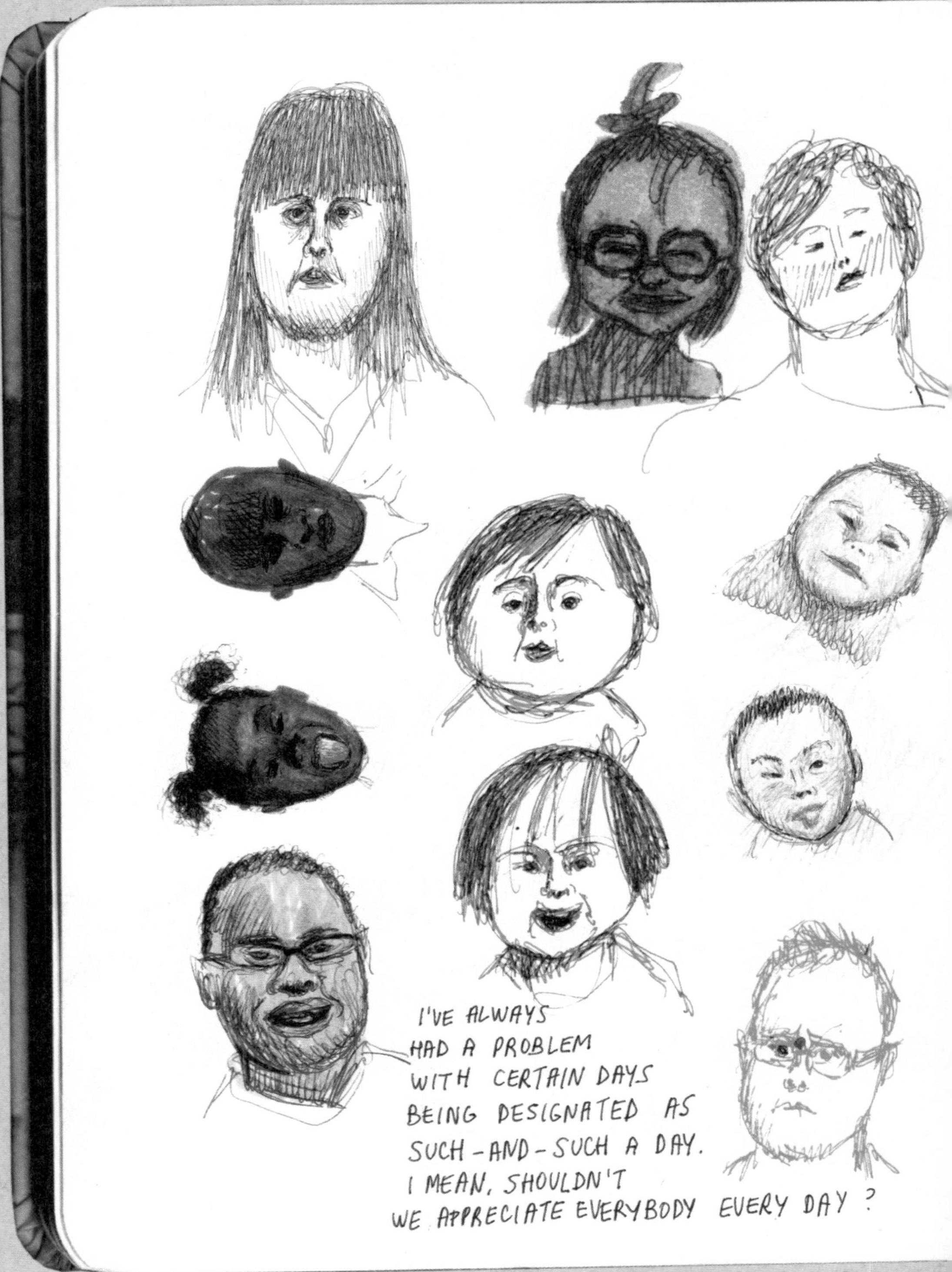
I'VE ALWAYS
HAD A PROBLEM
WITH CERTAIN DAYS
BEING DESIGNATED AS
SUCH-AND-SUCH A DAY.
I MEAN, SHOULDN'T
WE APPRECIATE EVERYBODY EVERY DAY?

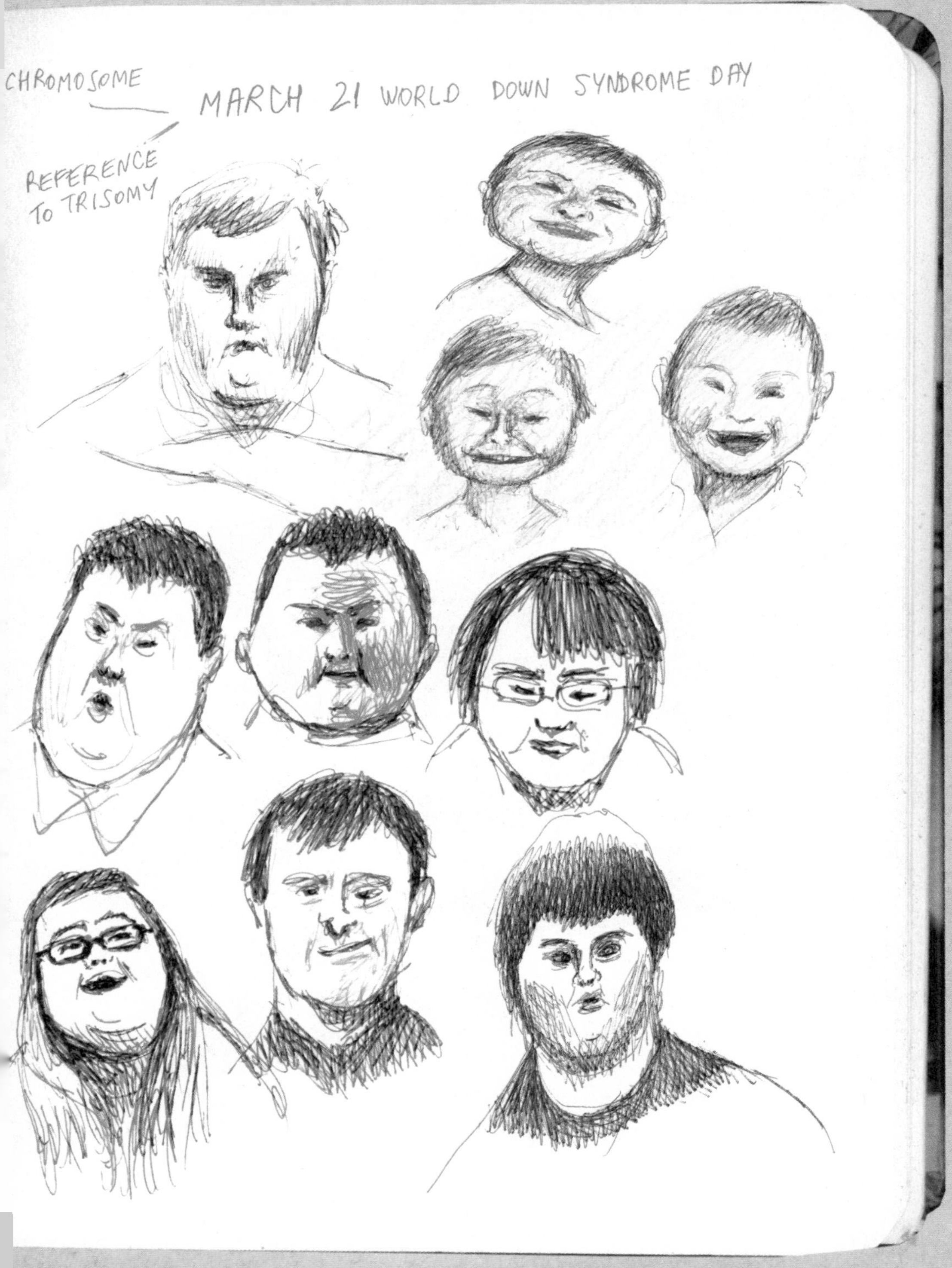
CHROMOSOME
MARCH 21 WORLD DOWN SYNDROME DAY
REFERENCE TO TRISOMY

When I started this book, I got interested in Down syndrome around the world. What was it like in Africa, Asia, elsewhere?

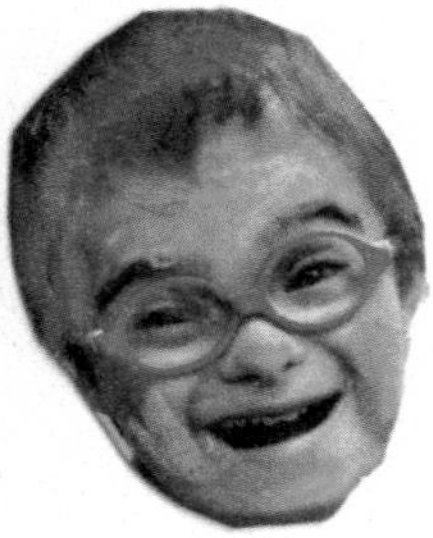

DIFFERENCE

A QUALITY, CHARACTERISTIC OR CIRCUMSTANCE THAT MAKES TWO PEOPLE OR THINGS NOT THE SAME.

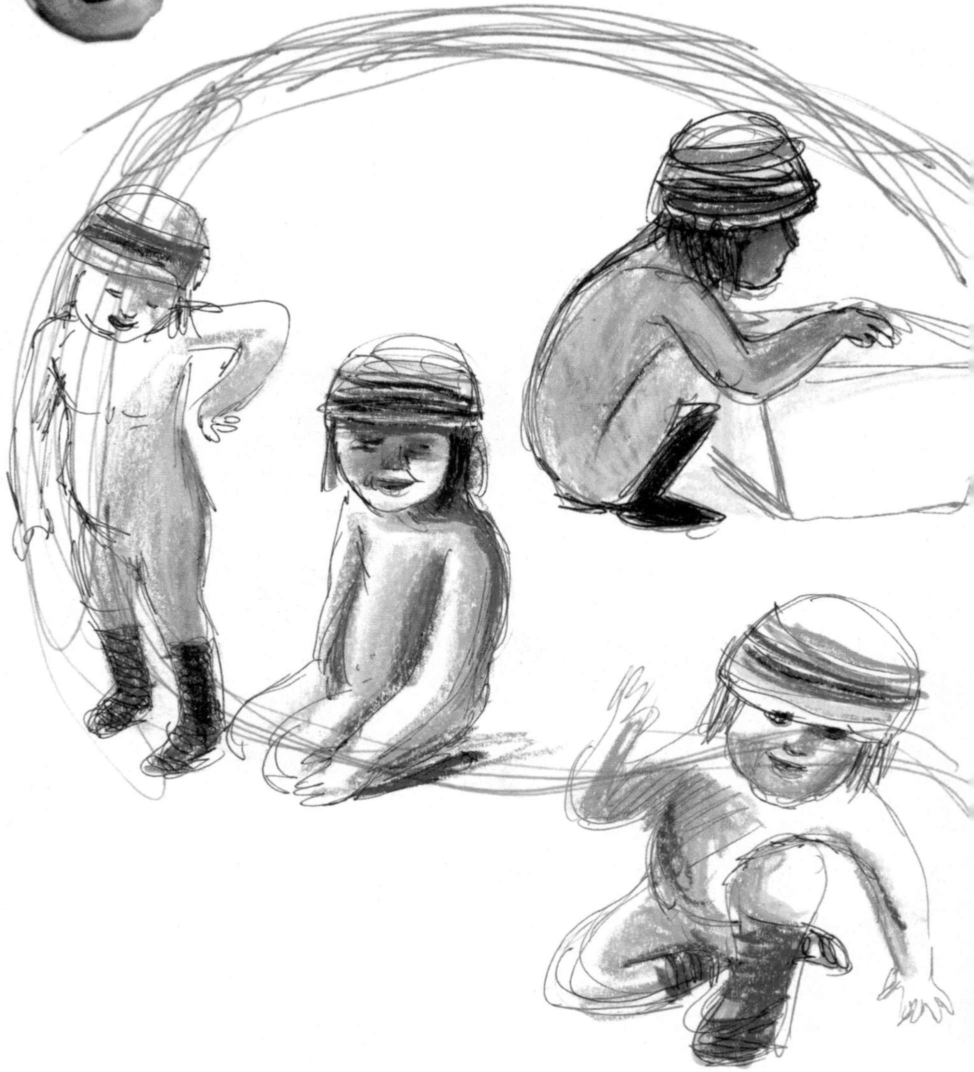

WHAT ARE YOUR REAL NEEDS, MALLKO?
ALL THE ANSWERS LEAD ME TO THE SAME
CONCLUSION [LOVE]

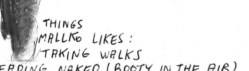

THINGS
MALLKO LIKES:
TAKING WALKS
READING NAKED (BOOTY IN THE AIR)
THE BEACH
EATING POPCORN
PLAYING WITH TRAINS, CARS,
DINOSAURS
~~PLAYING~~ PLAYING BALL
HELPING IN THE KITCHEN
MESSING UP ALL THE CLOSETS
JUMPING OUT TO SCARE YOU
PLAYING THE DRUM, FLUTE, GUITAR
DRAWING
PLAYING ON THE COMPUTER
WATCHING CARTOONS
READING PICTURE BOOKS
BADGERING AND PESTERING

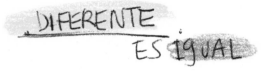

DIFERENTE ES IGUAL

IN BEING DIFFERENT,
WE ARE ALL THE SAME

PREGUNTA ASK

ENCUENTRA

FIND

FOLLOW

SIGUE

APRENDE

LEARN

CAMBIA

CHANGE

BUSCA

SEARCH

CUESTIONA

QUESTION

EQUIVÓCATE

MAKE MISTAKES

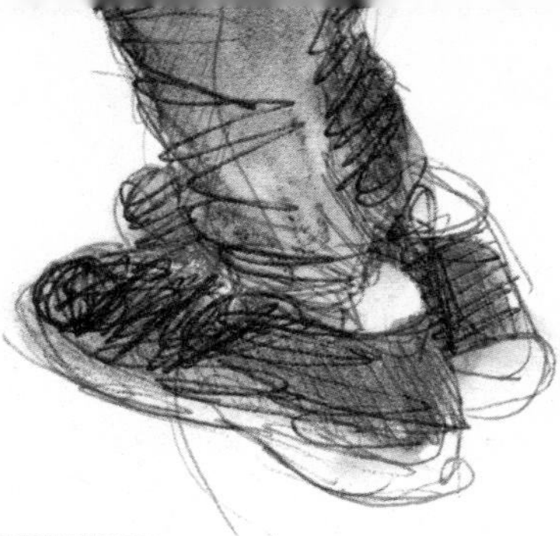

He loves to put on my sneakers,
his mom's sandals,
And his brother Theo's shoes.

It seems he wants to keep his feet planted
firmly on the ground.

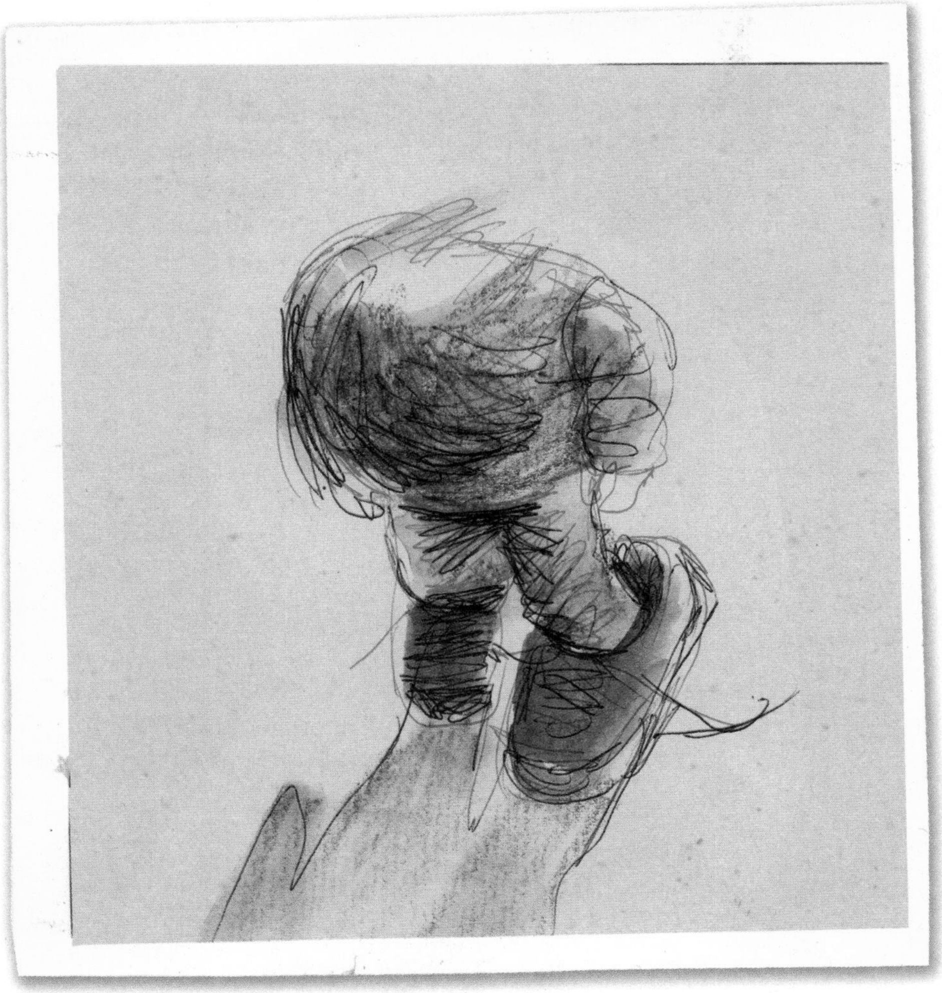

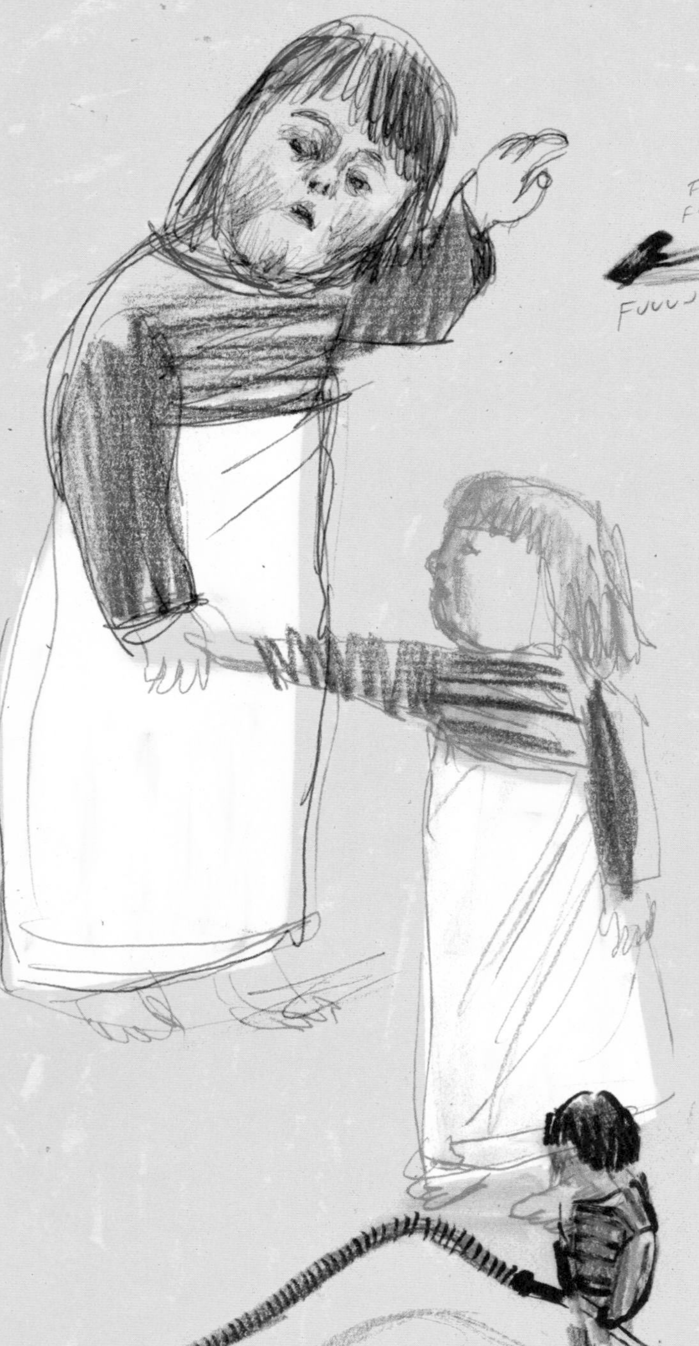

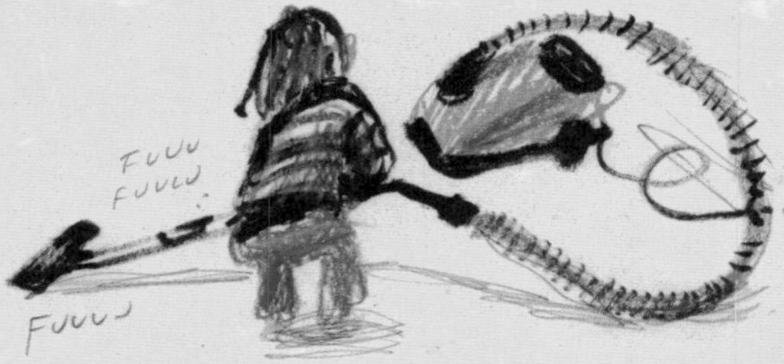
FUUU
FUUUU
FUUUU

He loves to help out.
He's fascinated by the vacuum cleaner because with the push of a button a light comes on and it starts to roar.
He's discovered that he can vacuum himself with the end that sucks in the air.

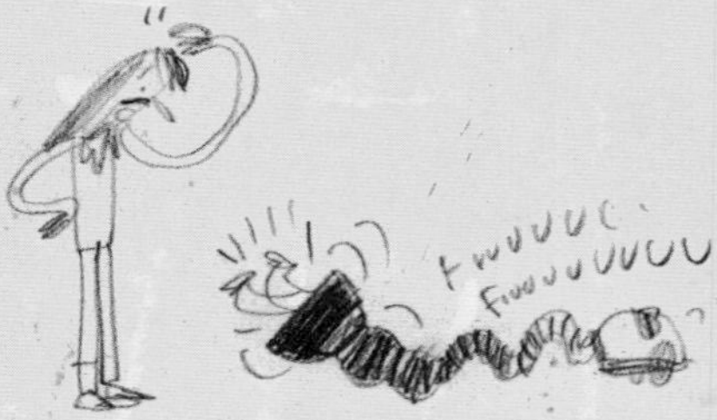

The action-reaction principle: press a button, a light comes on, there's a noise, the thing starts to work.

This action can be repeated again and again.

I PUT ON
THE CAP
I TAKE OFF
THE CAP

To the rhythm of the music
(Lila Downs singing *La cucaracha*),
he plays "put on the cap, take off the cap."

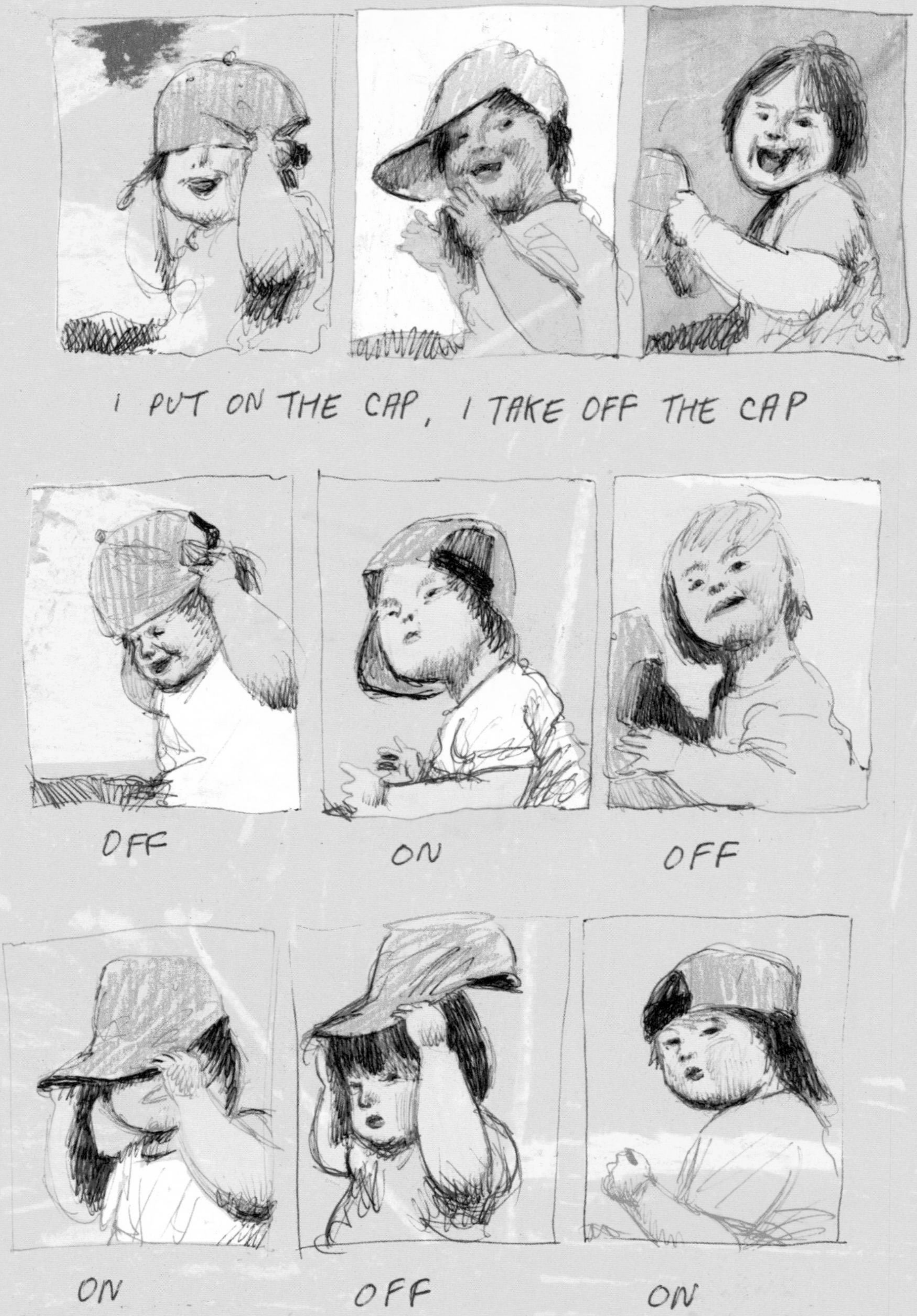
I PUT ON THE CAP, I TAKE OFF THE CAP
OFF
ON
OFF
ON
OFF
ON

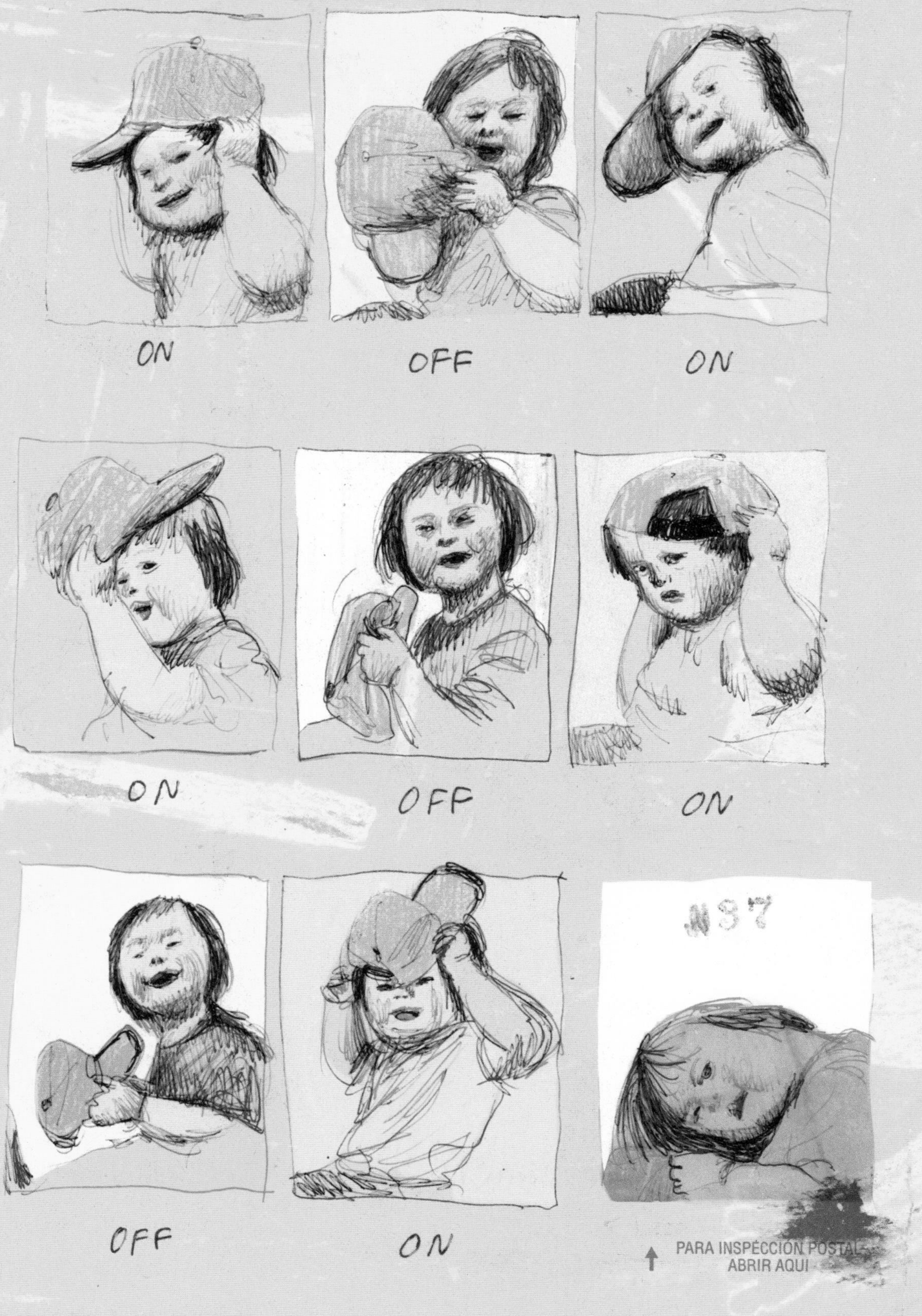
ON
OFF
ON
ON
OFF
ON
OFF
ON
N37
PARA INSPECCIÓN POSTAL
ABRIR AQUI

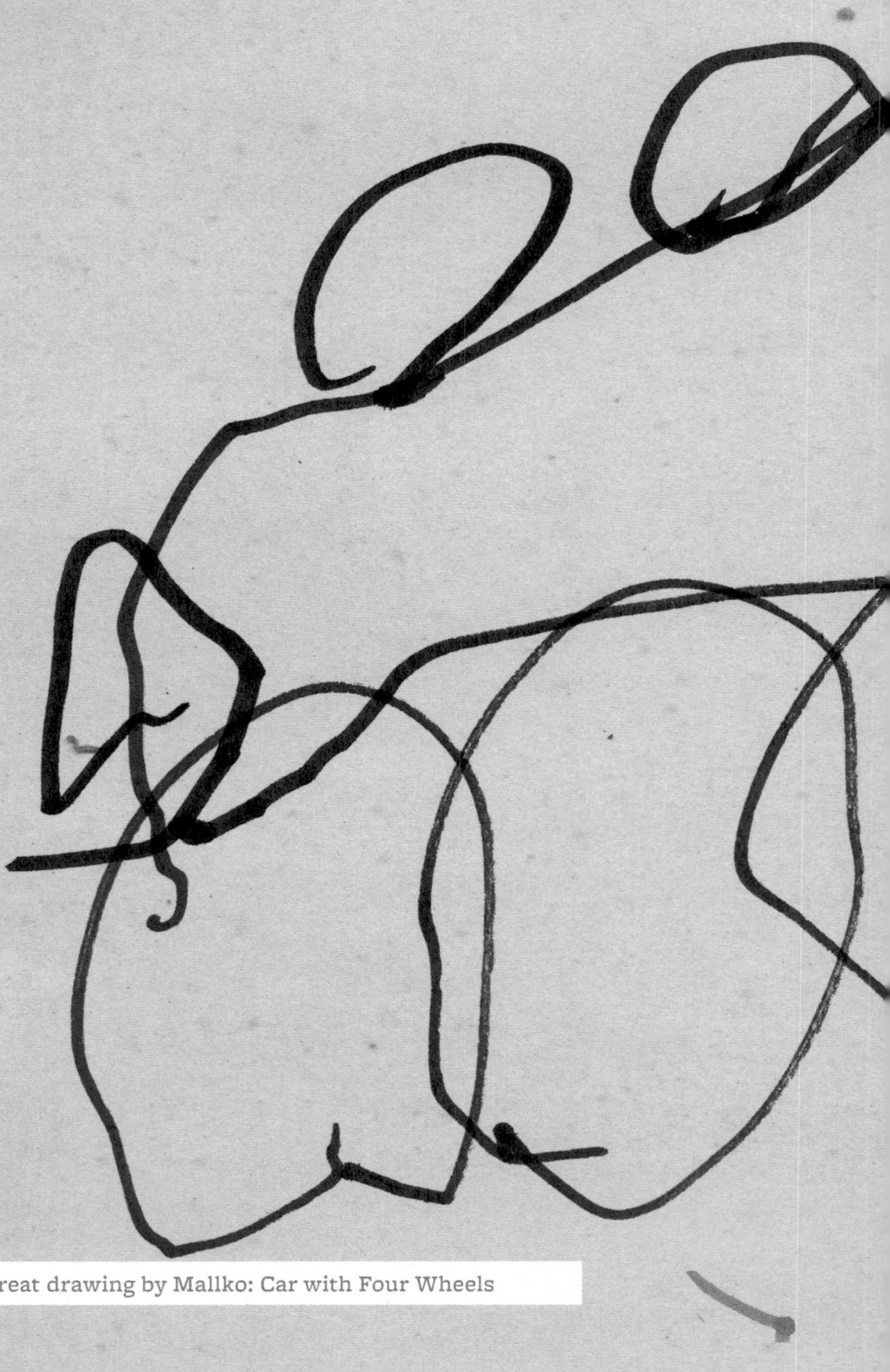

A great drawing by Mallko: Car with Four Wheels

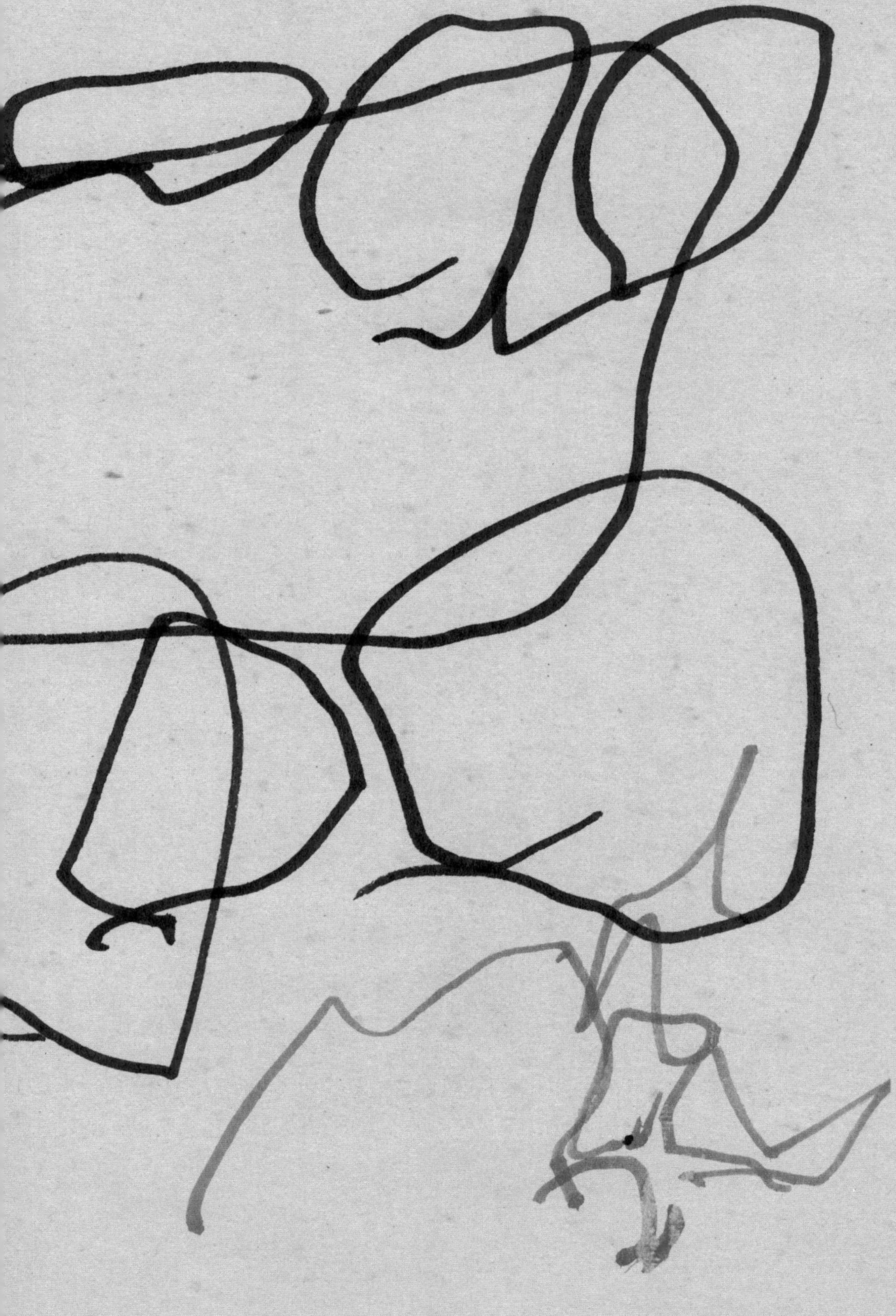

PIN PON PIN PON PIN

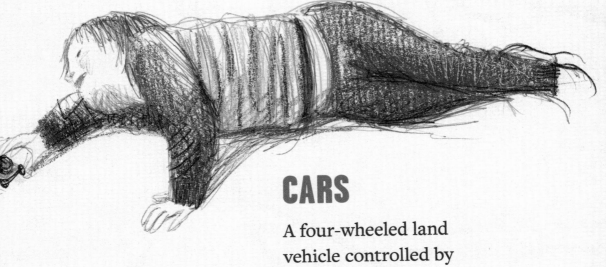

CARS

A four-wheeled land
vehicle controlled by
a steering wheel.

Mallko loves them and spends
a lot of time playing with them.

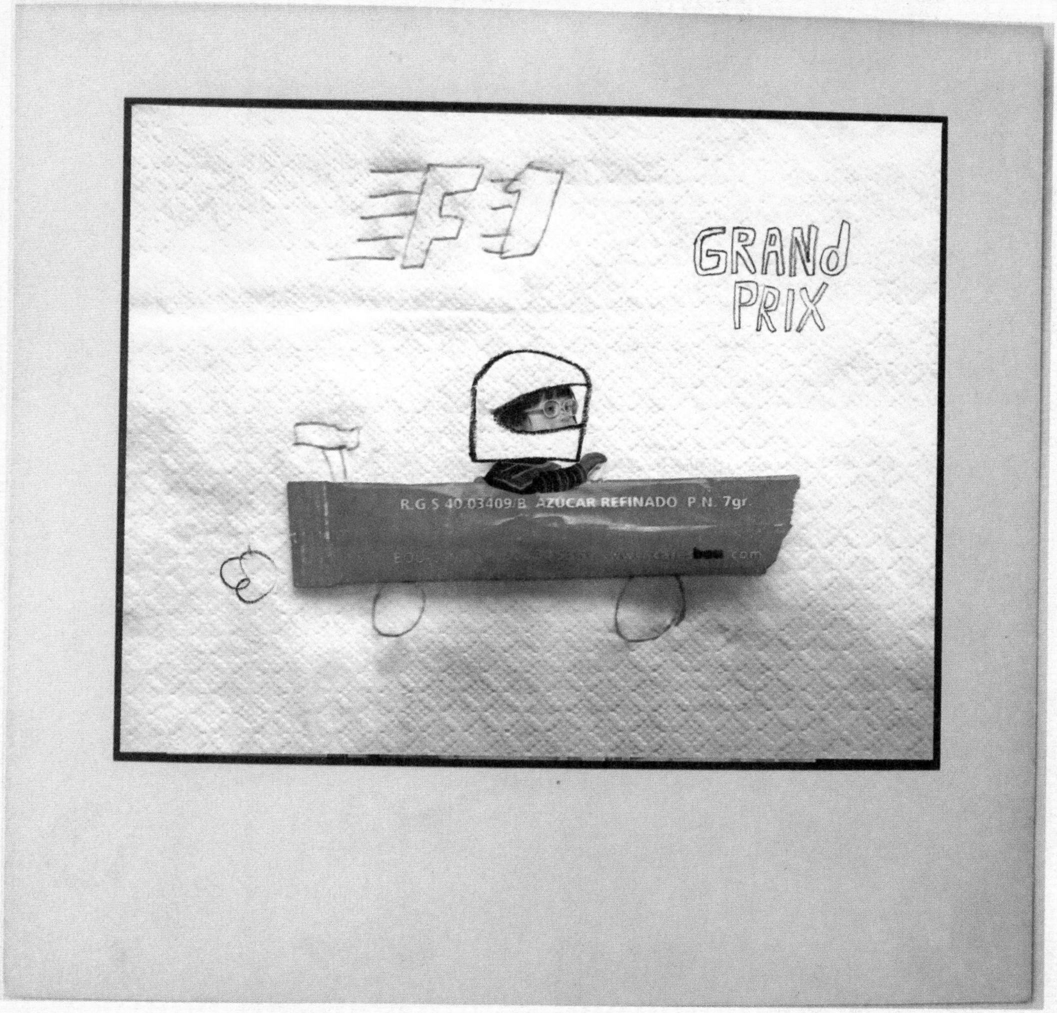
F1
GRAND PRIX
R.G.S 40.03409/B. AZUCAR REFINADO P.N. 7gr.

My father had a spare parts shop all his adult life.
So it's no surprise that those genes were transmitted to
Mallkito from his grandpa. I can't even change a spark plug.

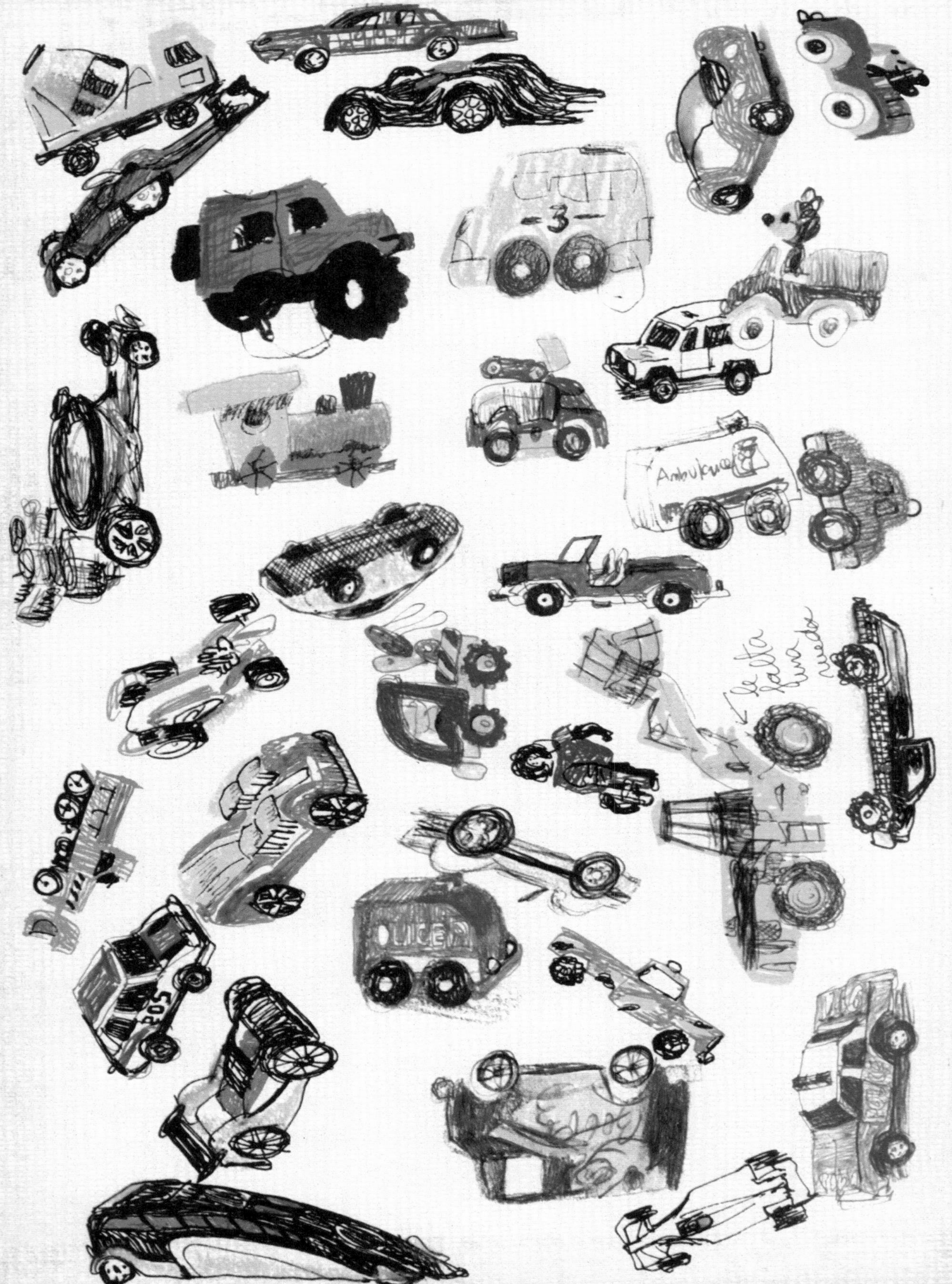
-3-
Ambulance

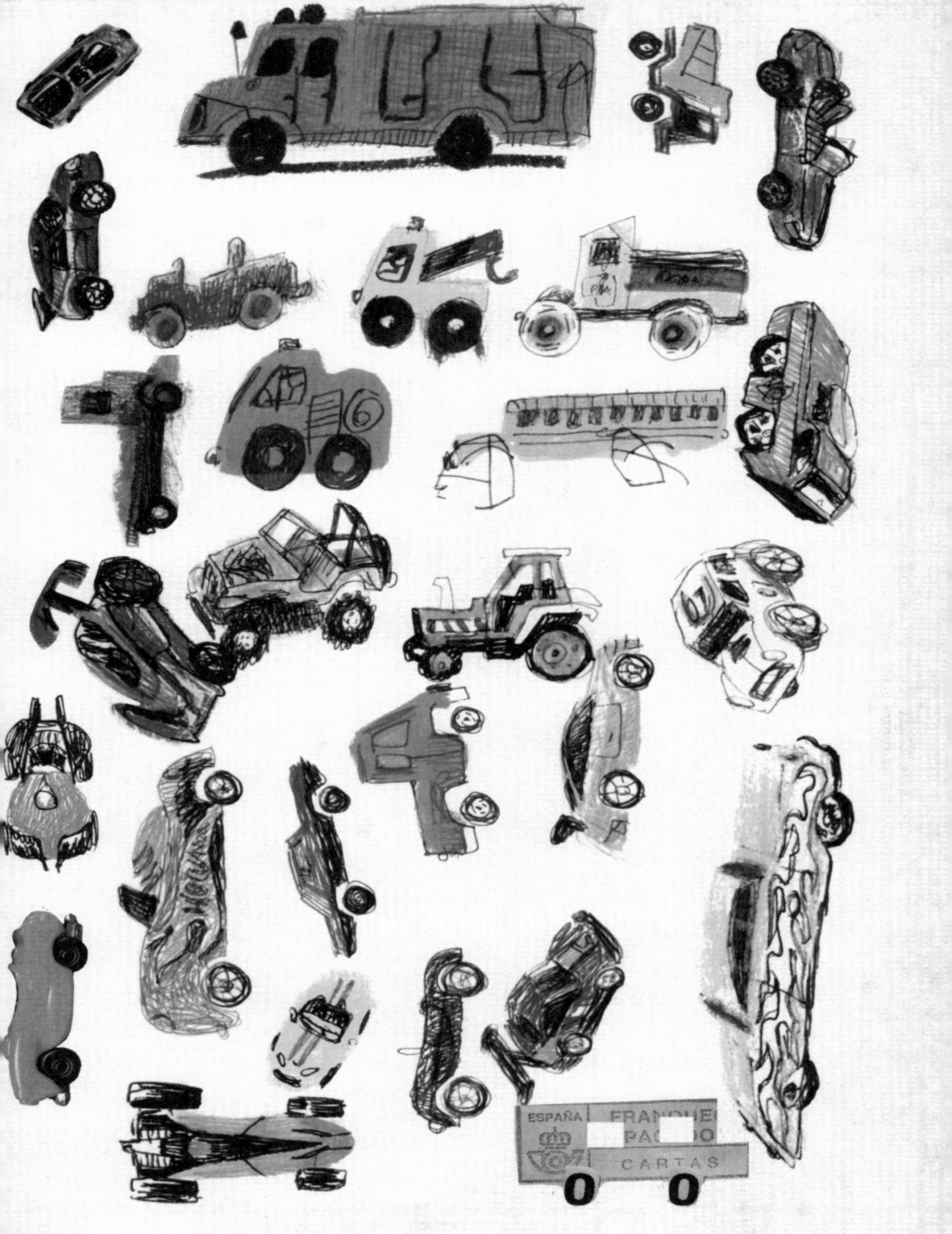
ESPAÑA
CARTAS

You like hugs and kisses.

LOVE

Tenderness or affection

for someone.

Be a little light for the world.

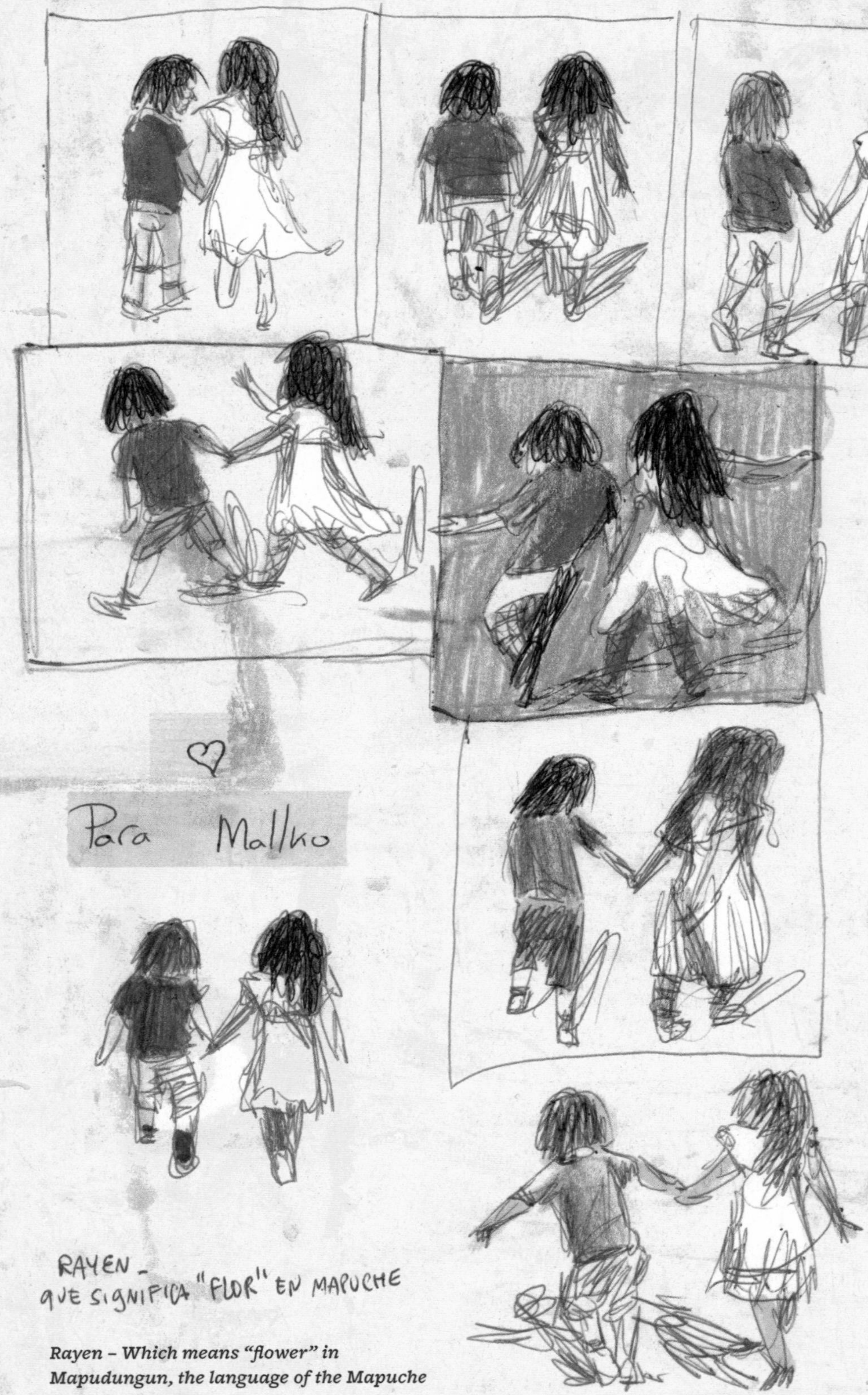
Para Mallko
RAYEN -
QUE SIGNIFICA "FLOR" EN MAPUCHE

Rayen – Which means "flower" in Mapudungun, the language of the Mapuche

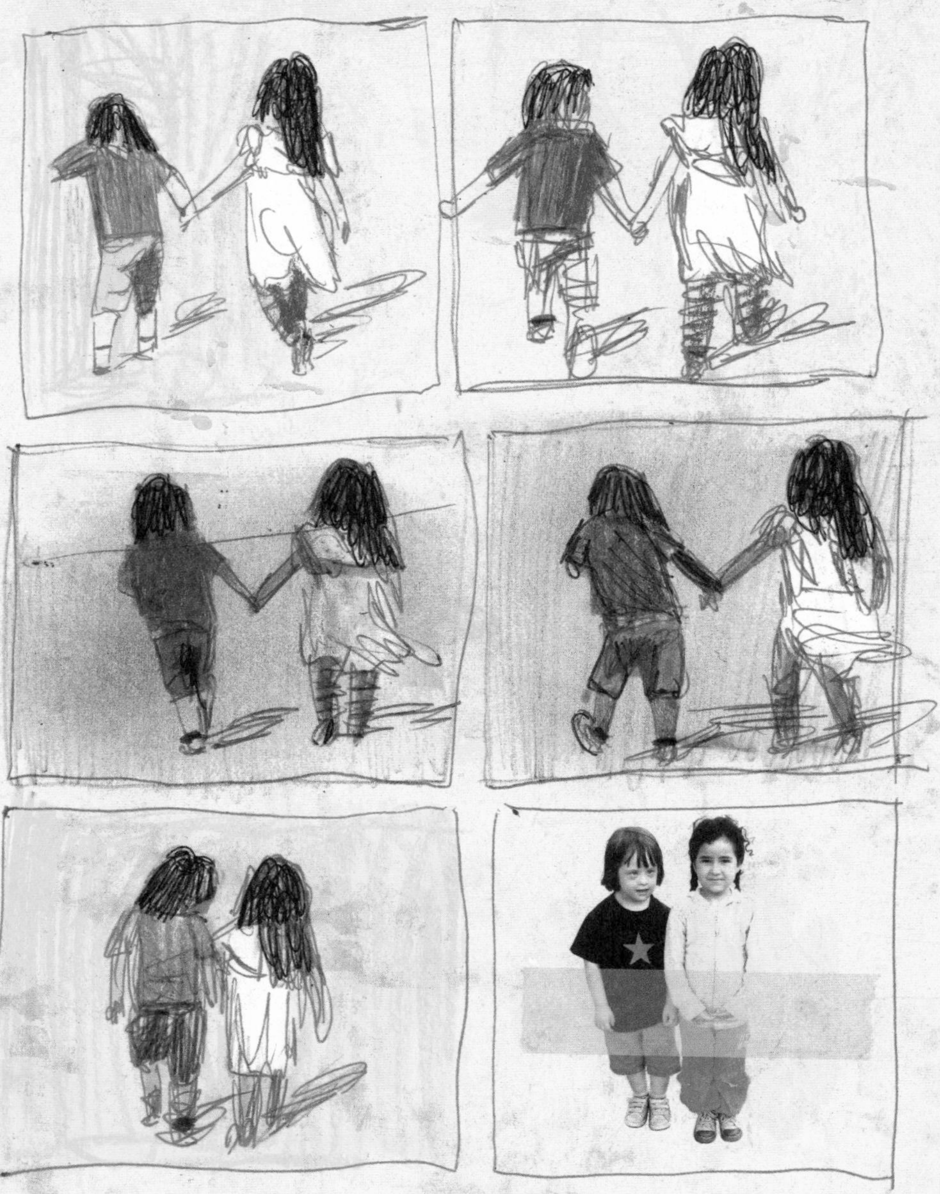

Dicen que puede ser que seas "especial" entre nosotros

Sabemos que eres Especial! Hemos convivido a tu lado estos días y nos has maravillado. Eres dulce, Eres tierno, bonito y bueno.

Cuando estamos a tu lado nos sentimos en el Cielo

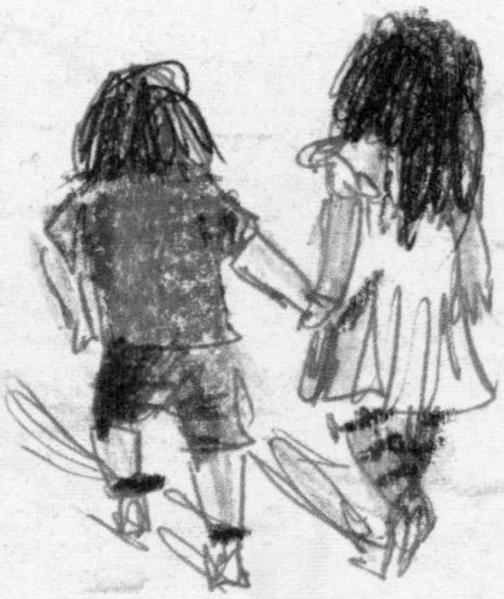

They say that you're special. We know you're special. From all our time together, we're in awe. You're sweet, tender, beautiful, and good. We're in heaven when we're with you.

MALLKO

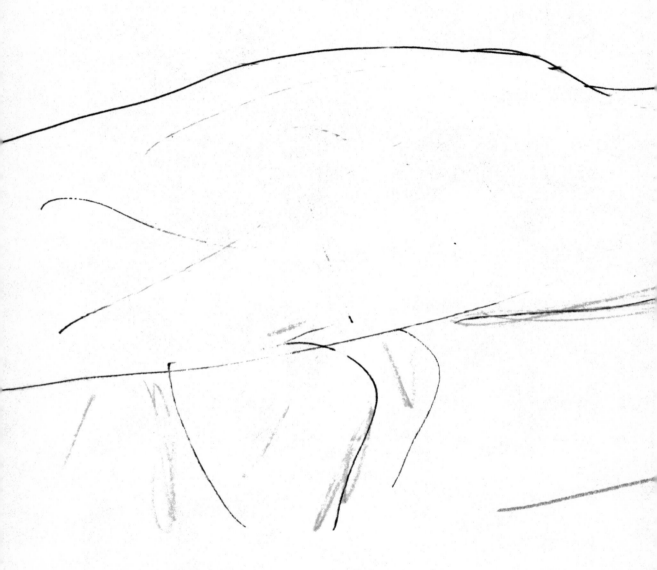

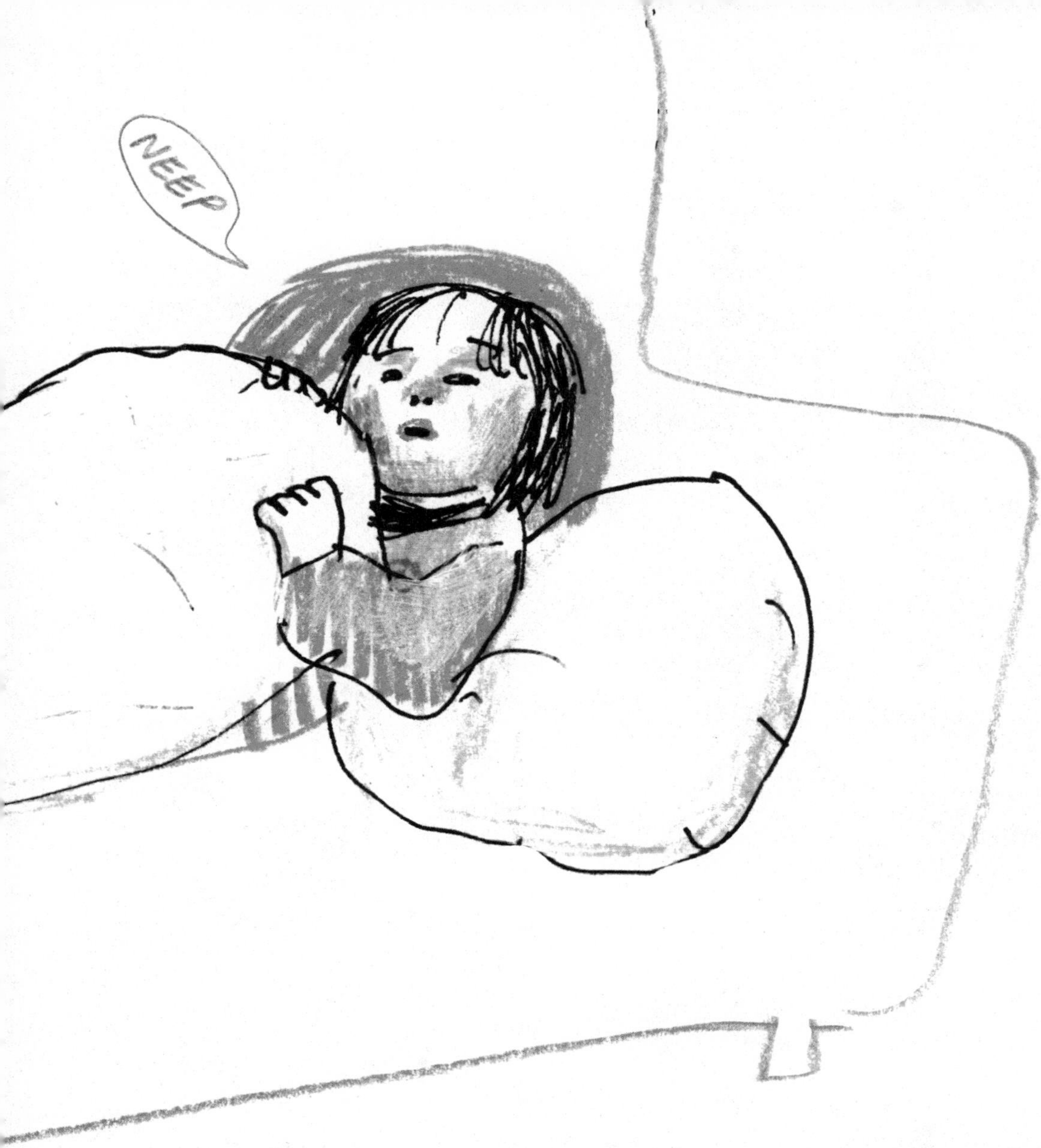
NEEP

MALLKO GO SLEEP
IN YOUR BED.

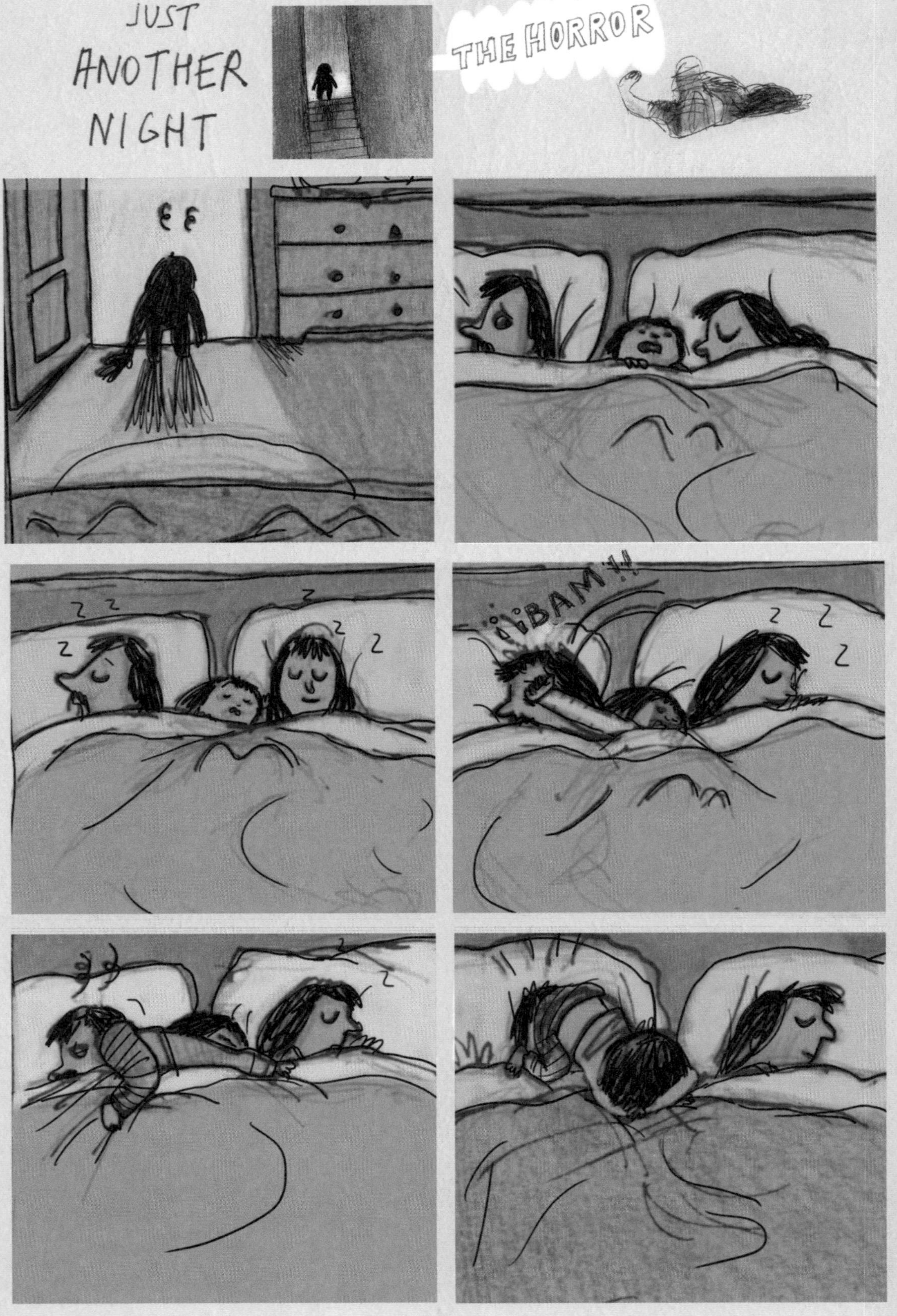
JUST ANOTHER NIGHT
THE HORROR
¡¡BAM!!

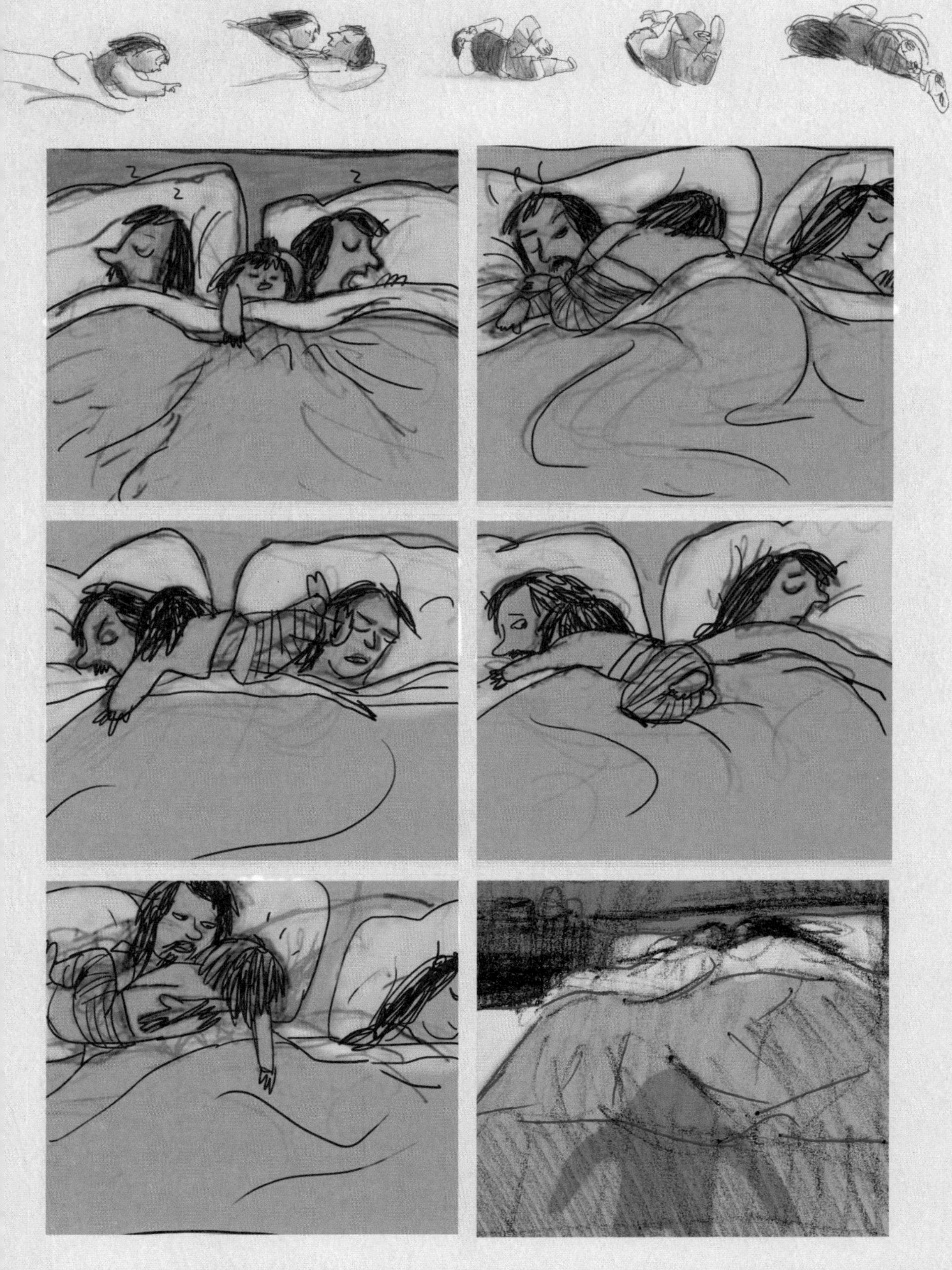
z
z
z

YOO HOOO!!!
DADDY, HUNGRY
HELLO

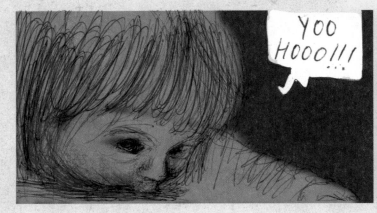

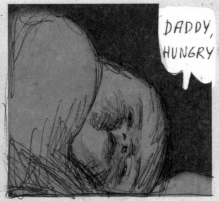

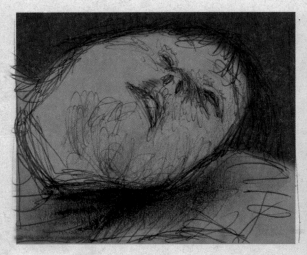

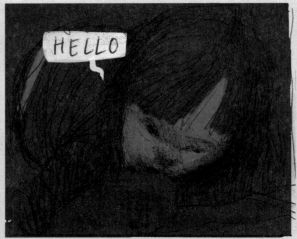

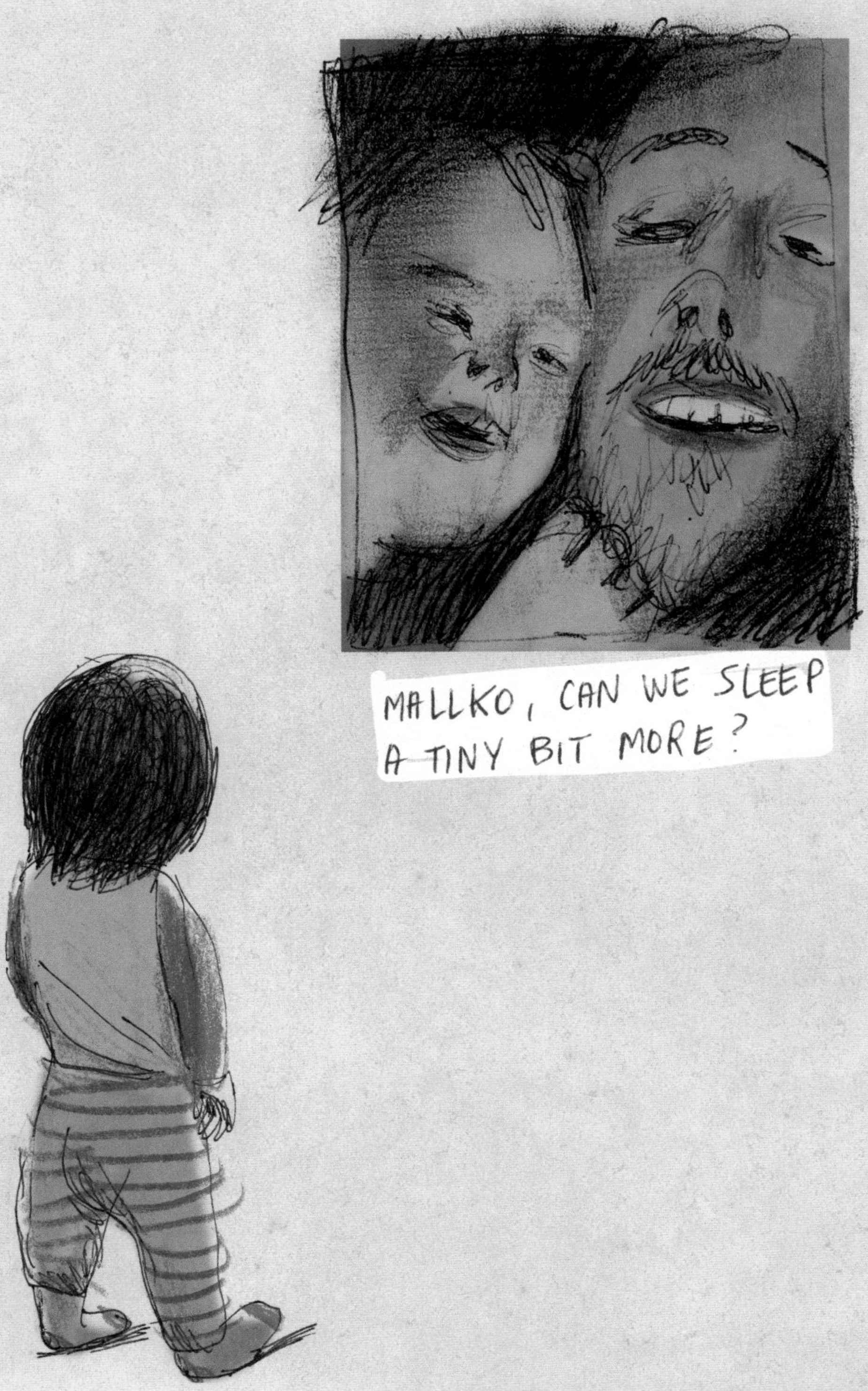
MALLKO, CAN WE SLEEP
A TINY BIT MORE?

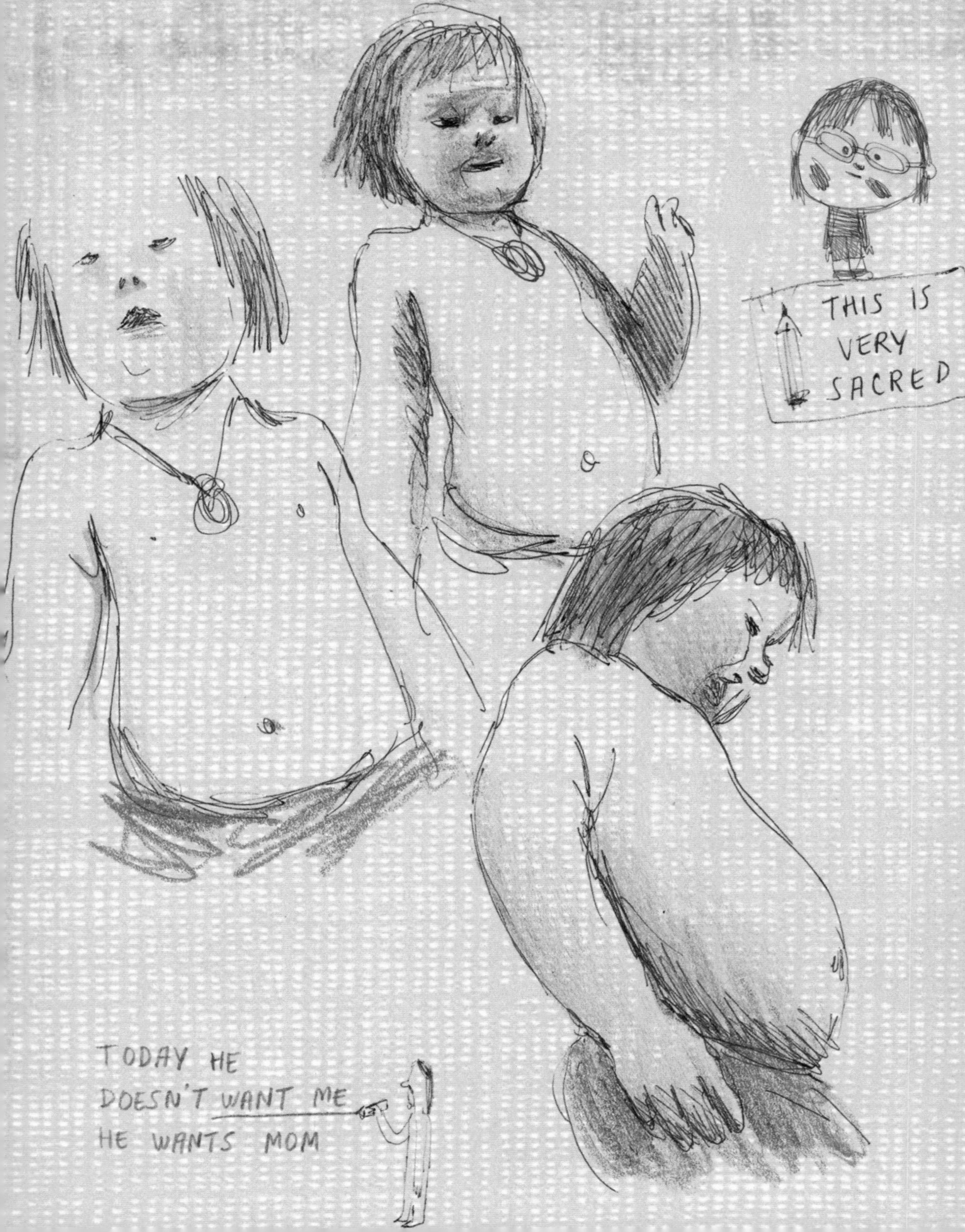
THIS IS VERY SACRED
TODAY HE DOESN'T WANT ME HE WANTS MOM

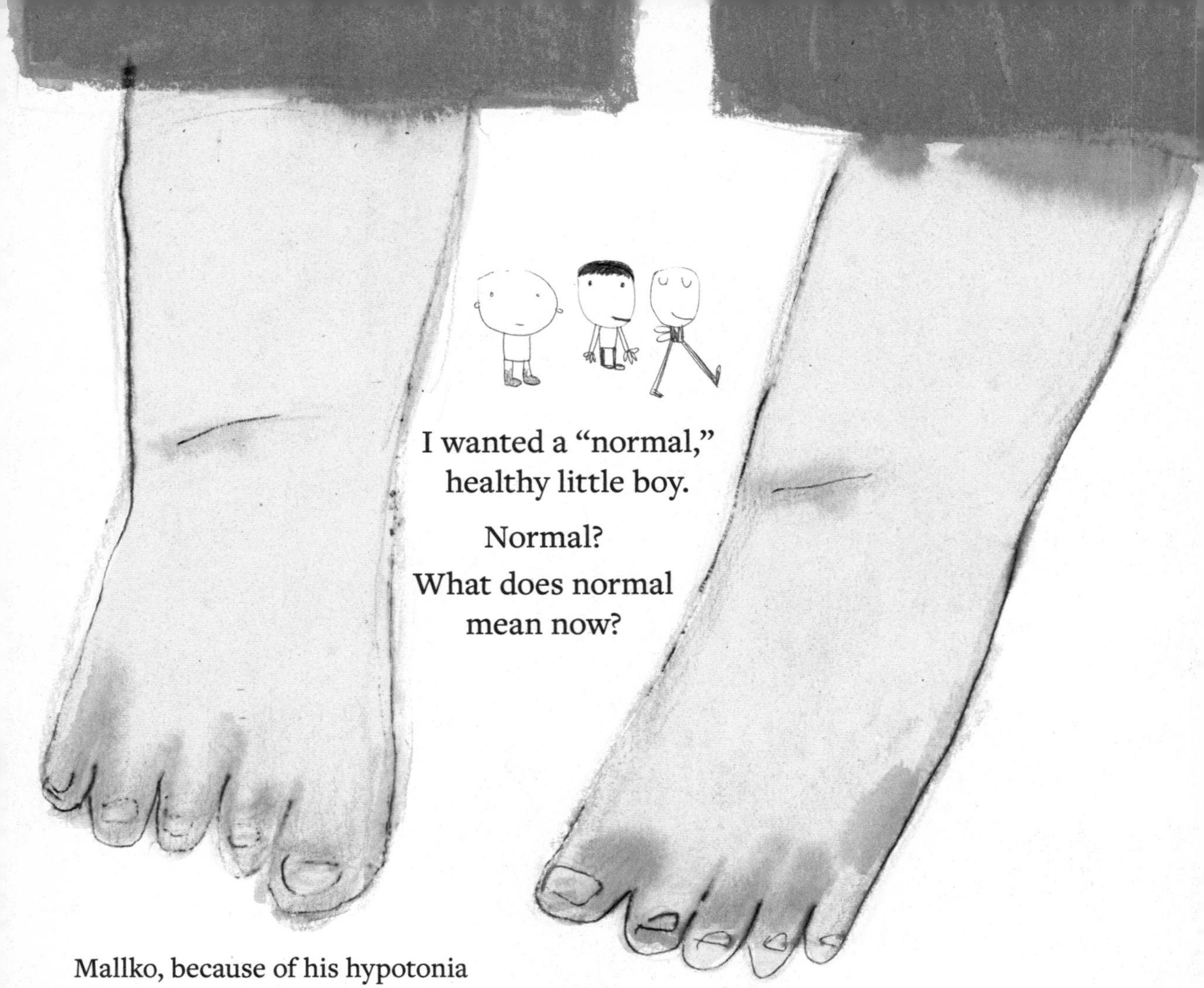

I wanted a "normal,"
healthy little boy.

Normal?

What does normal
mean now?

Mallko, because of his hypotonia (floppiness), is extremely flexible, like a yogi. When he doesn't want to move he falls down like a bag of sand.

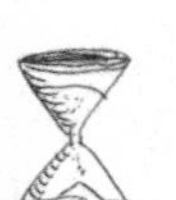

The bag of sand

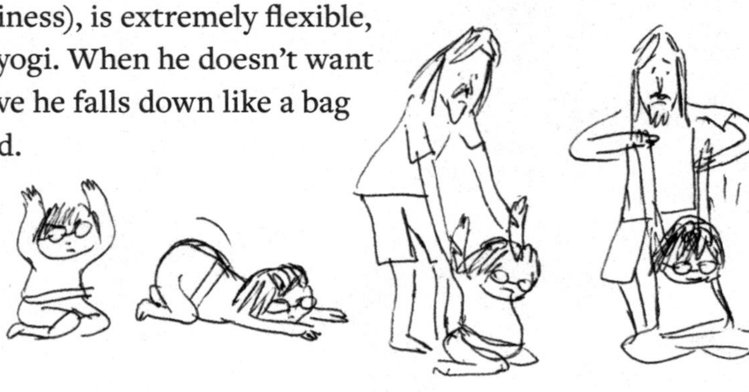

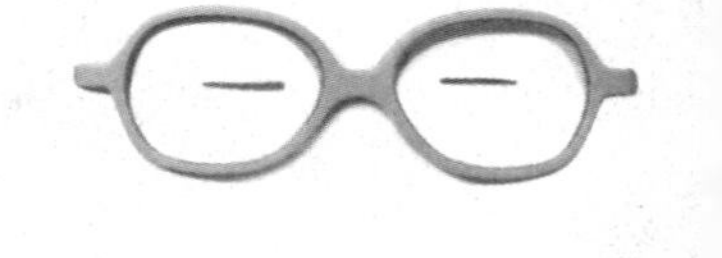
HE PUT ON HIS
GLASSES

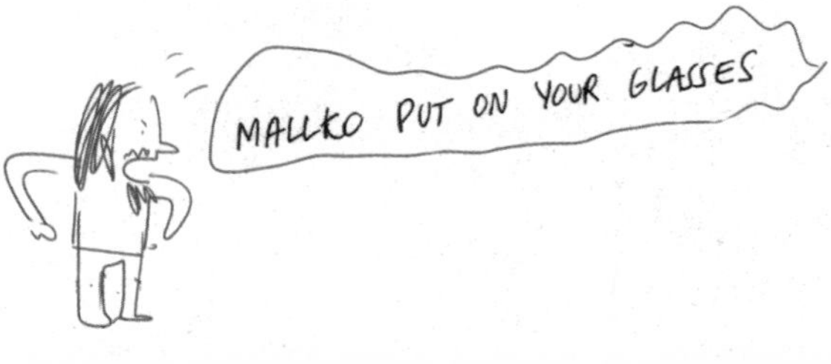
MALLKO PUT ON YOUR GLASSES

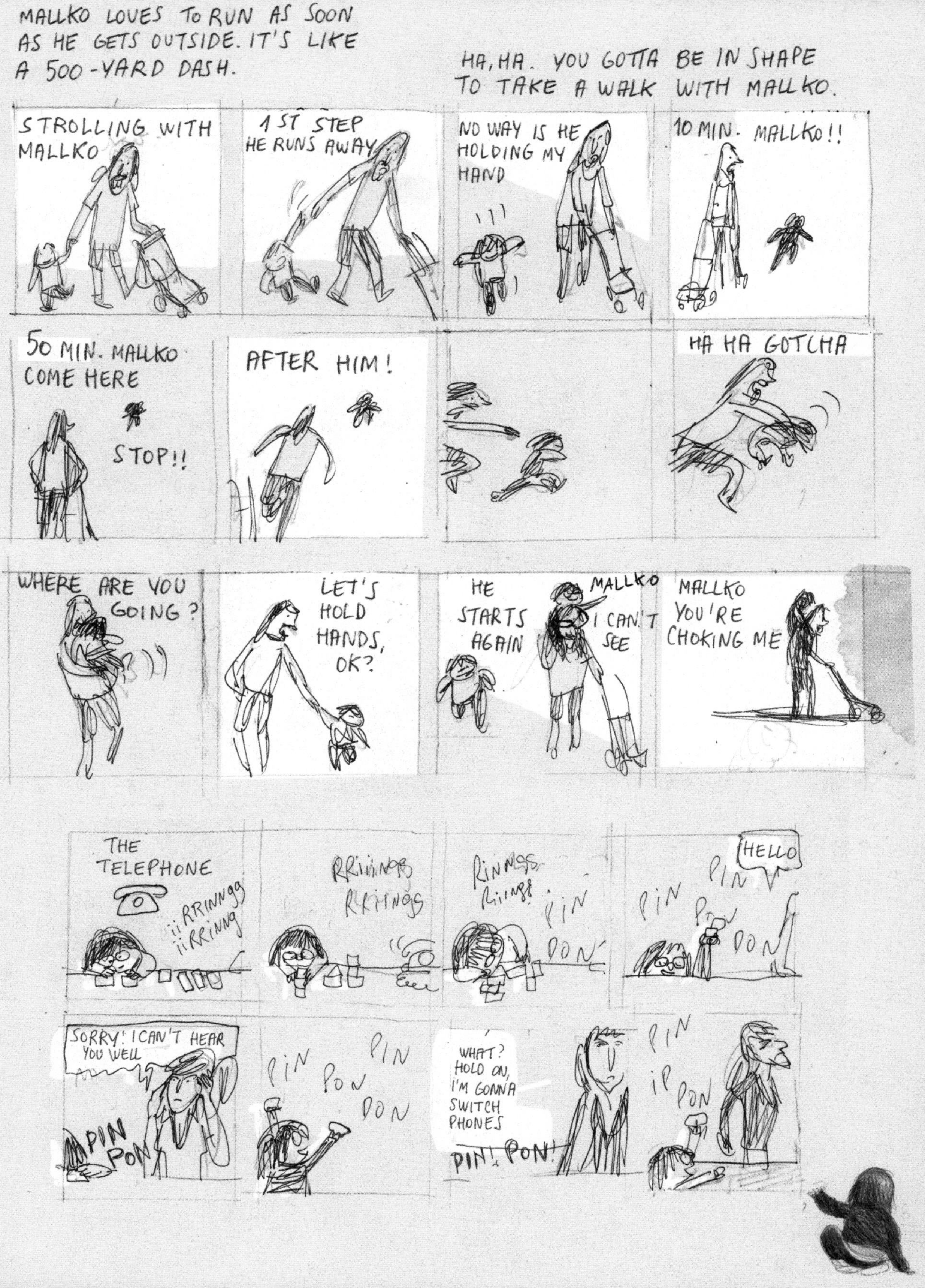
MALLKO LOVES TO RUN AS SOON AS HE GETS OUTSIDE. IT'S LIKE A 500-YARD DASH.
HA, HA. YOU GOTTA BE IN SHAPE TO TAKE A WALK WITH MALLKO.
STROLLING WITH MALLKO
1ST STEP HE RUNS AWAY
NO WAY IS HE HOLDING MY HAND
10 MIN. MALLKO!!
50 MIN. MALLKO COME HERE
STOP!!
AFTER HIM!
HA HA GOTCHA
WHERE ARE YOU GOING?
LET'S HOLD HANDS, OK?
HE STARTS AGAIN
MALLKO
I CAN'T SEE
MALLKO YOU'RE CHOKING ME
THE TELEPHONE
¡¡RRINNGG ¡¡RRING
RRIiiiNGS
RRIiiNGS
RINNGS
RiiNGS
PIN
DON
PIN
PIN
PON
DON
HELLO
SORRY! I CAN'T HEAR YOU WELL
PIN PON
PIN
PIN
PON
DON
WHAT? HOLD ON, I'M GONNA SWITCH PHONES
PIN! PON!
PIN
IP
PON

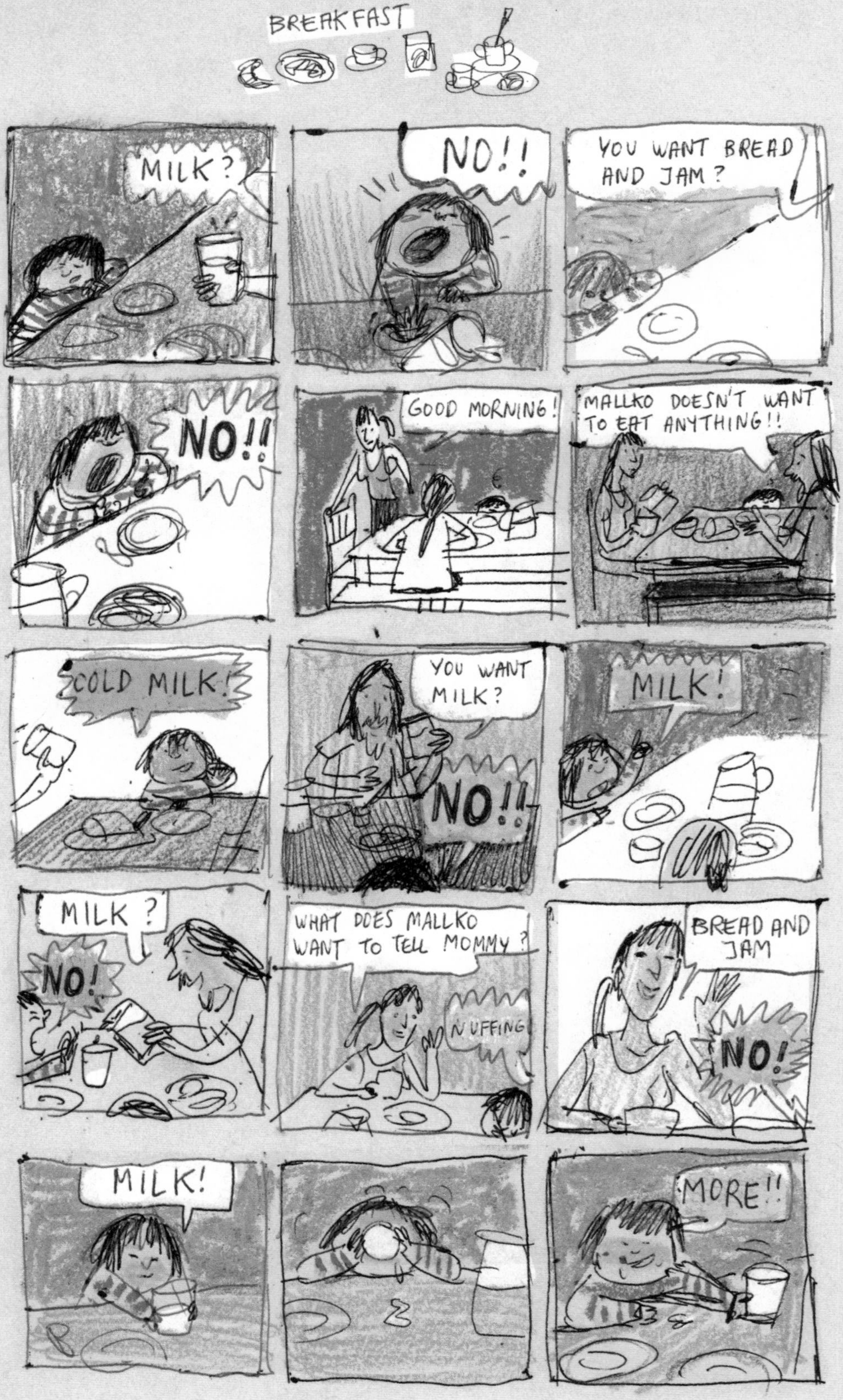
BREAKFAST
MILK?
NO!!
YOU WANT BREAD AND JAM?
NO!!
GOOD MORNING!
MALLKO DOESN'T WANT TO EAT ANYTHING!!
COLD MILK!
YOU WANT MILK?
NO!!
MILK!
MILK?
NO!
WHAT DOES MALLKO WANT TO TELL MOMMY?
NUFFING
BREAD AND JAM
NO!
MILK!
MORE!!

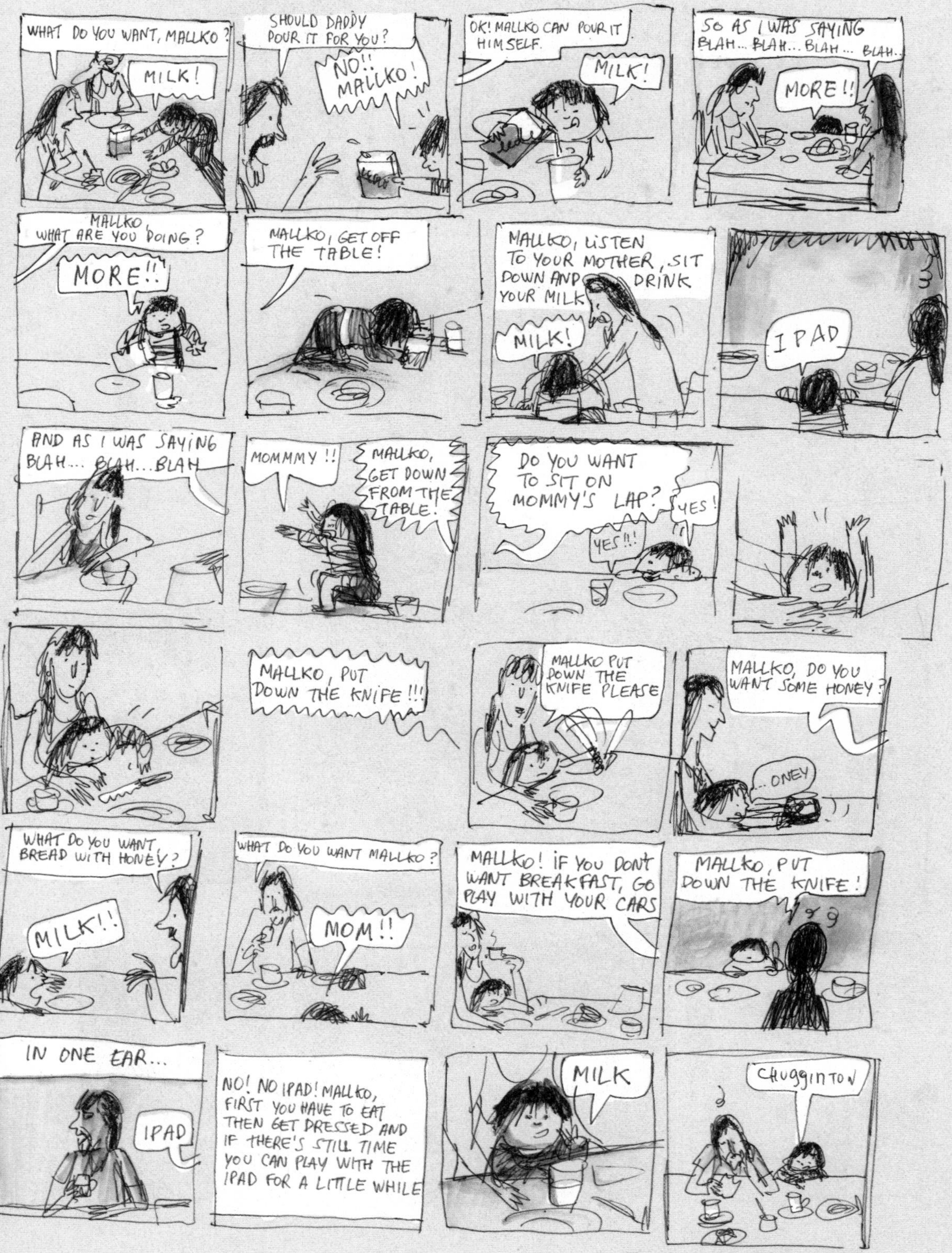
WHAT DO YOU WANT, MALLKO?
MILK!
SHOULD DADDY POUR IT FOR YOU?
NO!! MALLKO!
OK! MALLKO CAN POUR IT HIMSELF.
MILK!
SO AS I WAS SAYING BLAH... BLAH... BLAH... BLAH...
MORE!!
MALLKO, WHAT ARE YOU DOING?
MORE!!
MALLKO, GET OFF THE TABLE!
MALLKO, LISTEN TO YOUR MOTHER, SIT DOWN AND DRINK YOUR MILK
MILK!
IPAD
AND AS I WAS SAYING BLAH.... BLAH...BLAH
MOMMMY!!
MALLKO, GET DOWN FROM THE TABLE!
DO YOU WANT TO SIT ON MOMMY'S LAP?
YES!
YES!!!
MALLKO, PUT DOWN THE KNIFE!!!
MALLKO PUT DOWN THE KNIFE PLEASE
MALLKO, DO YOU WANT SOME HONEY?
...ONEY
WHAT DO YOU WANT, BREAD WITH HONEY?
MILK!!
WHAT DO YOU WANT MALLKO?
MOM!!
MALLKO! IF YOU DON'T WANT BREAKFAST, GO PLAY WITH YOUR CARS
MALLKO, PUT DOWN THE KNIFE!
IN ONE EAR...
IPAD
NO! NO IPAD! MALLKO, FIRST YOU HAVE TO EAT THEN GET DRESSED AND IF THERE'S STILL TIME YOU CAN PLAY WITH THE IPAD FOR A LITTLE WHILE
MILK
CHUGGINTON

Chugginton = a cartoon about trains

BATHTIME

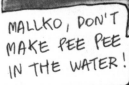

MALLKO !! IT'S BATHTIME

MALLKO, DON'T MAKE PEE PEE IN THE WATER !

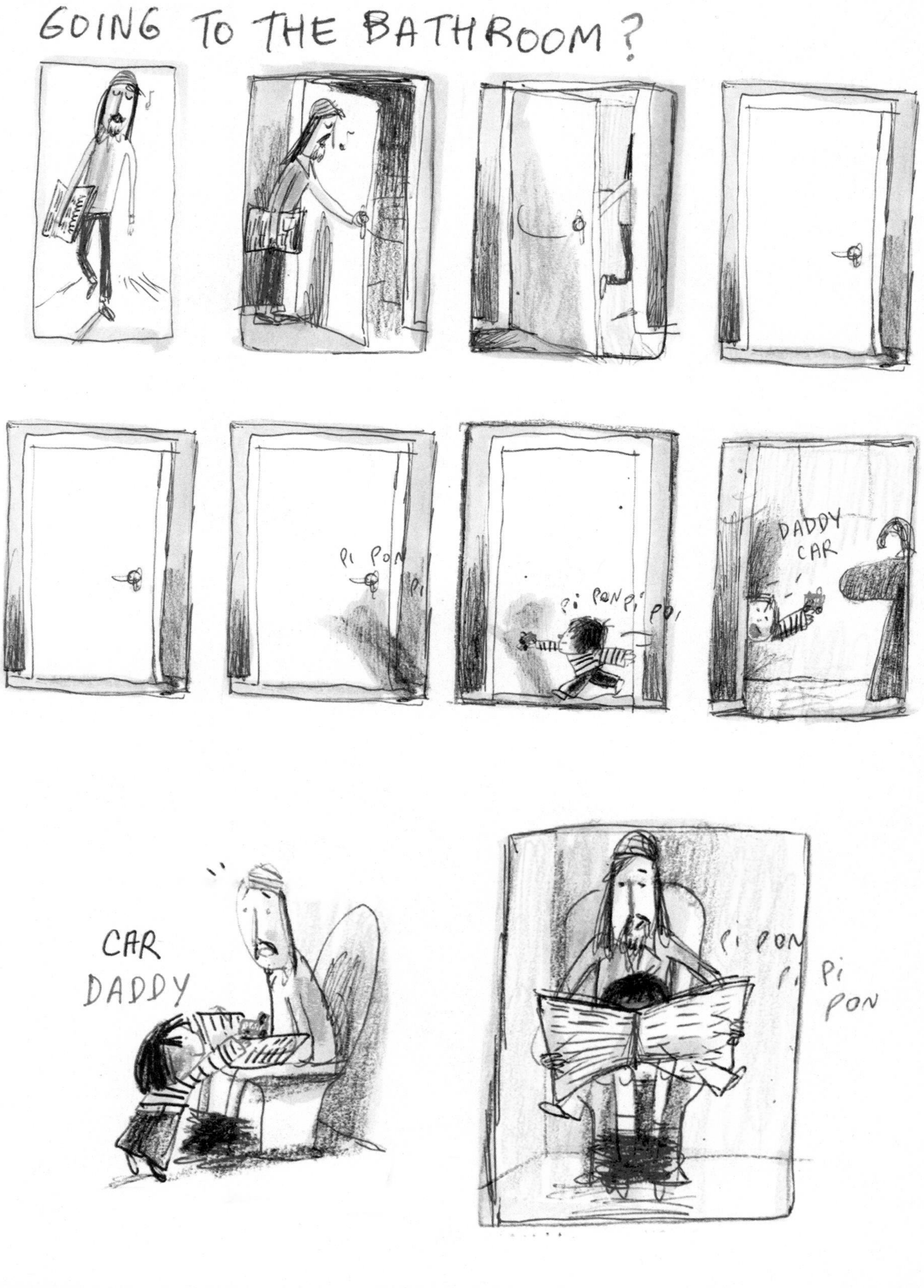

GOING TO THE BATHROOM?
PI PON
PI
PI PON PI PO
DADDY CAR
CAR DADDY
PI PON
PI PI
PON

When he gets angry,
he puts on his angry face.
It's very important to
put on the angry face.
He also knows how to
make a sad face.

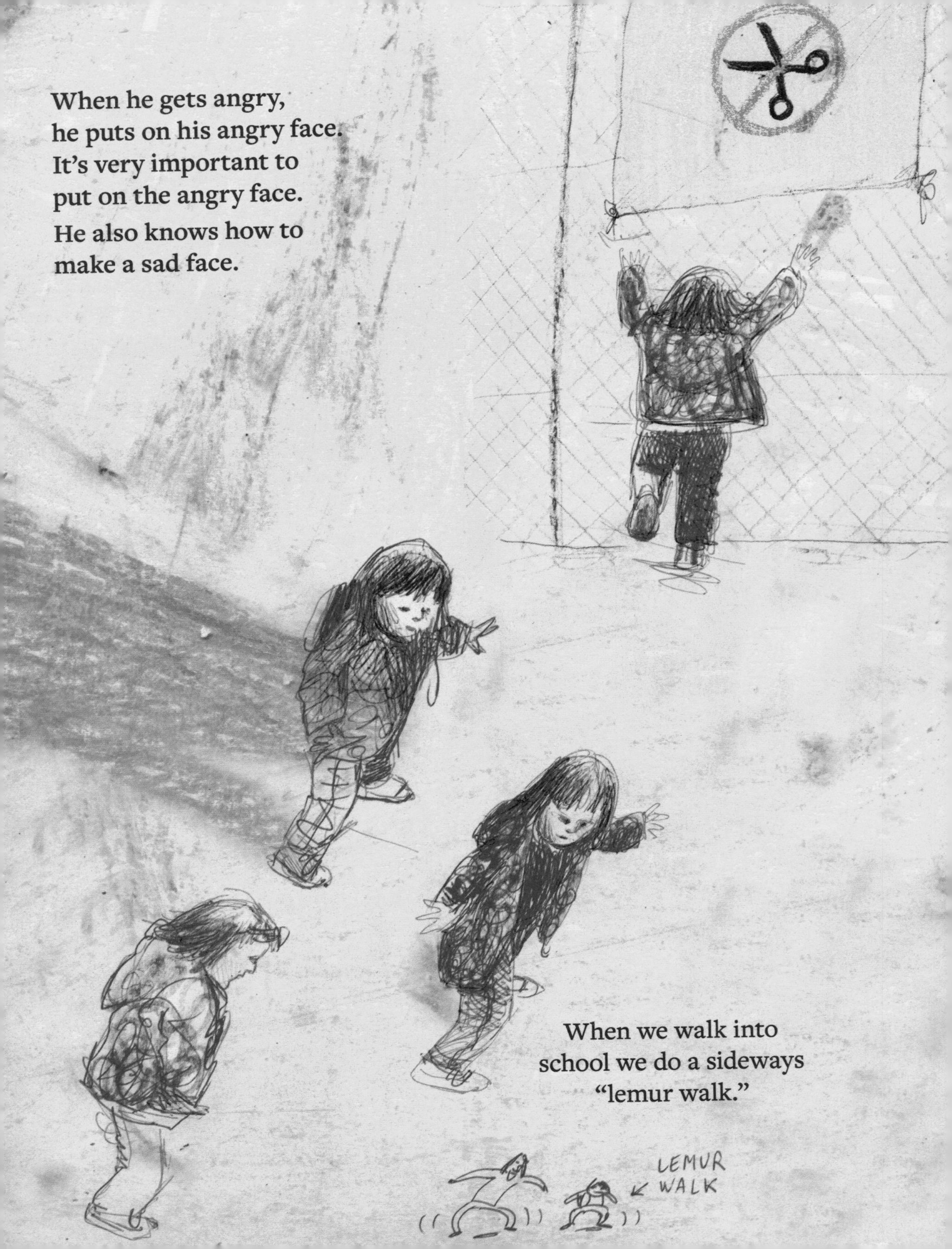
LEMUR
WALK

When we walk into
school we do a sideways
"lemur walk."

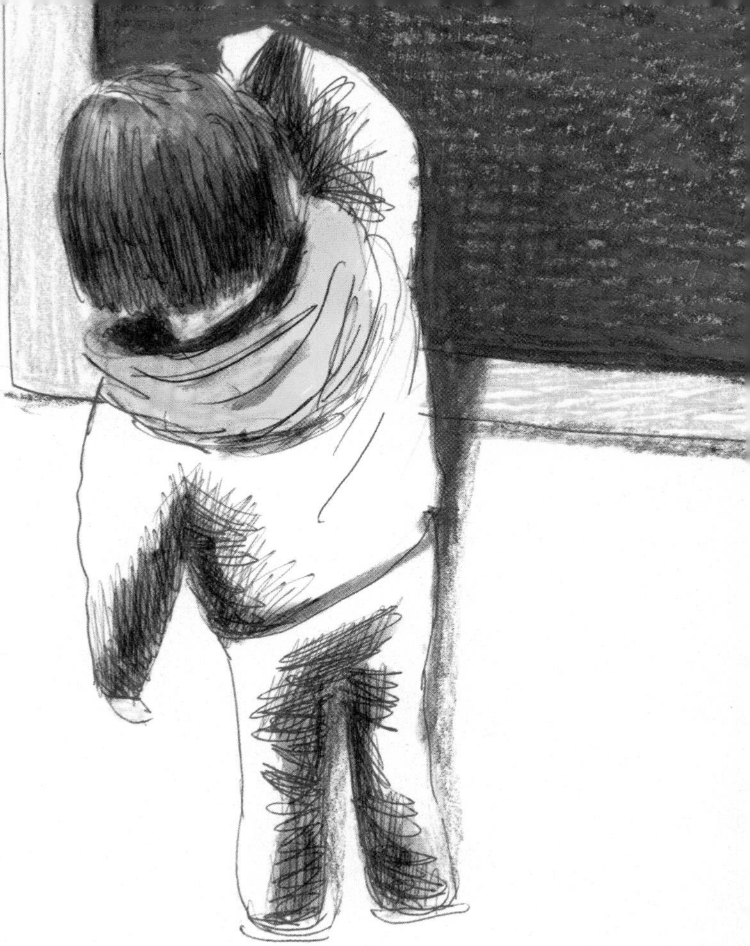

SCHOOL

A public institution of learning

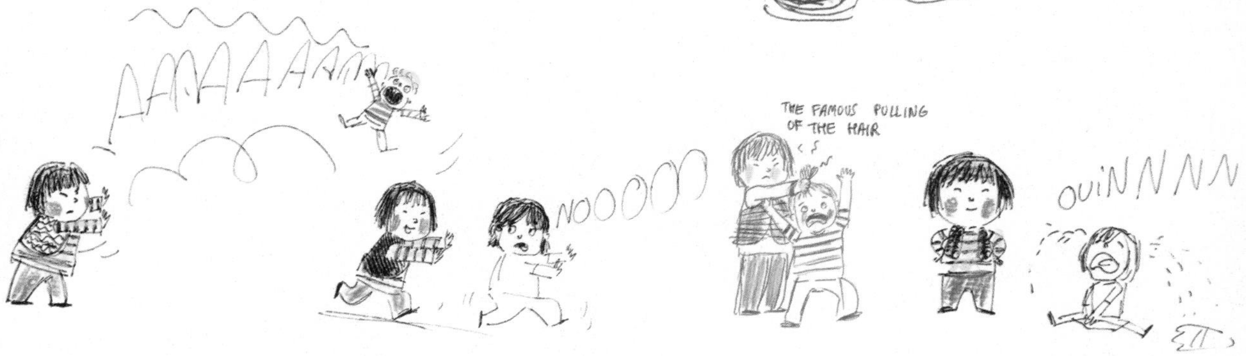
NOOOOO
THE FAMOUS PULLING OF THE HAIR
OUiNNNN

In his first year of school, Mallko was docile and affectionate.
His way of relating to other kids was pulling their hair. Or pushing them.
Because it really got his attention if they cried or shouted.
So in the beginning, Mallko used this kind of play to relate to others.

Of course, Mallko can learn with everyone else. For both the children and their parents, it's an opportunity to relate to someone who's really different as an equal.

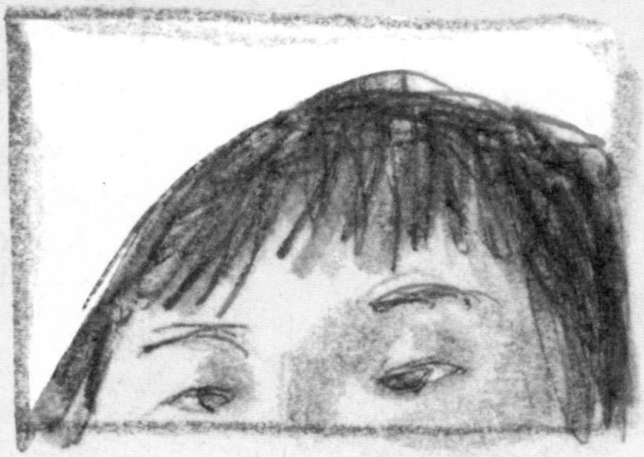

MALLKO'S EYES ARE LIKE TWO LITTLE FISH.

THREE, THREE

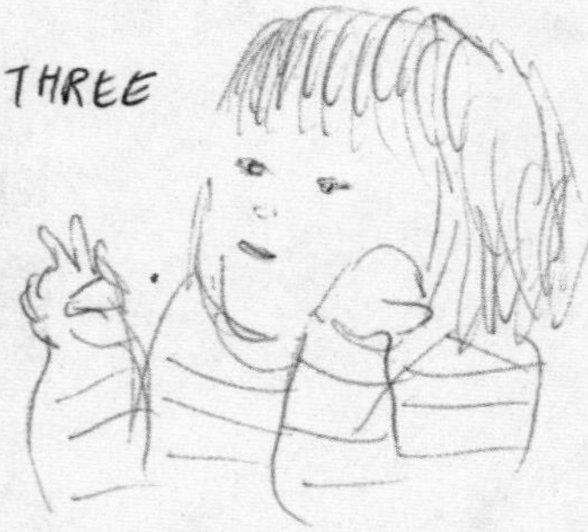

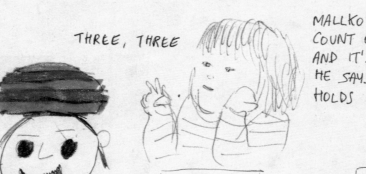

MALLKO'S TRYING TO COUNT ON HIS FINGERS, AND IT'S REALLY FUNNY. HE SAYS THREE AND HOLDS UP TWO FINGERS.

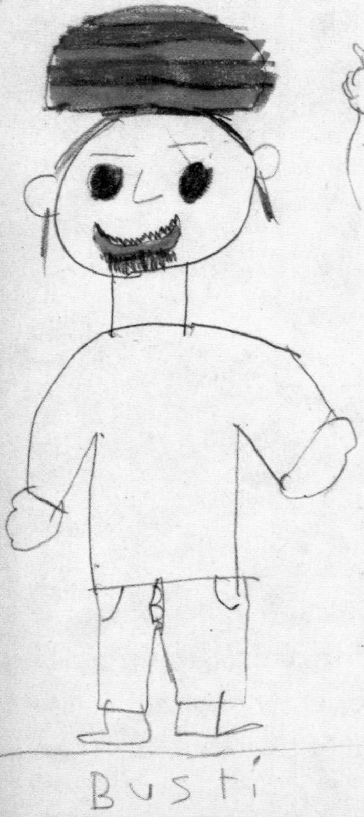
BUSTI

I'M SCARED!

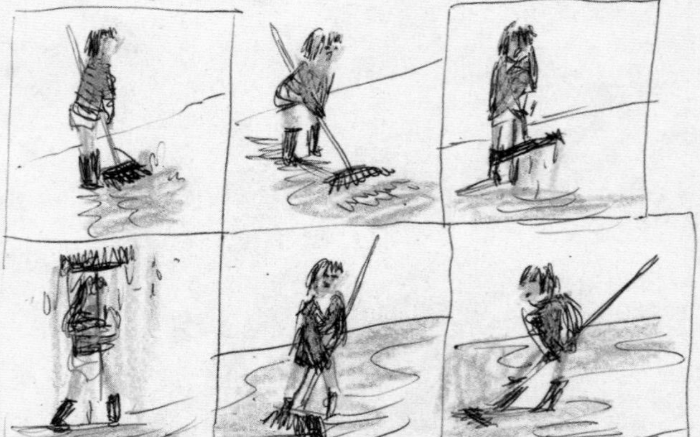

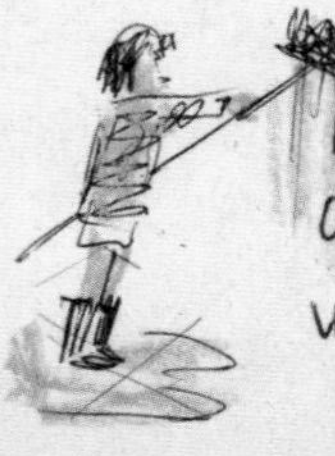

MALLKO LOVES TO HELP OUT BY MOPPING THE PATIO. WHO CAN RESIST HELP LIKE THI

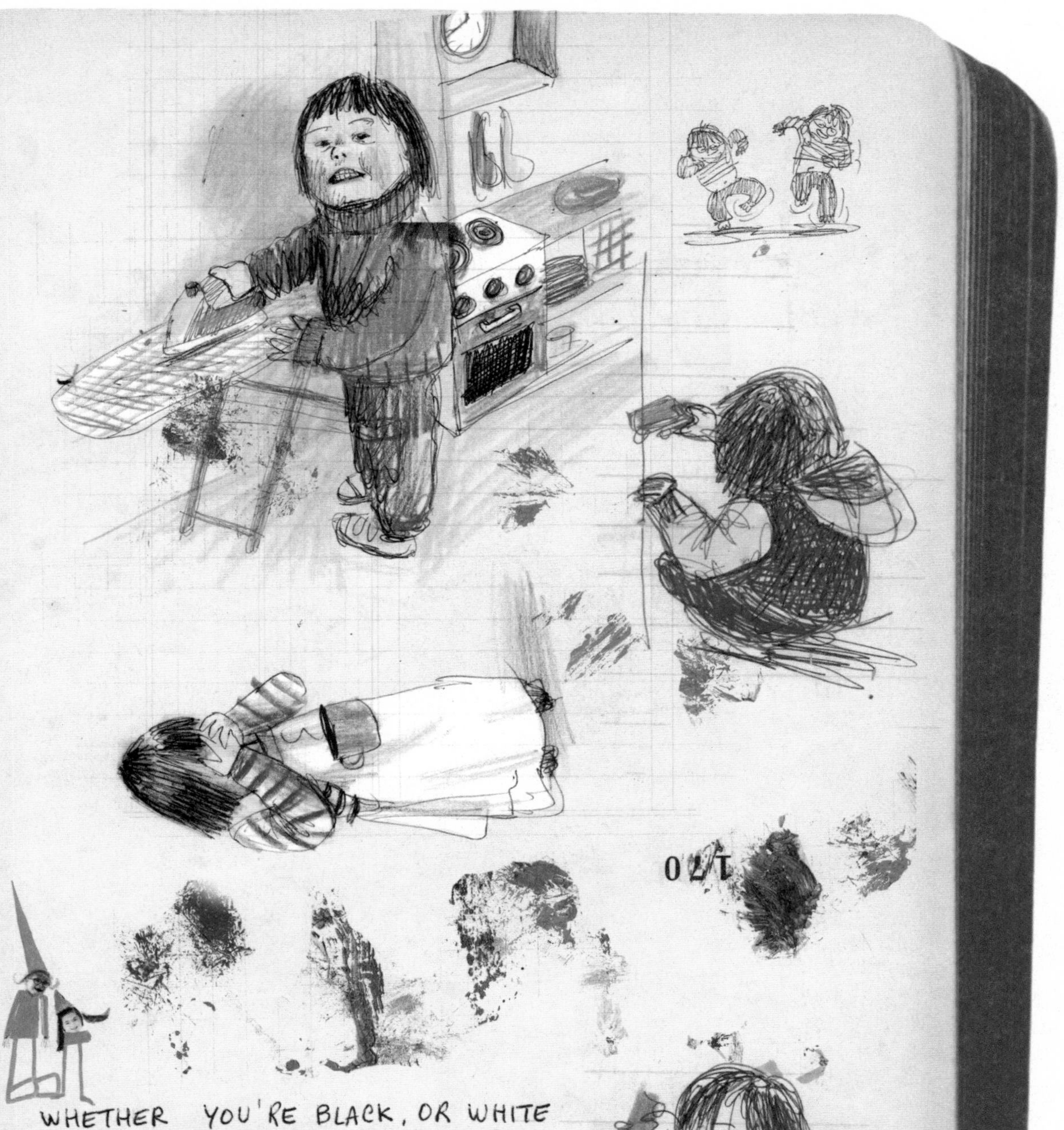

WHETHER YOU'RE BLACK, OR WHITE
WHETHER YOU'RE BIG OR SMALL
WHETHER YOUR HAIR IS BLOND OR BROWN
WHETHER YOU'RE AN OLD OR NEW STUDENT
YOU ARE THE CENTER OF THIS CENTER
OF THIS CENTER, YOU'RE THE CENTER

(Excerpt from the Eladi Homs school song)

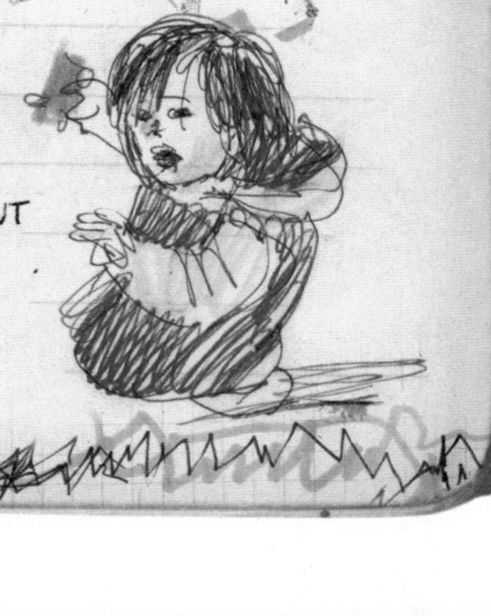

My mother asks me if all kids with Down
syndrome have bowl haircuts and why
I don't give him a more modern look.

THE TRUTH IS
I LET MY HAIR
GROW TO COPY
THE GUY FROM
THE RED HOT
CHILI PEPPERS!

This page is dedicated to Clarita,
my mother, who still tells me,
even though I'm over 50:
"Son, get a haircut, they're going
to put you behind bars."

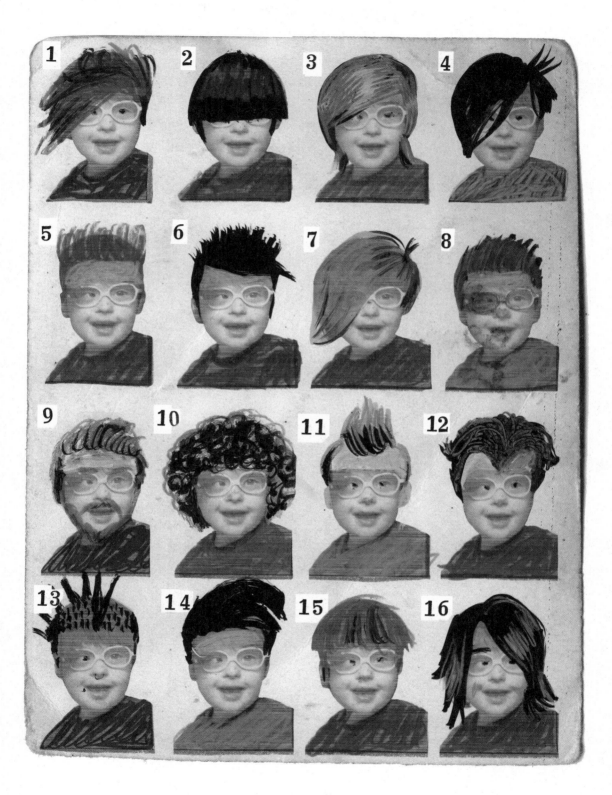

MONDAY, AUGUST 27   11:00 AM

WE ARE AT TERRAZA HOSPITAL, WE HAVE TO DO AN ECHOCARDIOGRAM, MALLKO'S SLEEPING, UNAWARE OF ANYTHING AROUND HIM. THE DAY IS HOT AND STICKY.

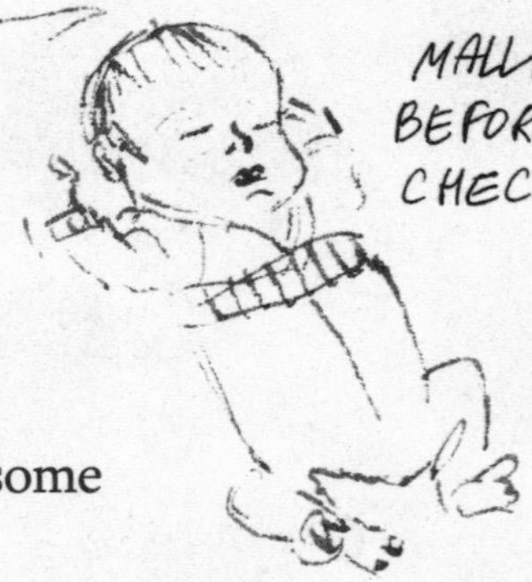

MALLKO SLEEPING BEFORE HIS HEART CHECK-UP

HOSPITAL-DOCTORS

People with Down syndrome usually have some cardiopathy or heart problems.

When we had to do Mallko's check-up, Juanma, a biologist friend who works with eagles, especially imperial eagles, sent me a rock in the shape of a heart that he found on the beach in New Zealand. It is exactly identical to the heart of an imperial eagle. Really. Luckily, Mallko's heart was just fine. Thank goodness.

The coronary grooves are marked in blue

The two sides of the stone heart

Mallko Papá

This stone is like the heart of the male imperial eagle. In birds of prey, the front of the heart is rounded, while the back is slightly flat.

Magic is in the heart

The more it gives, the more it has.

The more it shrinks, the more it expands later

The younger it is, the faster it beats

The older it is, the more it softens

The more you use it, the more it grows

The more it hurts, the more it heals

When it beats for two, soon it will beat for three

If it beats for three, it beats for everyone

When it stops beating, others beat for it

Magic is in the heart

A huge hug, Mallko

His eagle heart is fine.

Magic is in the heart

The more it gives, the more it has.

The more it shrinks, the more it expands later

The younger it is, the faster it beats

The older it is, the more it softens

The more you use it, the more it grows

The more it hurts, the more it heals

When it beats for two, soon it will beat for three

If it beats for three, it beats for everyone

When it stops beating, others beat for it

Magic is in the heart

A huge hug, Maliko

His eagle heart is fine.

La magia está en el Corazón

Cuanto más se da, más se tiene.
Cuanto más se encoge, más grande
se hace luego
Cuanto más niño, más deprisa late
Cuanto más viejo, más se ablanda
Cuanto más se ejercita, más crece
Cuanto más duele, más cura.
Cuando late por dos, ya laten tres
Si late por tres, late por todos
Cuando deja de latir, otros laten por él
La magia está en el corazón

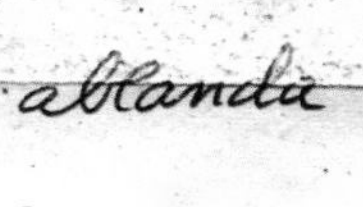

Un Cariño Gigante, Malko

JH + Ursula + Adi

SU CORAZÓN DE ÁGUILA ESTÁ BIEN.

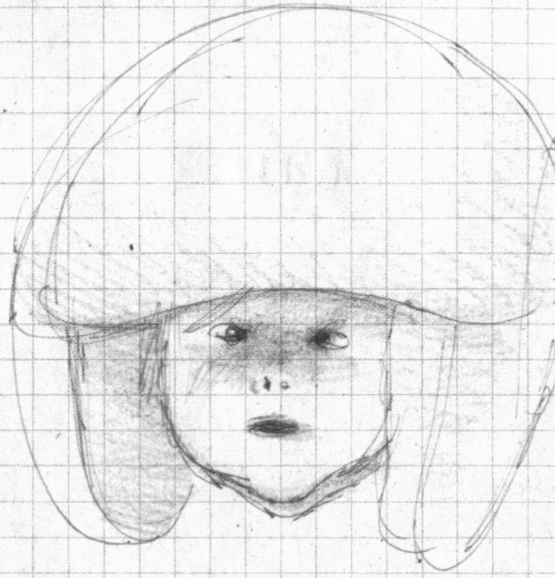

Pediatra, Homeópata, NEUROPEDIATRA, Logopeda, Endocrinologa, Quiropráctico, Fisioterapeuta, Psicólogo ...

Pediatrician, homeopath, neuropediatrician, speech therapist, endocrinologist, chiropractor, physical therapist, psychologist...

→ son: Gabriela D, Álvaro L P, Dra ARELLANO, Chus, Rosaángela T, Guillaume L, Lali, Neus...

Y pensar que antes, era una radical de la homeopatía y de los remedios naturales.

✿ Mallko me enseñó a ver el lado bueno a la medicina alopática.

And to think that I used to be a radical proponent of homeopathy and natural remedies. Mallko taught me to see the good side of mainstream medicine.

We deal with things by putting them into categories. The second something doesn't fit the way we want it to, we get scared and pull back.

Zinnat® 250 mg / 5 ml

granulado para suspensión oral en frasco

Cefuroxima

L-Thyroxin Henning Tropfen

100 Mikrogramm / milliTropfen zum einnehmen, Lösung

CEPATOL-H
medicamento Homeopático

LABCATAL X 3

P **S** **MANGANÈSE**
Phosphate Azufre **CUIVRE**

CALCAREA CARBONICA 30 CH

todos los domingos por las noches.

Mallko

HUBO UNA ÉPOCA EN QUE MALLKO
TOMABA MÁS DE 7 COSAS DISTINTAS
ENTRE REMEDIOS NATURALES Y
MEDICAMENTOS ALOPÁTICOS.

There was a period when Mallko was taking more than seven different things, both natural remedies and allopathic medicines.

All the world's children have a gift.

Each has their own and grows up unlike any other, making each child a piece of heaven on earth.

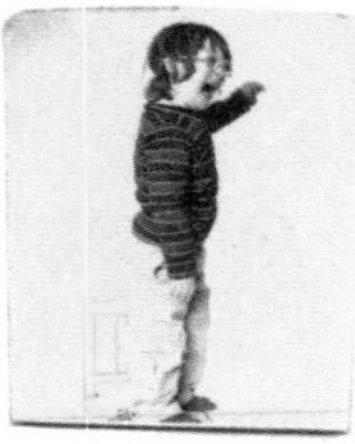

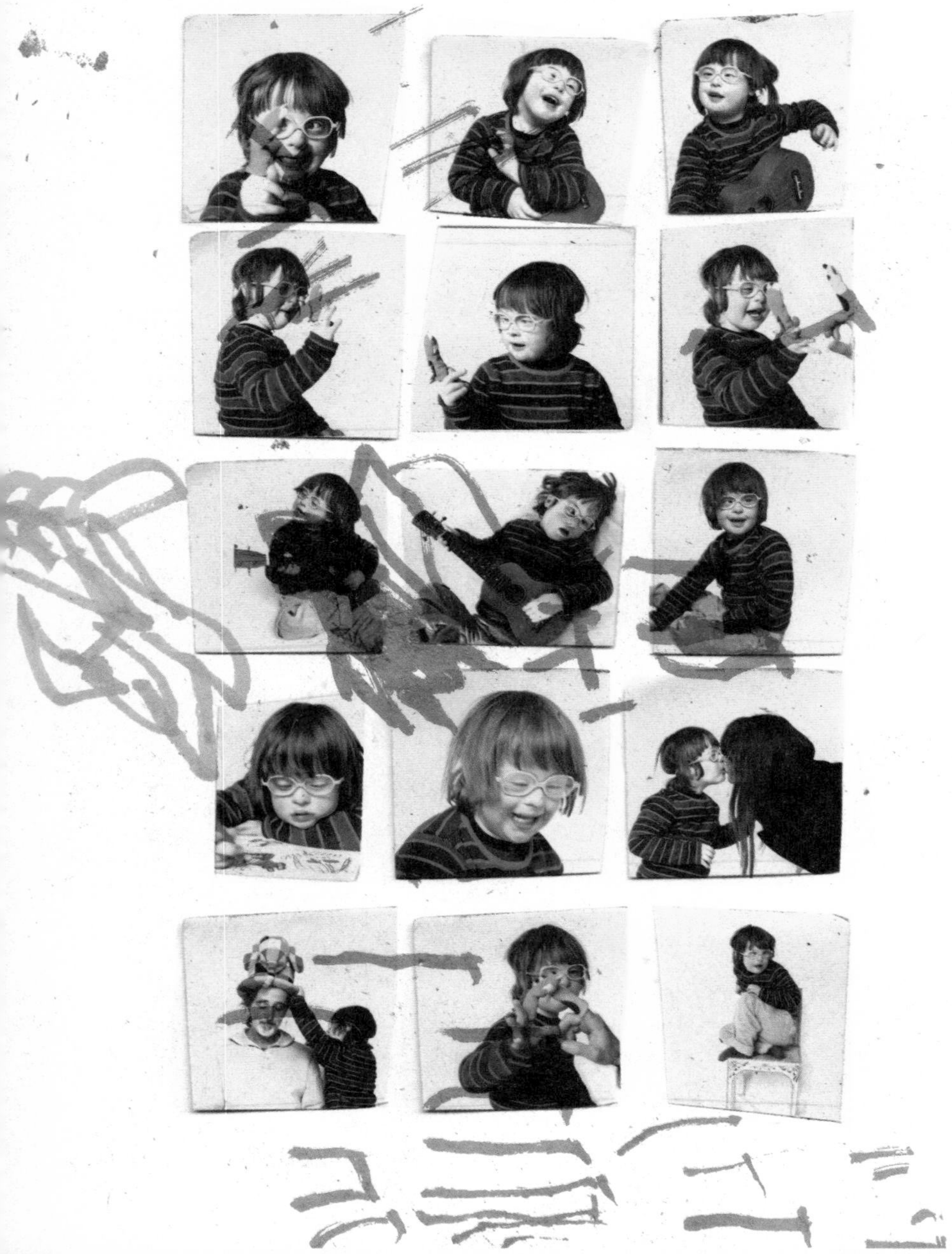

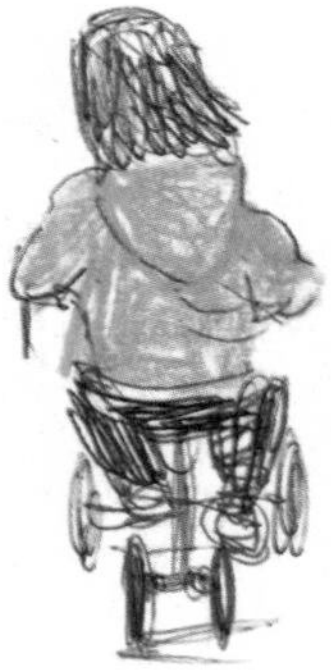

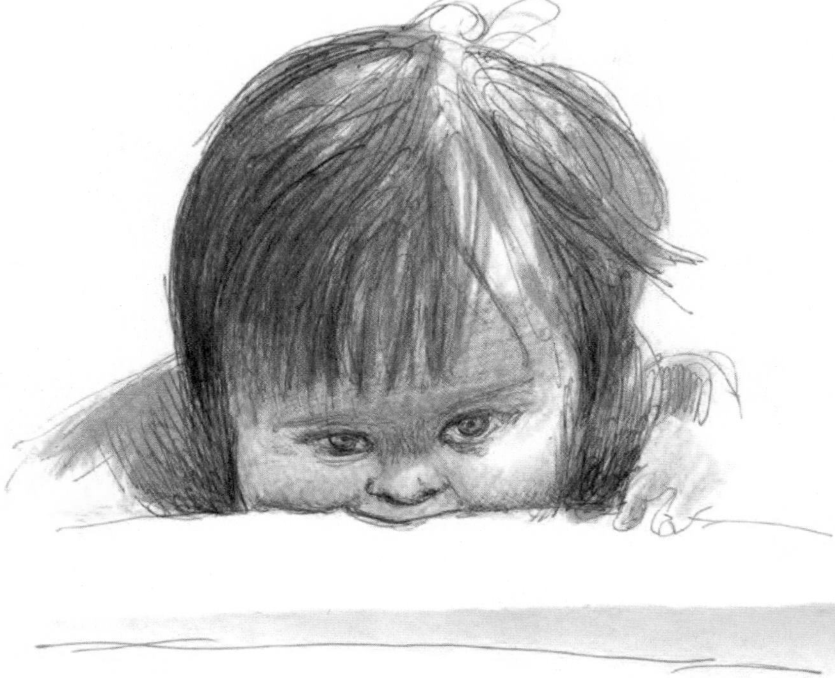

PLAY IS SACRED

EL PAÍS DELS GELATS

MALLKO

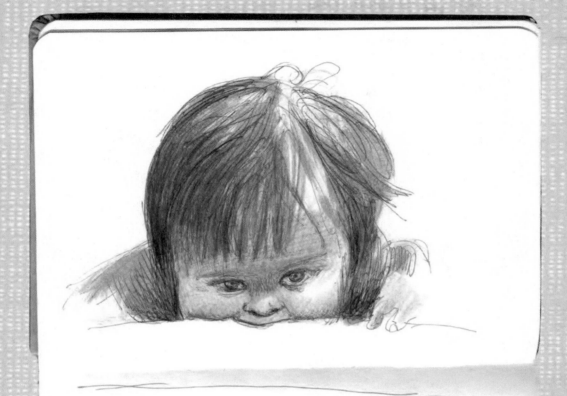

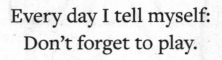
Every day I tell myself:
Don't forget to play.

That's how Mallko started
to relate to others.

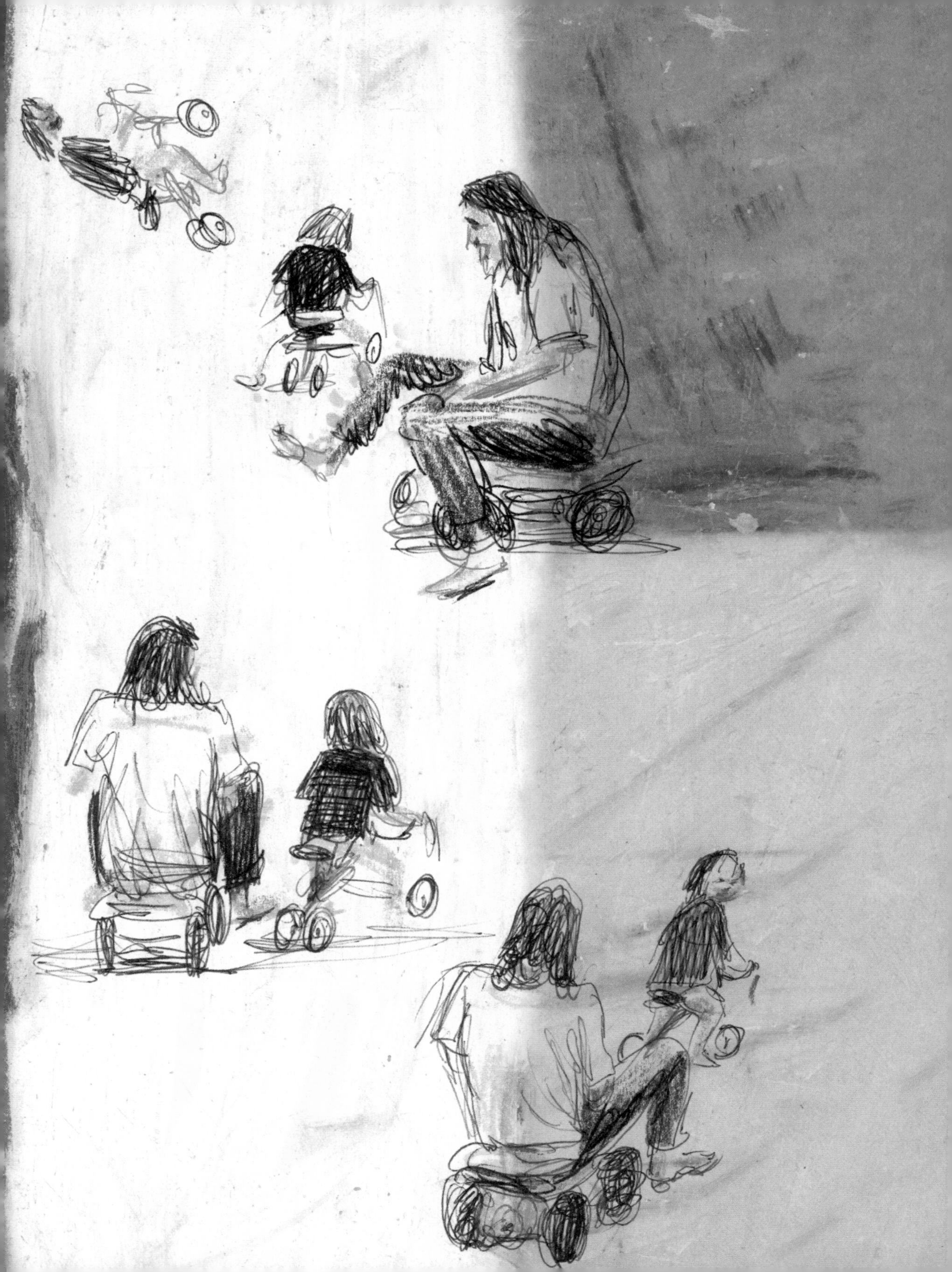

MESSI-MALLKO

The other day in the park, Mallko grabbed a boy's ball
and we started to play.

Every once in a while, I would throw the ball to the boy,
so he wouldn't feel like we'd taken it from him.

The boy's dad told his son "throw the ball to the little girl."

Once, twice, three times.

The fourth time I said: "He's a boy."

Then the dad said again, "Throw the ball to the little girl."

So I got more serious and said, "He's a boy."

"Oh, sorry," said the man. "Since he has long hair, I thought
he was a girl."

I said "I've got long hair too."

TO SHOUTS OF
MESSI - MALLKO
WE PLAY SOCCER
WITH A BASKETBALL

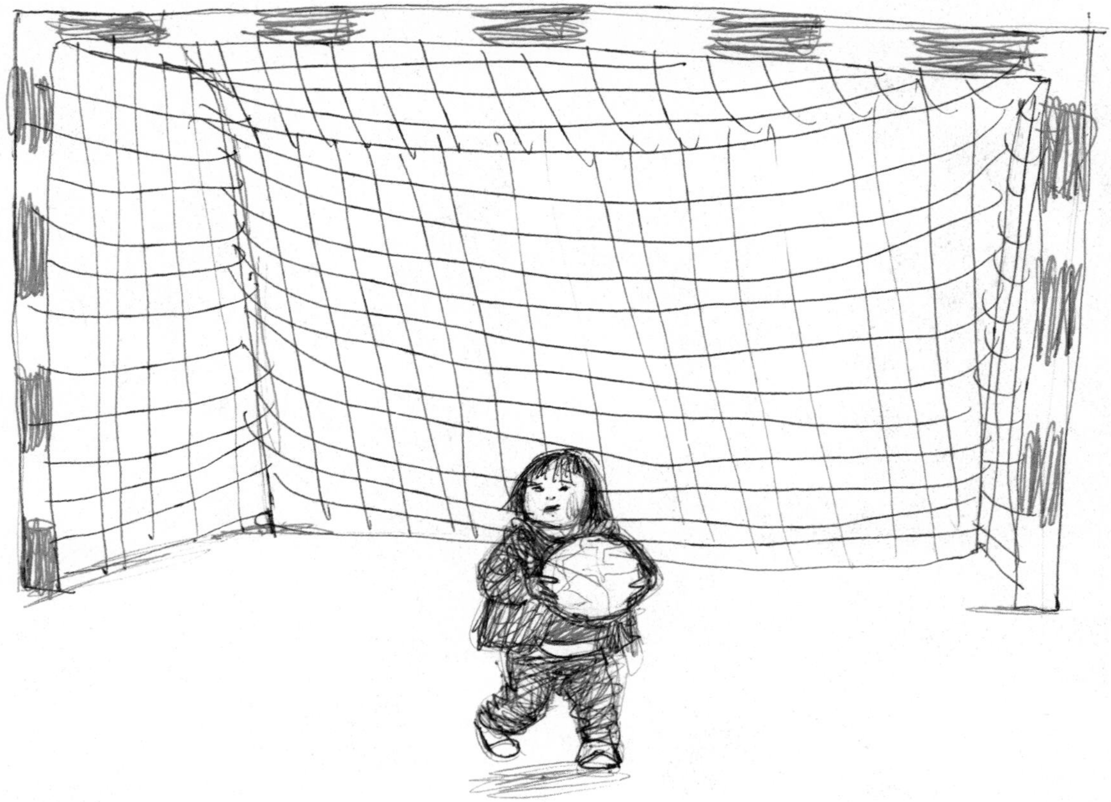

MALLKO LIKES TO PICK UP THE BALL AND STOP THE GAME

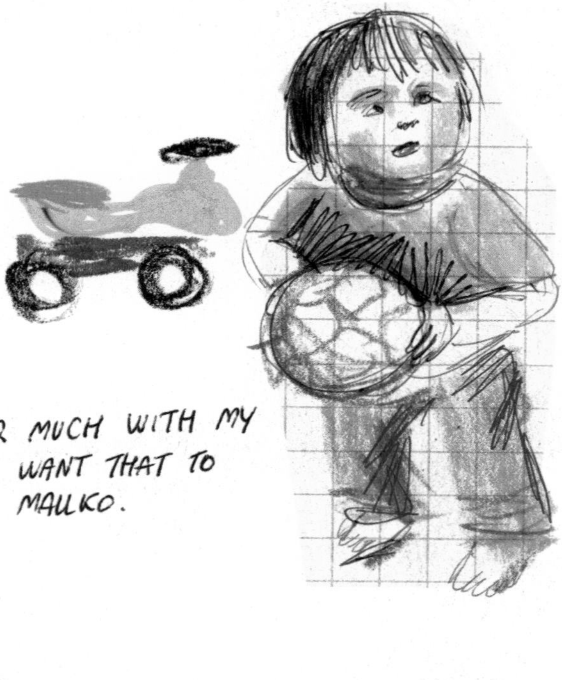

I DIDN'T PLAY SOCCER MUCH WITH MY FIRST SON, I DIDN'T WANT THAT TO HAPPEN AGAIN WITH MALLKO.

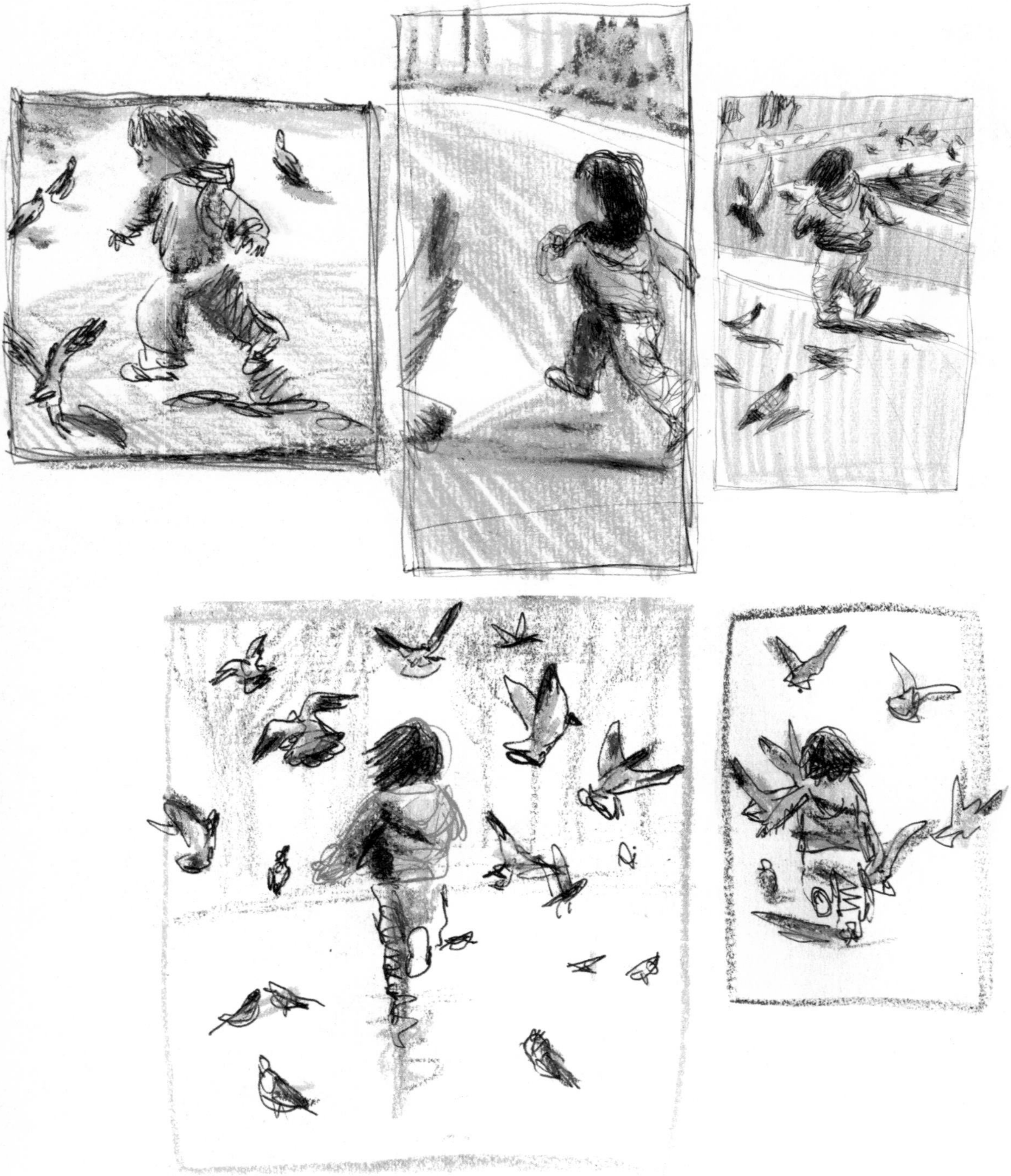

When Mallko sees a pigeon, he goes crazy and starts shouting and chasing it. Now imagine there are 1,000 pigeons.

It's like he goes into a trance, testing my patience.

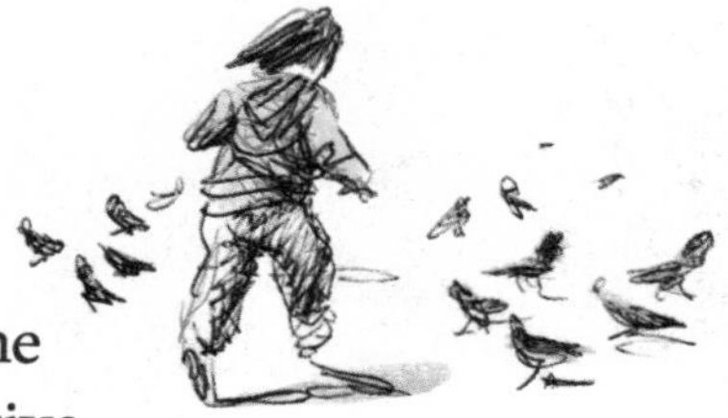
HE STARTS UP AGAIN

ONE CALM AFTERNOON IN THE PLAZA CATALUNYA

Anne and I had agreed that I would take Mallko into town. We live a half-hour from the center of Barcelona. To get there, I have to drive and park at the train station—that is, if I can find a spot. Then we take the train to Barcelona.

When we get there, we go to the Plaza Catalunya—a plaza filled with tourists and pigeons. The pigeons are super fat because they're constantly being fed. And there aren't just a few, but thousands. Some even land on your hand to eat and will let you take their picture.

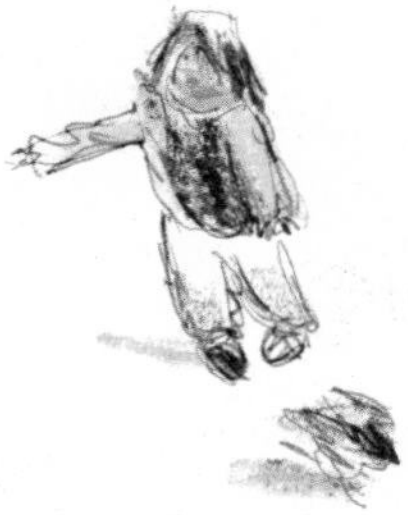

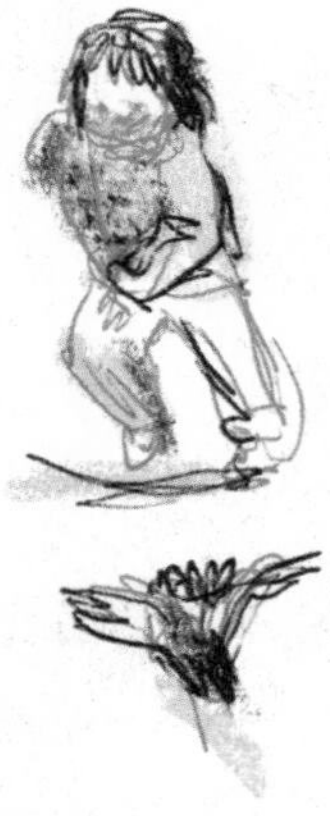

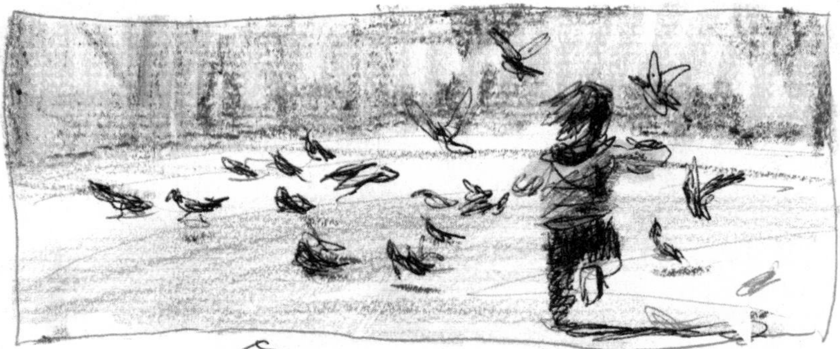

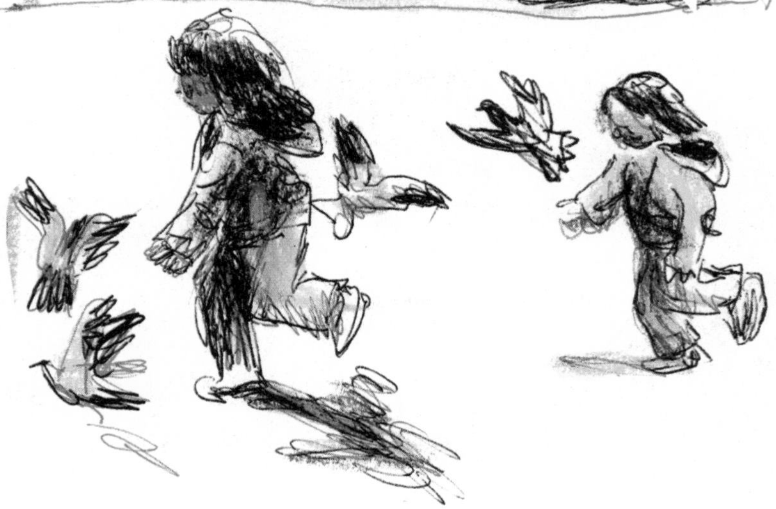

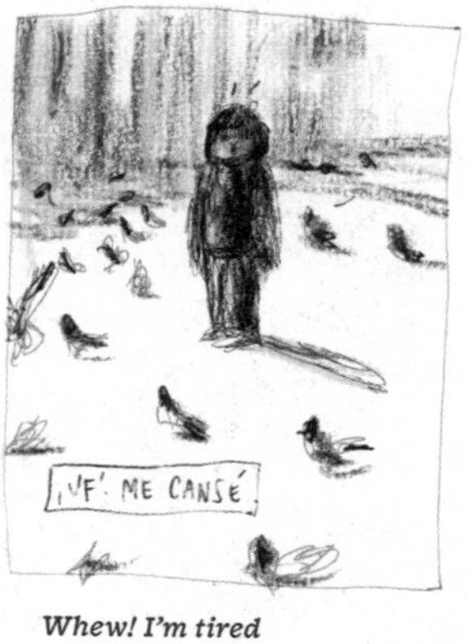
¡UF! ME CANSÉ

Whew! I'm tired

ILLNESS

Down syndrome is not an illness.

VARIOUS
TYPES OF
DAD VEHICLES

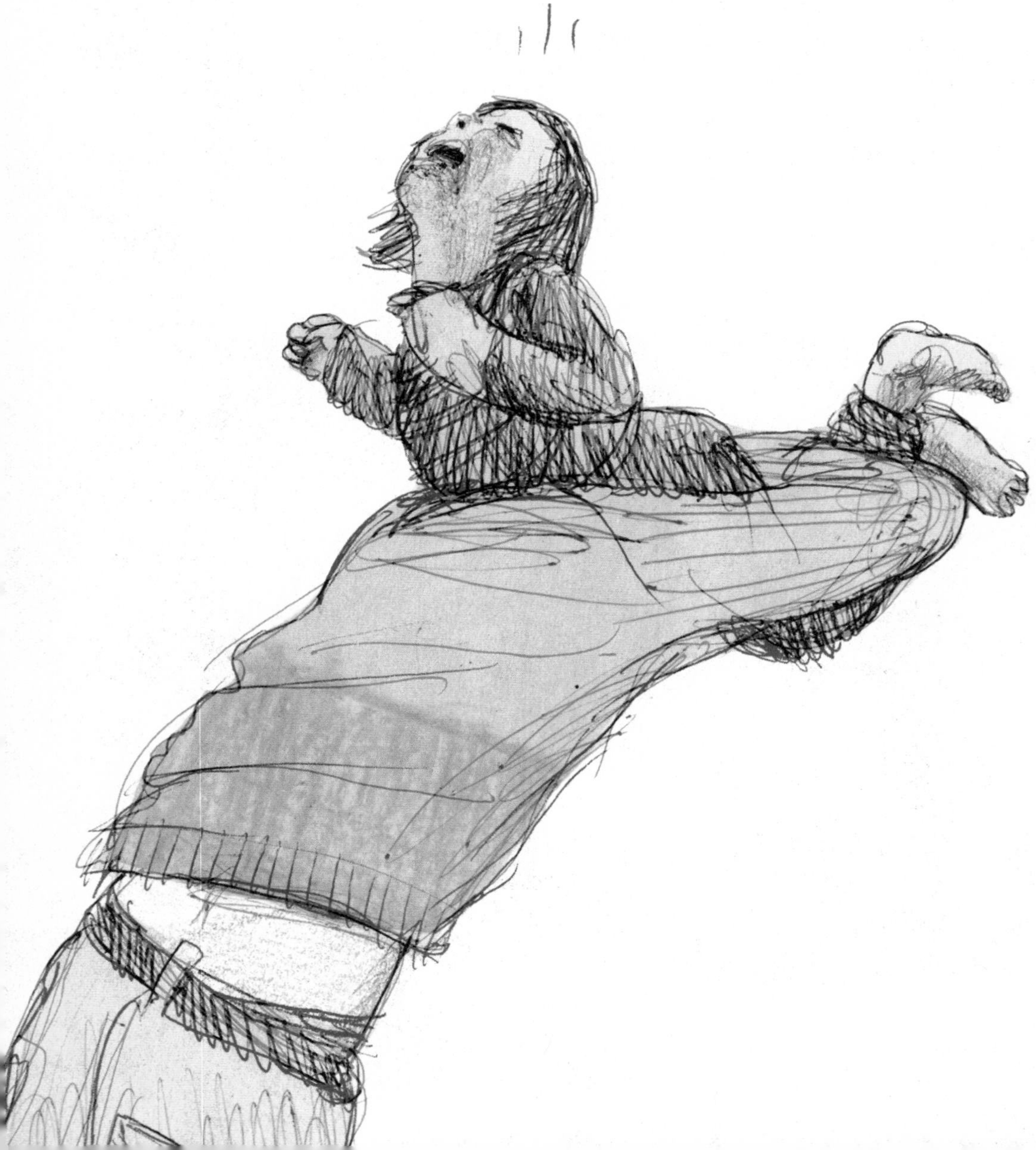

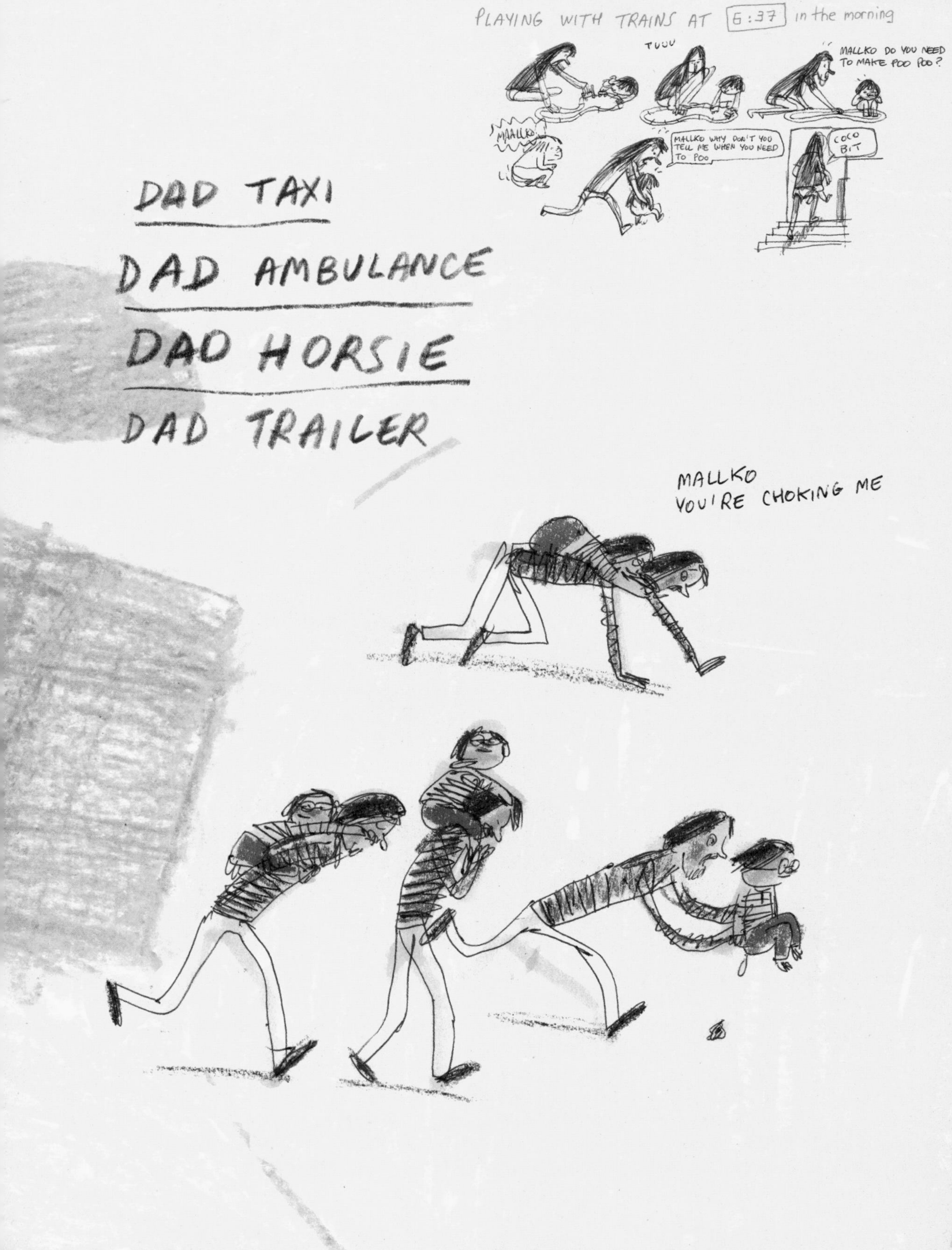

PLAYING WITH TRAINS AT 6:37 in the morning
TUUU
MALLKO DO YOU NEED TO MAKE POO POO?
MAALLKO
MALLKO WHY DON'T YOU TELL ME WHEN YOU NEED TO POO
COCO BIT
DAD TAXI
DAD AMBULANCE
DAD HORSIE
DAD TRAILER
MALLKO YOU'RE CHOKING ME

FROZEN GUY

MALLKO HAS MANY POWERS.
ONE OF THEM IS HIS "FREEZE" RAY.
HE SHOOTS IT AT YOU, USUALLY ALONG
WITH A BOOOO! OR A SHOUT.
AND YOU BECOME FROZEN.
ONCE YOU ARE FROZEN
YOU HAVE TO WAIT
FOR HIM TO
UNFREEZE YOU.
THE MOST EFFECTIVE
METHOD IS
A KISS.
SOMETIMES HE'LL TRY
SOME OTHER
WAY, BOOO!
BUT
IF IT DOESN'T WORK
HE COMES OVER AND GIVES YOU A
KISS AND YOU THAW OUT.
AND IT STARTS ALL OVER AGAIN*

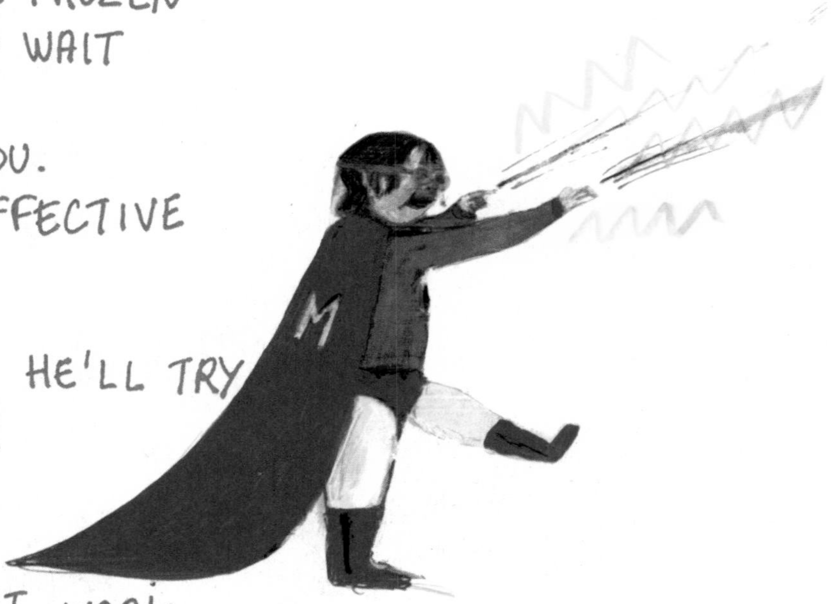
M

* (warning, the game can go on for several hours)

SOMETIMES HE GIVES YOU
THE FREEZE POWER
AND THEN YOU
FREEZE HIM
AND HE FREEZES UP
WITH HIS HEAD
TO ONE SIDE.

like this

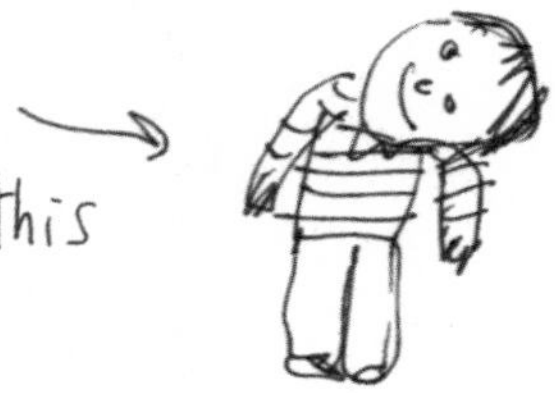

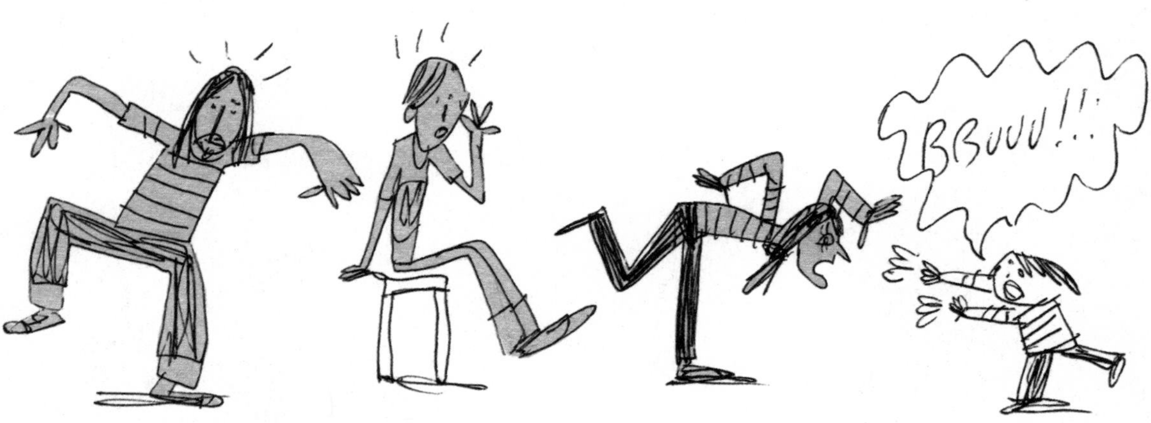
BBUUU!!!

Playing also helps you face pain and difficulties. A few years ago, we had to go through two operations: one to improve hearing and another to improve vision.

Mallko took it like a champ.

But when he came to from the anesthesia, he wanted to rip off the patch they'd put on his eye. So I put one on too. That way, we were the same and people stared at both of us in the street.

LOOK, MALLKO! DAD HAS AN OWIE IN HIS EYE TOO.

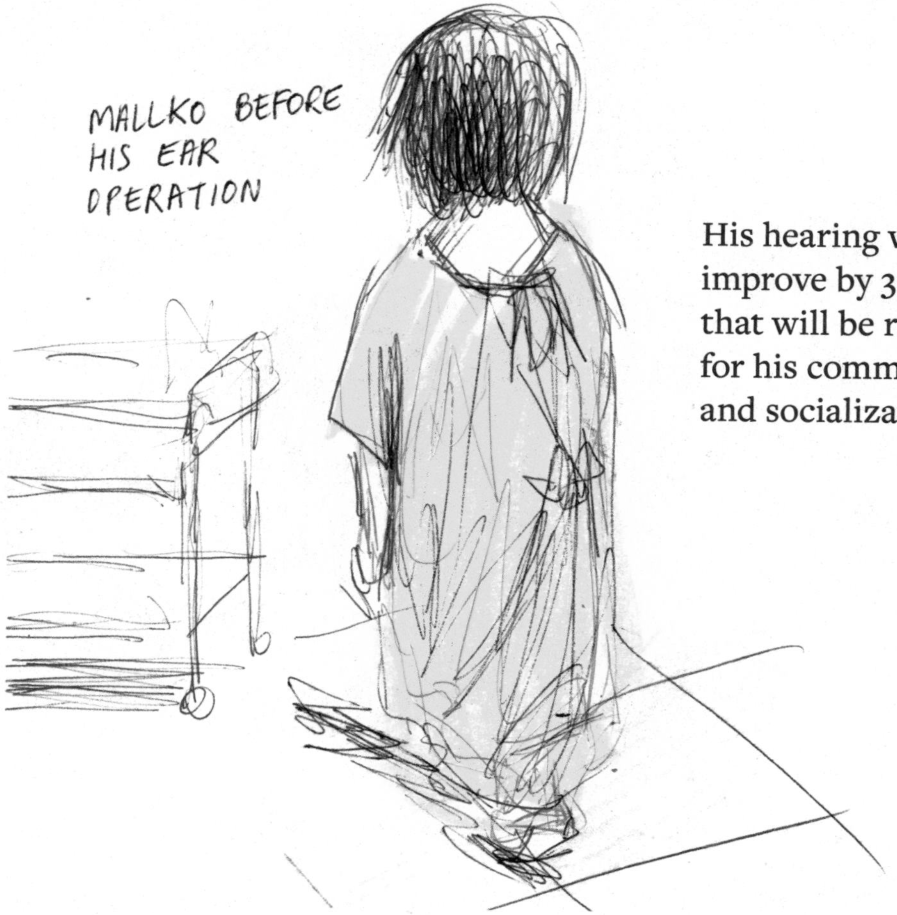
MALLKO BEFORE
HIS EAR
OPERATION

His hearing will improve by 30% and that will be really good for his communication and socialization.

What I like about Mallko is his good attitude. He's always playing—even before an operation.

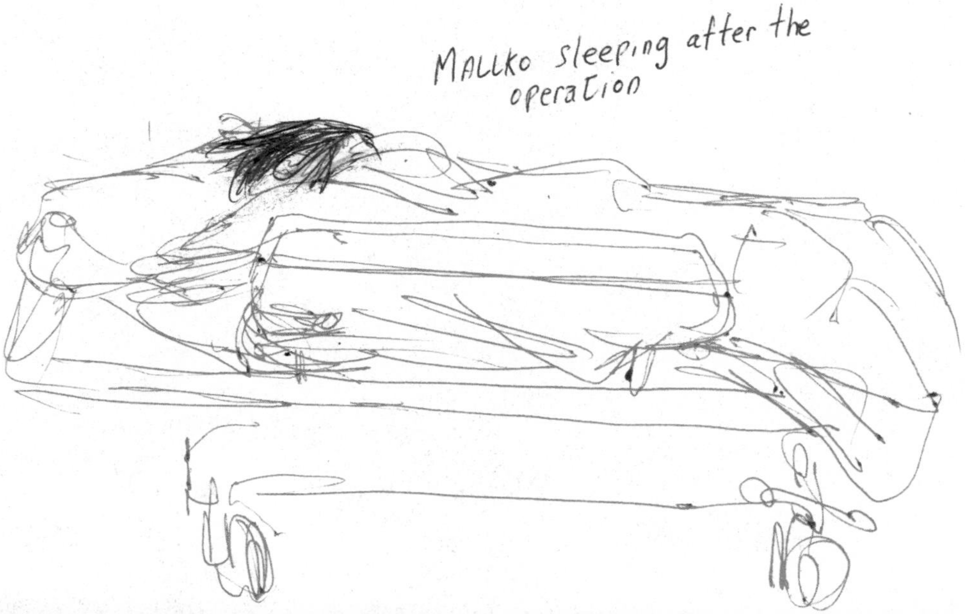
MALLKO sleeping after the
operation

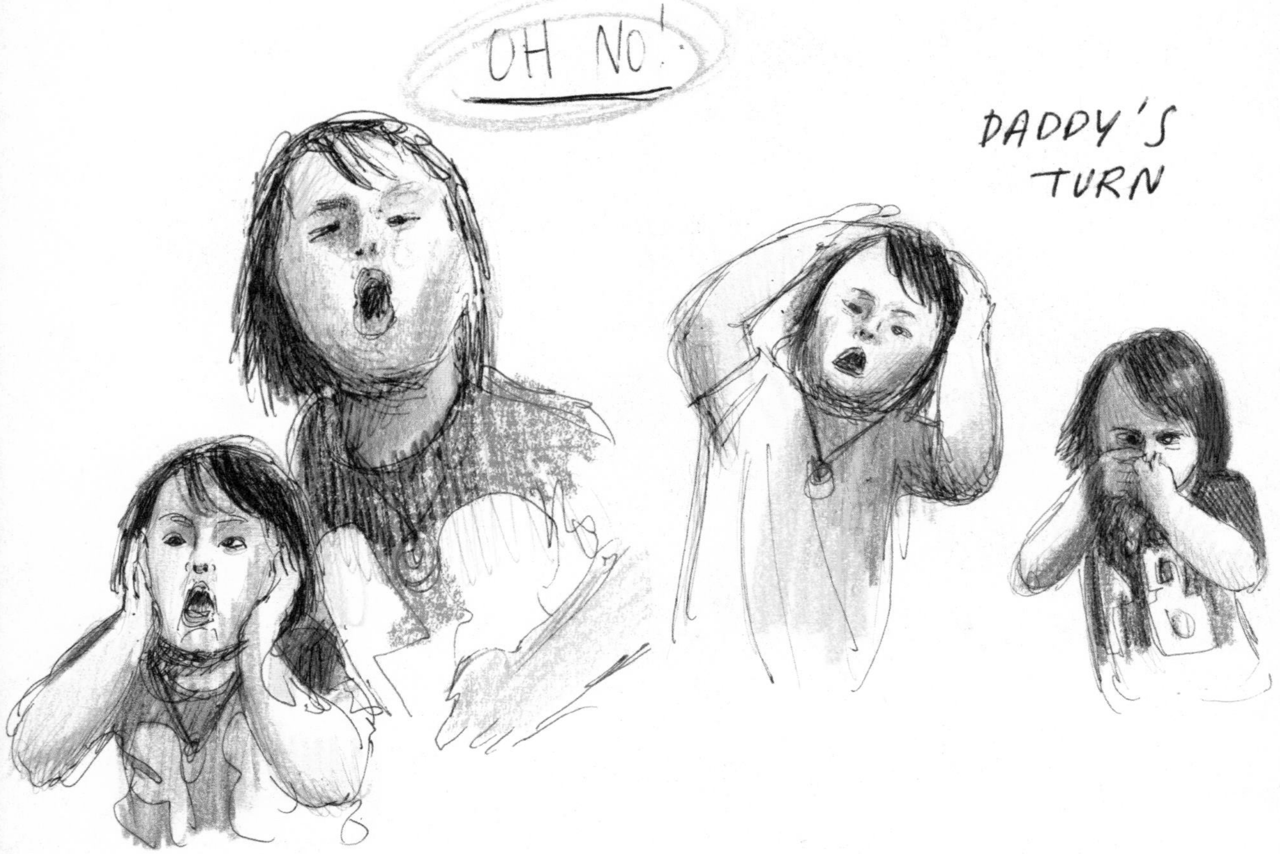
OH NO!
DADDY'S TURN

tren

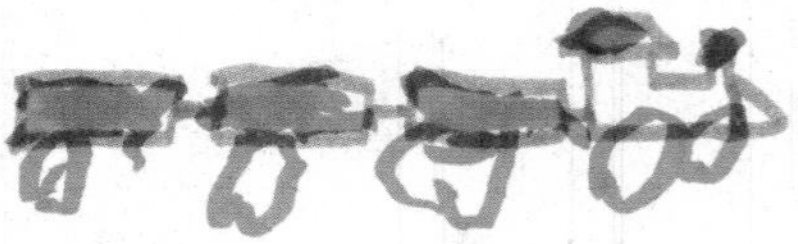

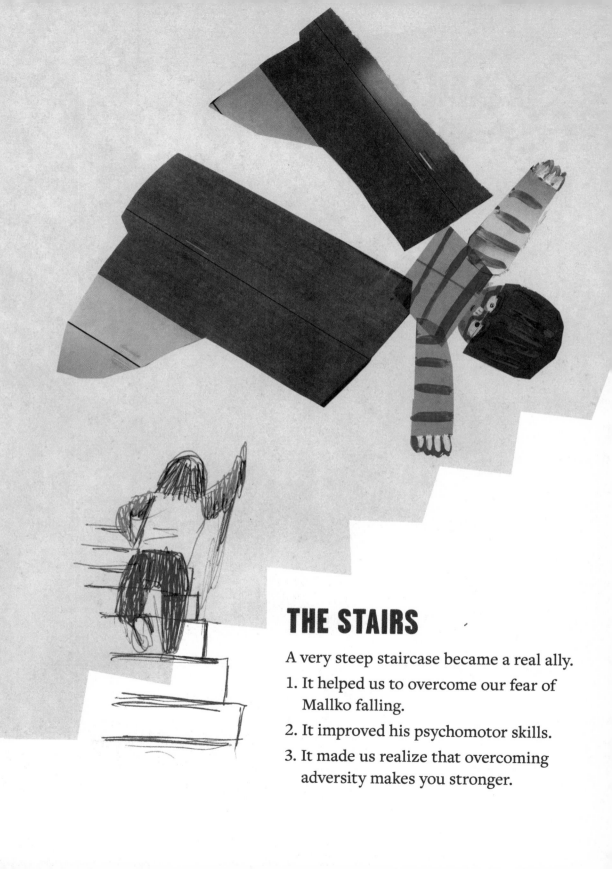

THE STAIRS

A very steep staircase became a real ally.

1. It helped us to overcome our fear of Mallko falling.

2. It improved his psychomotor skills.

3. It made us realize that overcoming adversity makes you stronger.

DISABILITY

~~DIS~~ ABILITY

EVERYBODY SAYS I'M "DISABLED"
BECAUSE THERE ARE LOTS OF THINGS I CAN'T
DO, OR THEY WON'T LET ME DO, BUT I...
UNDERSTAND "LOVE" JUST LIKE YOU.

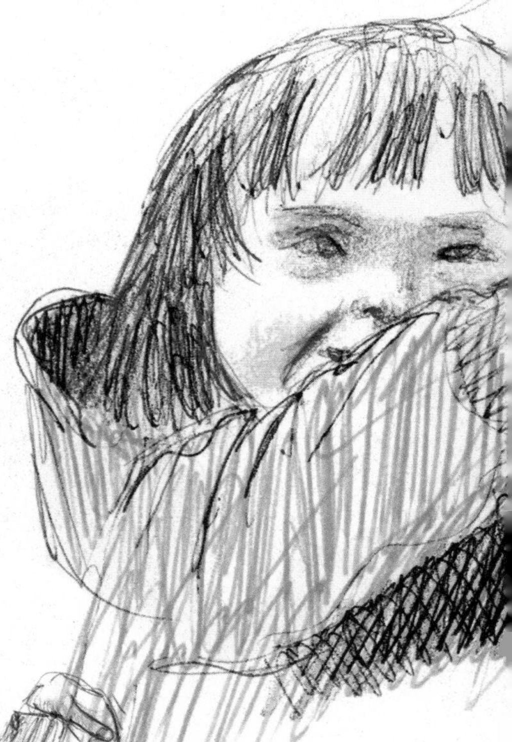

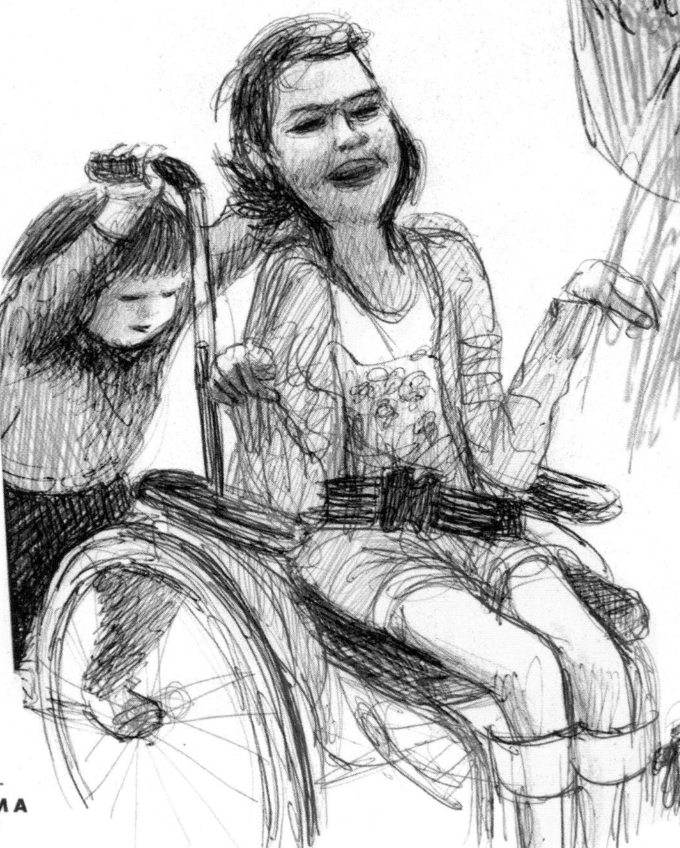

"Gusti, the publishing house is called Cromosoma [Chromosome] and has three O's on the logo. What a coincidence, right? Your son came to detonate your world and to teach you that love has no limits or conditions."

CROMOSOMA

" Gusti. la editorial se llama Cromosoma y
tiene 3 sobre el nombre, que sincronía
no...? tu hijo les viene a detonar o
enseñar, que el amor no tiene límite
ni condición "

Alberto Lapiccain

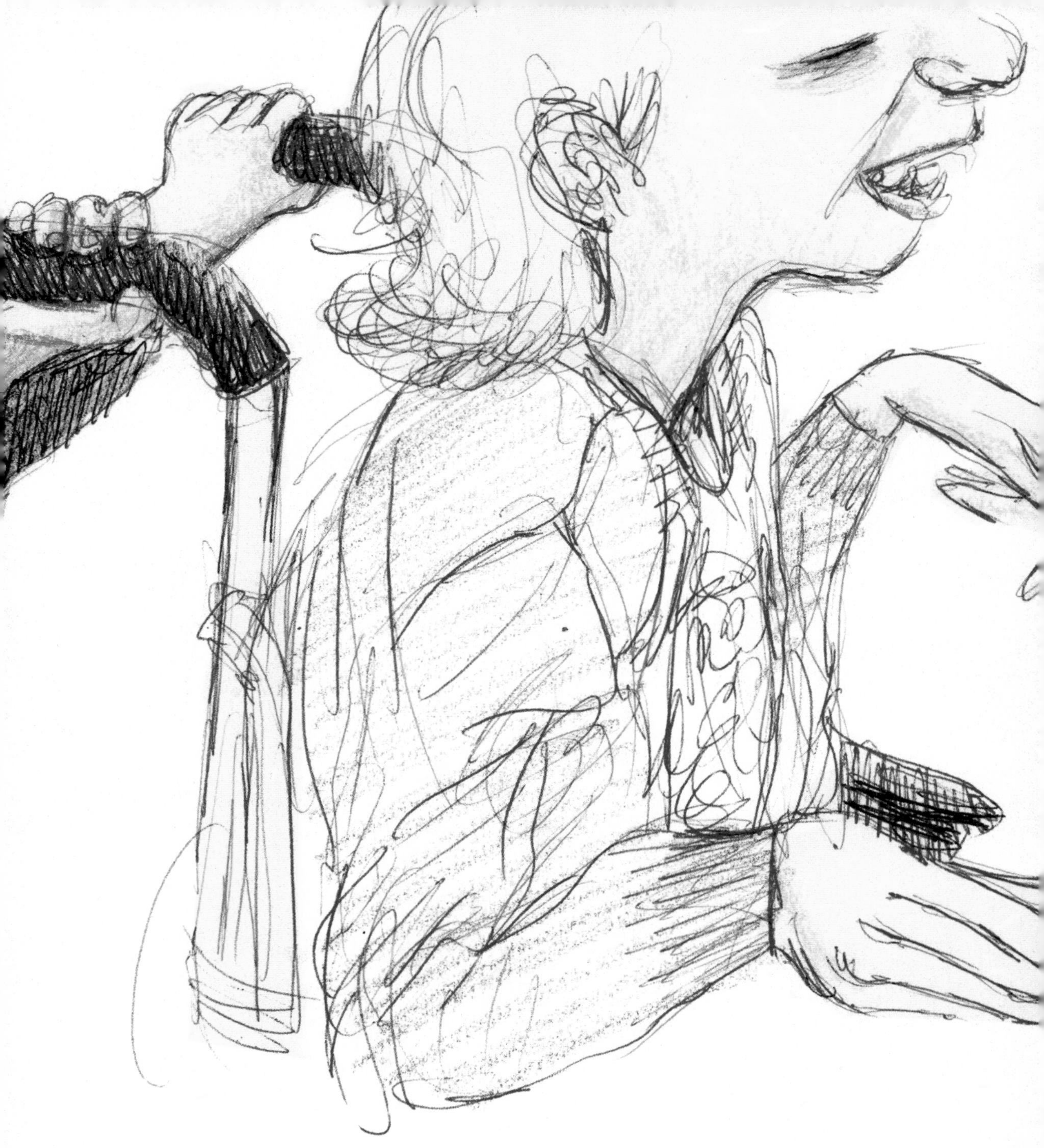

In one of the higher grades, there's Irene, who's in a wheelchair. Mallko is fascinated by it. Every time he gets the chance, he wheels her around the schoolyard.

THE STARS HAVE THE MARK OF GOD
GOODNESS HAS THE MARK OF GOD
FREEDOM HAS THE MARK OF GOD
HOPE HAS THE MARK OF GOD
SADNESS HAS THE MARK OF GOD
MUSIC HAS THE MARK OF GOD
YOUR BROTHER HAS THE MARK OF GOD
NATURE HAS THE MARK OF GOD
CHILDREN HAS THE MARK OF GOD
YOUR SON HAS THE MARK OF GOD

VUL 200

LA LA LA LA LA

Marca Registrada
por
The Gramophone
Company Ltd.

UNA COMPAÑÍA
DEL GRUPO M

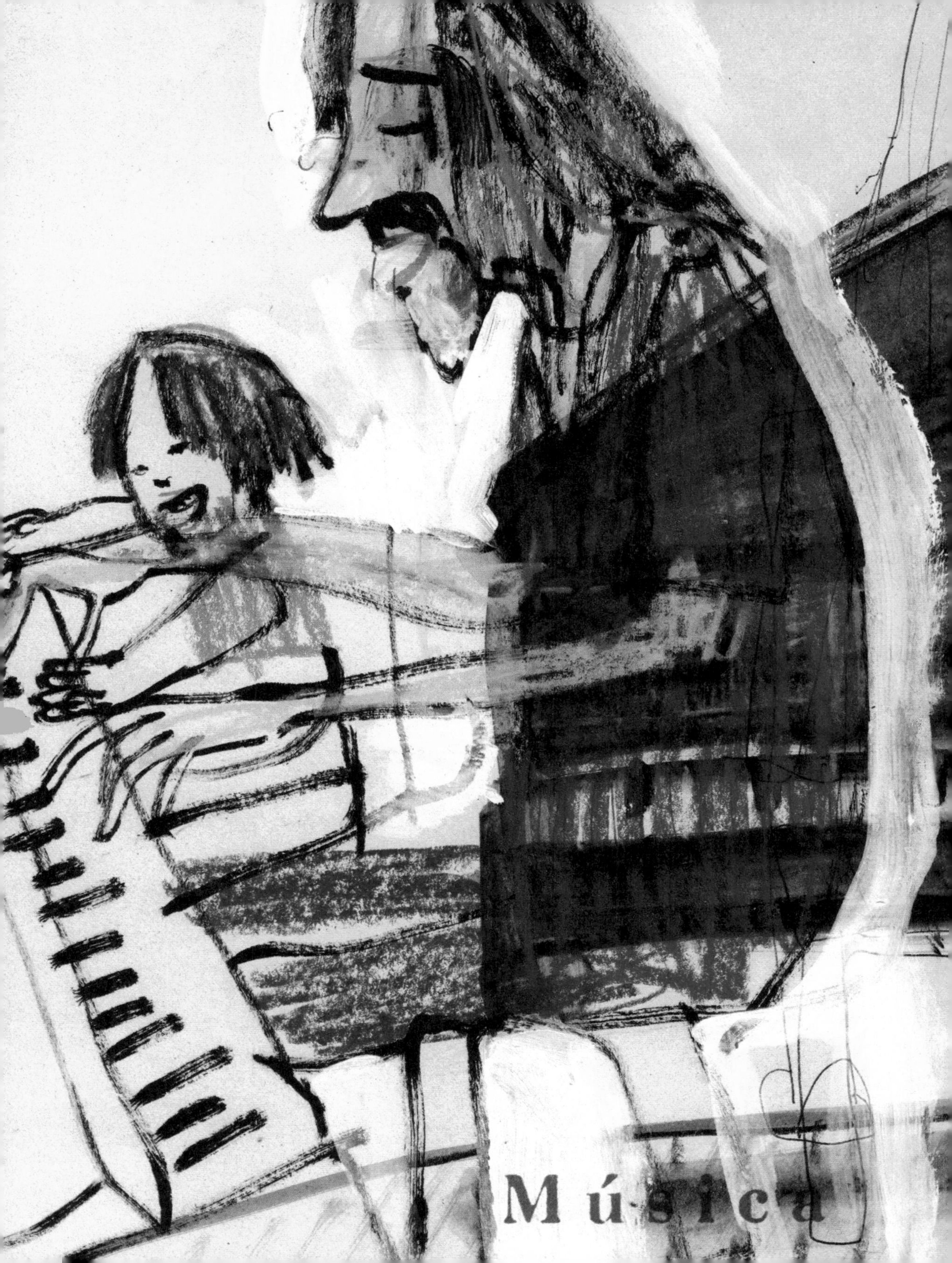

Música

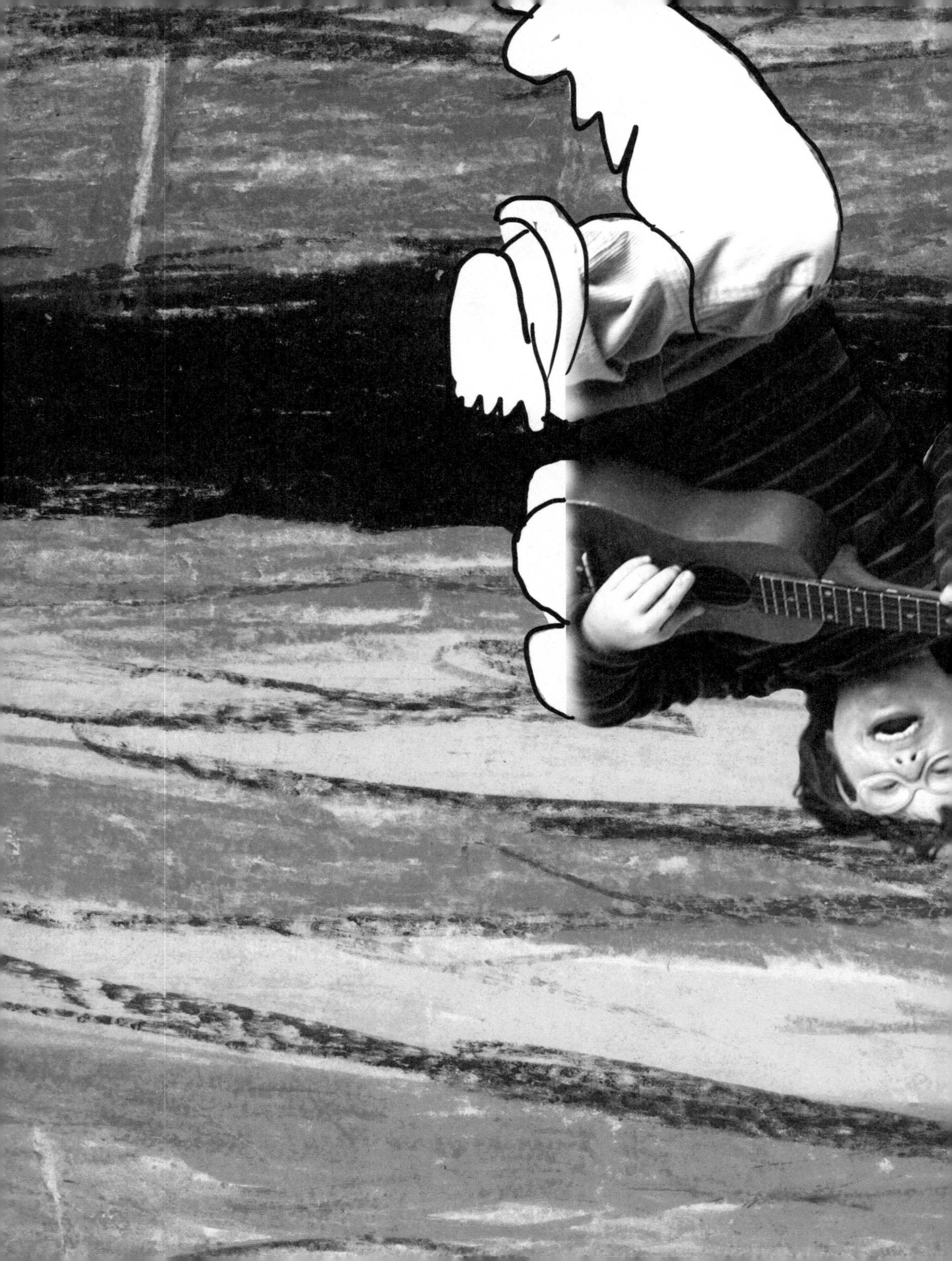

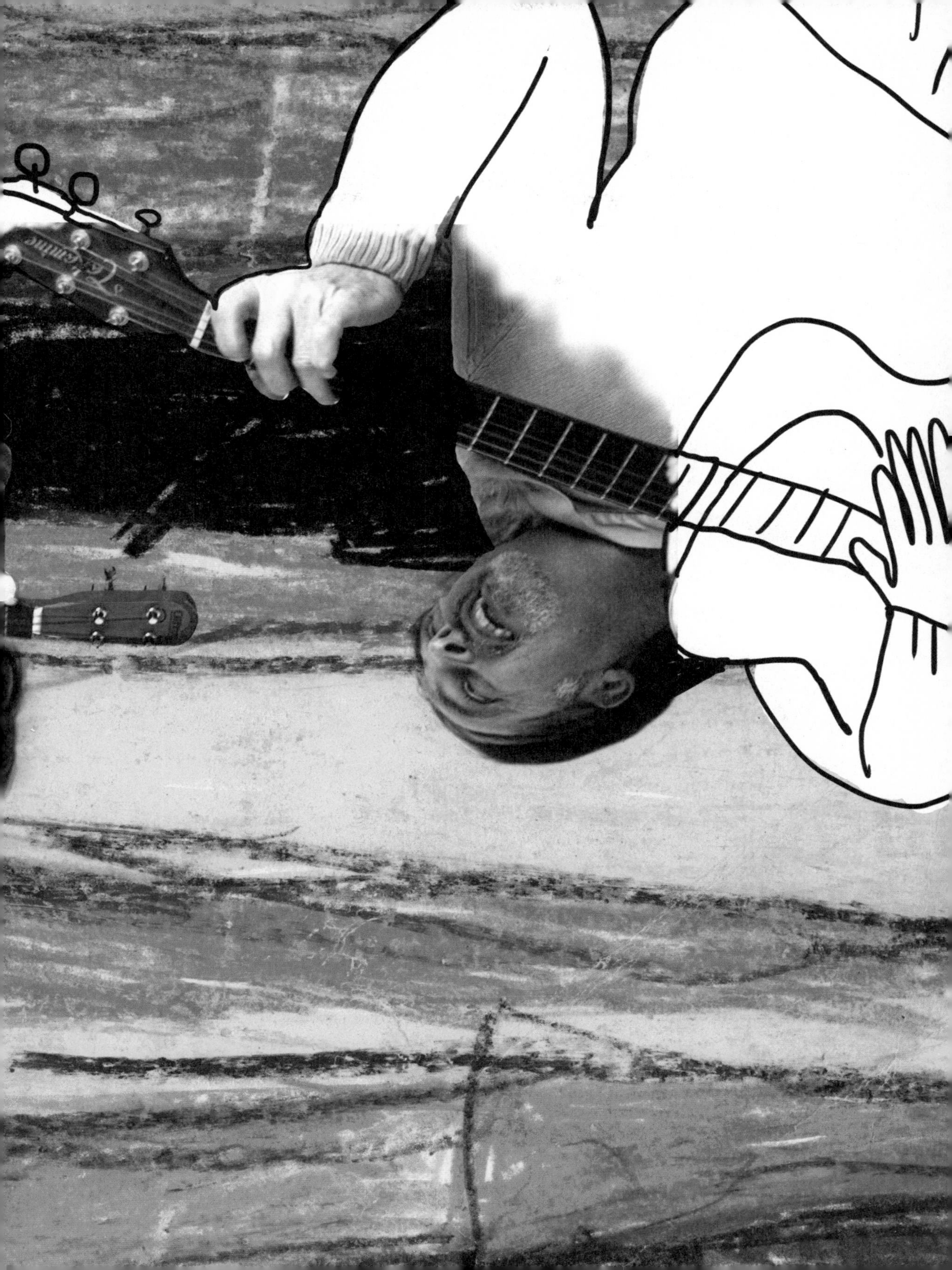

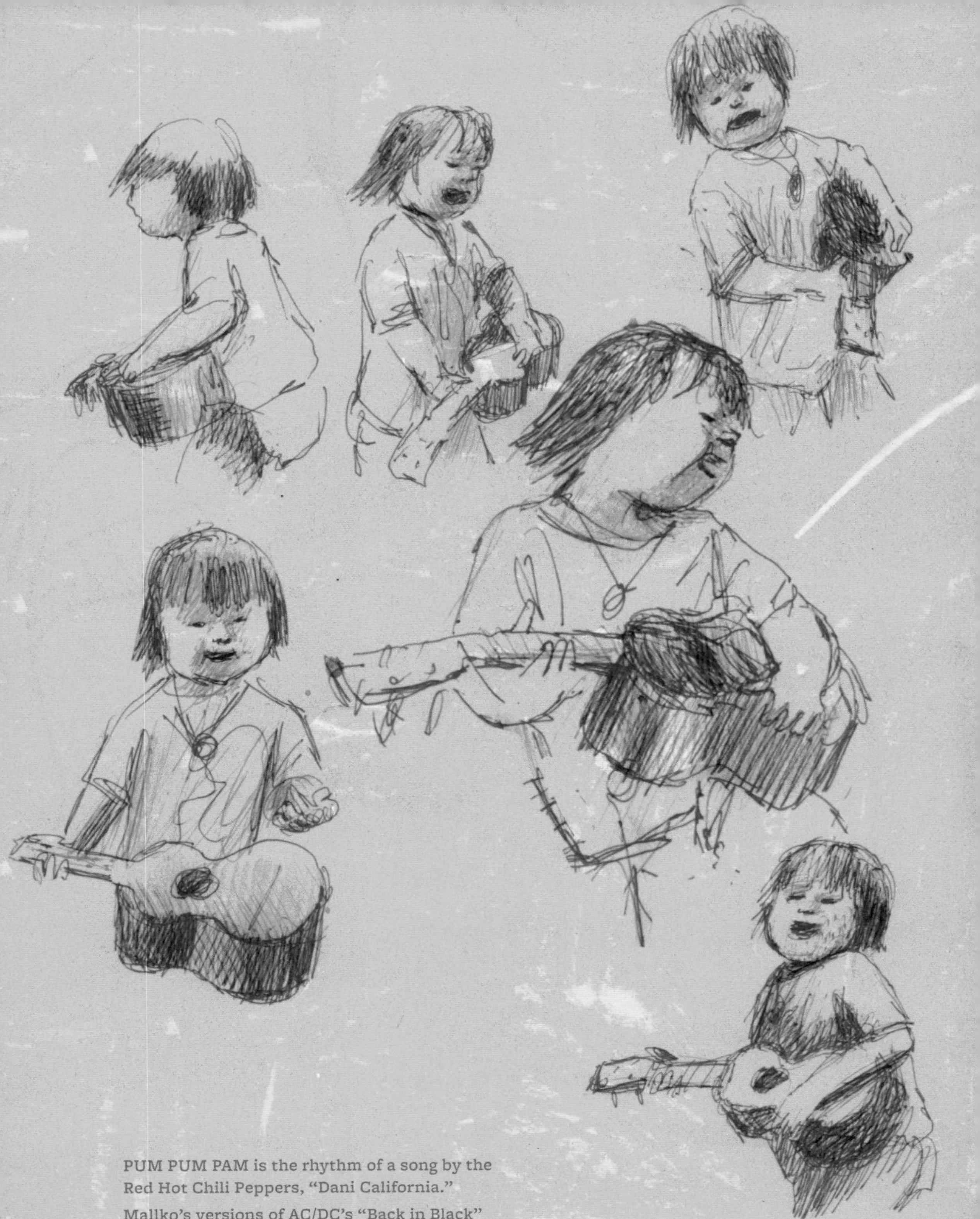

PUM PUM PAM is the rhythm of a song by the Red Hot Chili Peppers, "Dani California."

Mallko's versions of AC/DC's "Back in Black" and "Gangnam Style" are impossible to draw.

PUM PUM PAM
PUM PUM
PAM

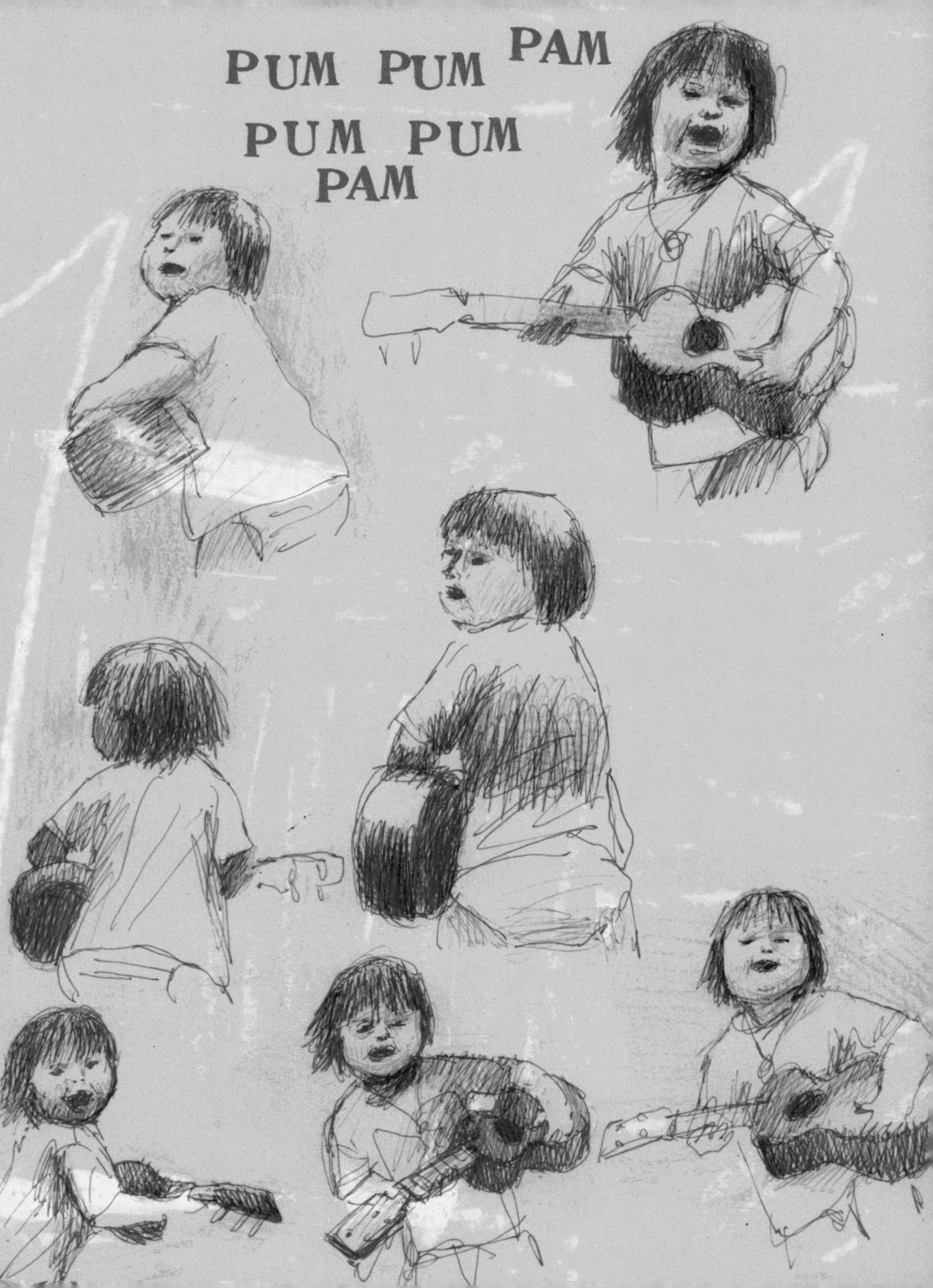

When we draw together
we enter our own universe—
of trains, cars, mom and dad.

Mallko likes to color in my
drawings and almost always
colors in the eyes.

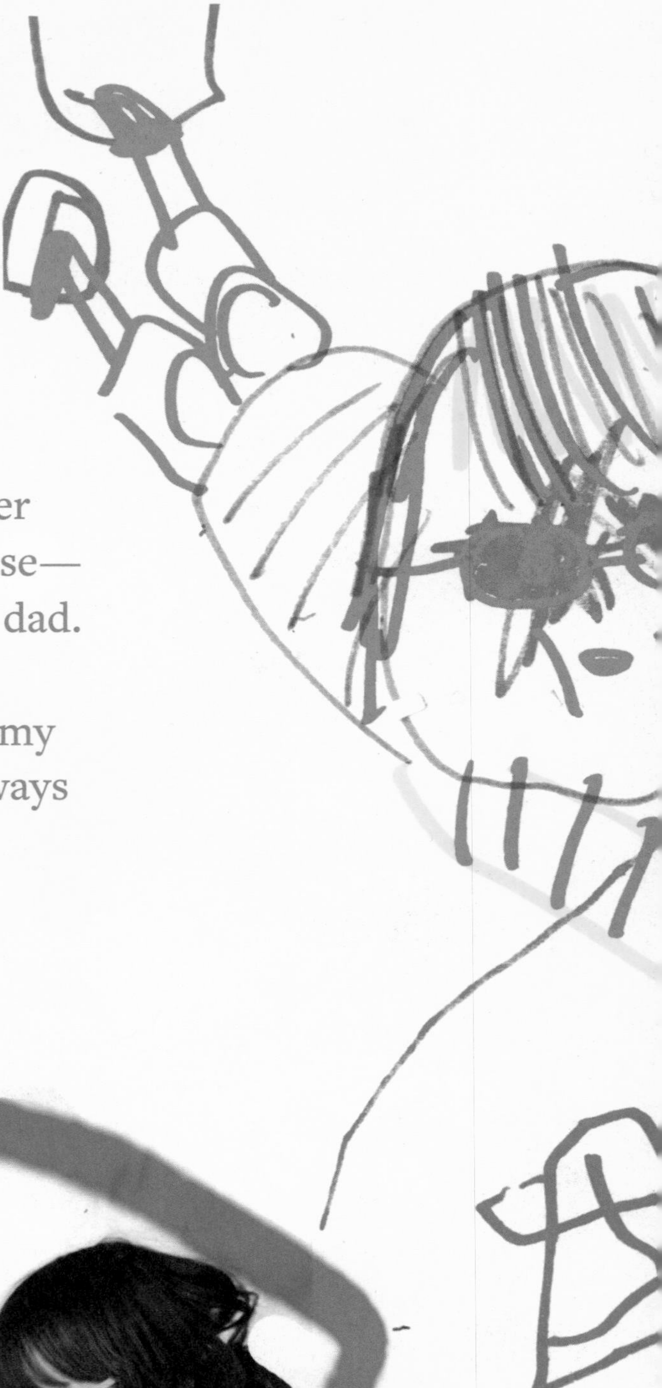

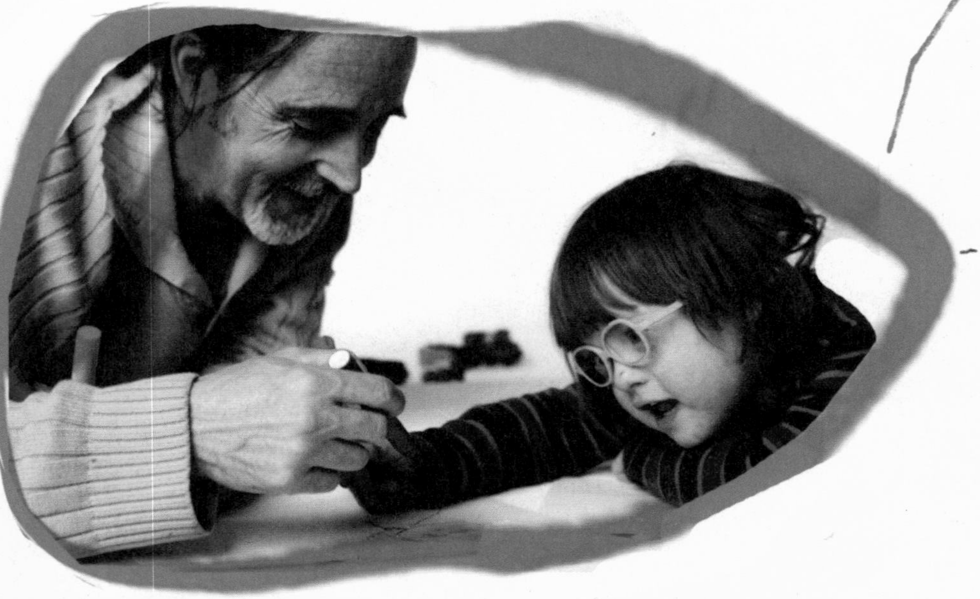

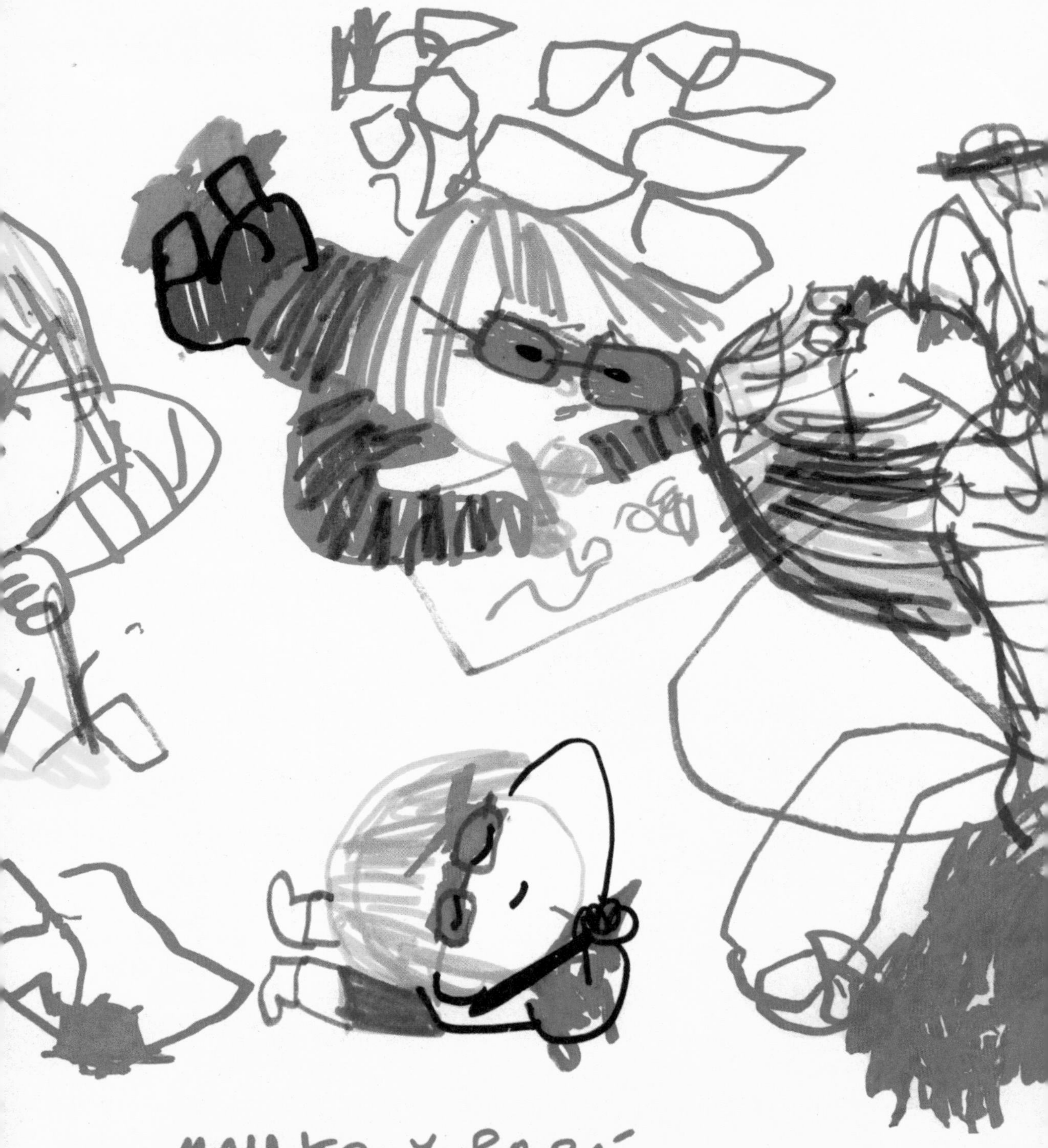

MALLKO Y PAPÁ
DIBUJANDO JUNTOS.

Mallko and dad drawing together

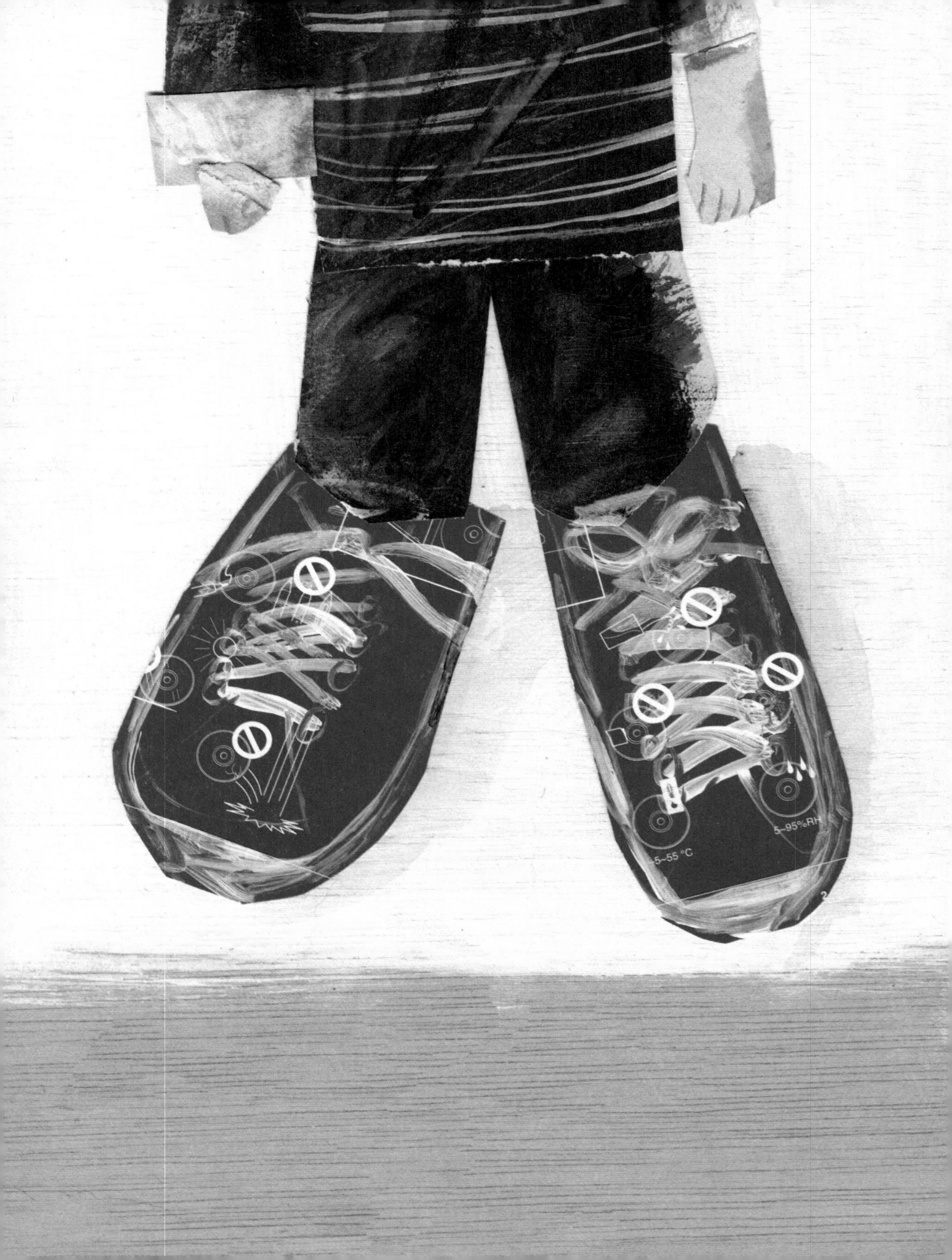
5–95%RH
5–55 °C

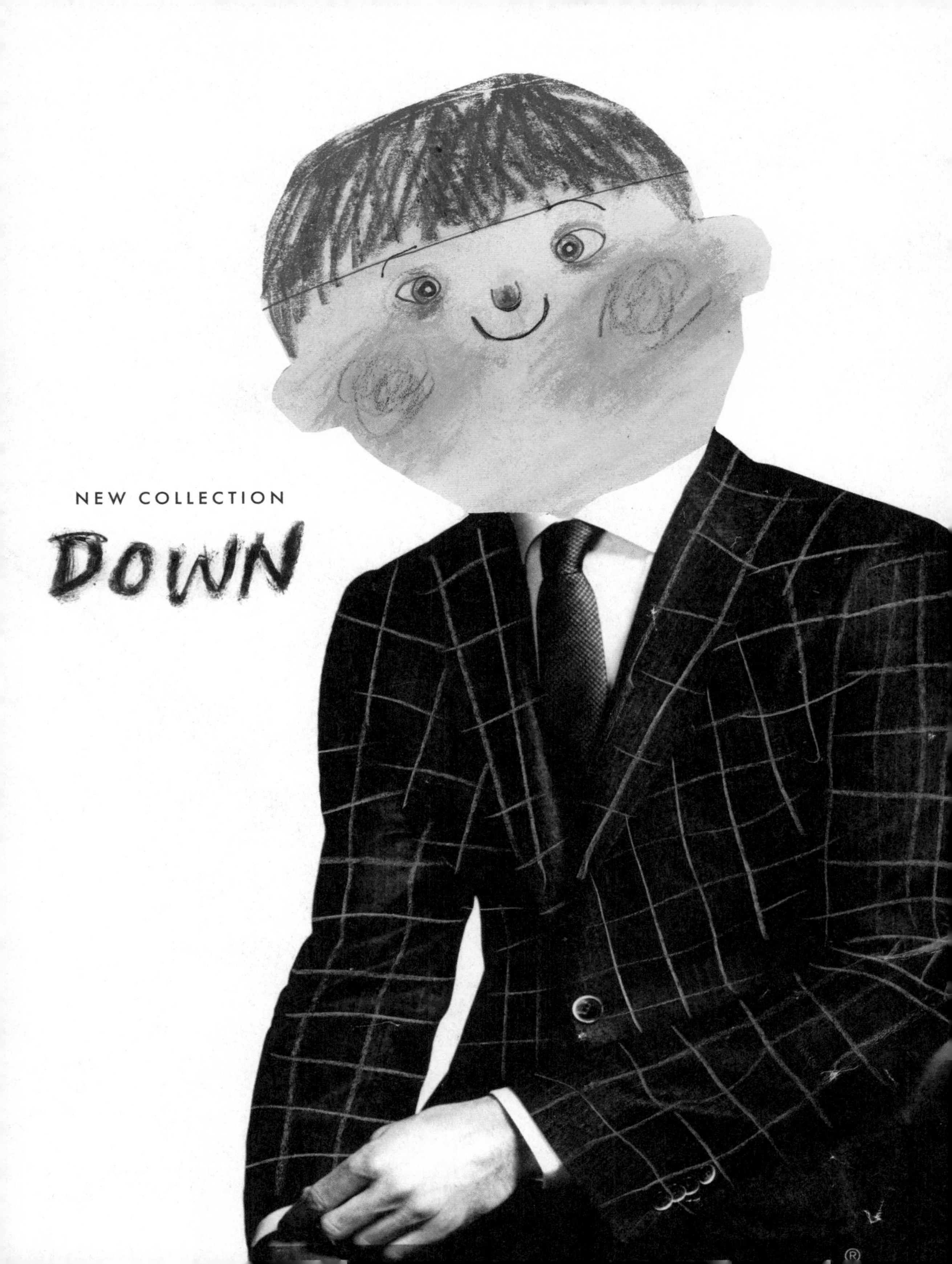
NEW COLLECTION
DOWN

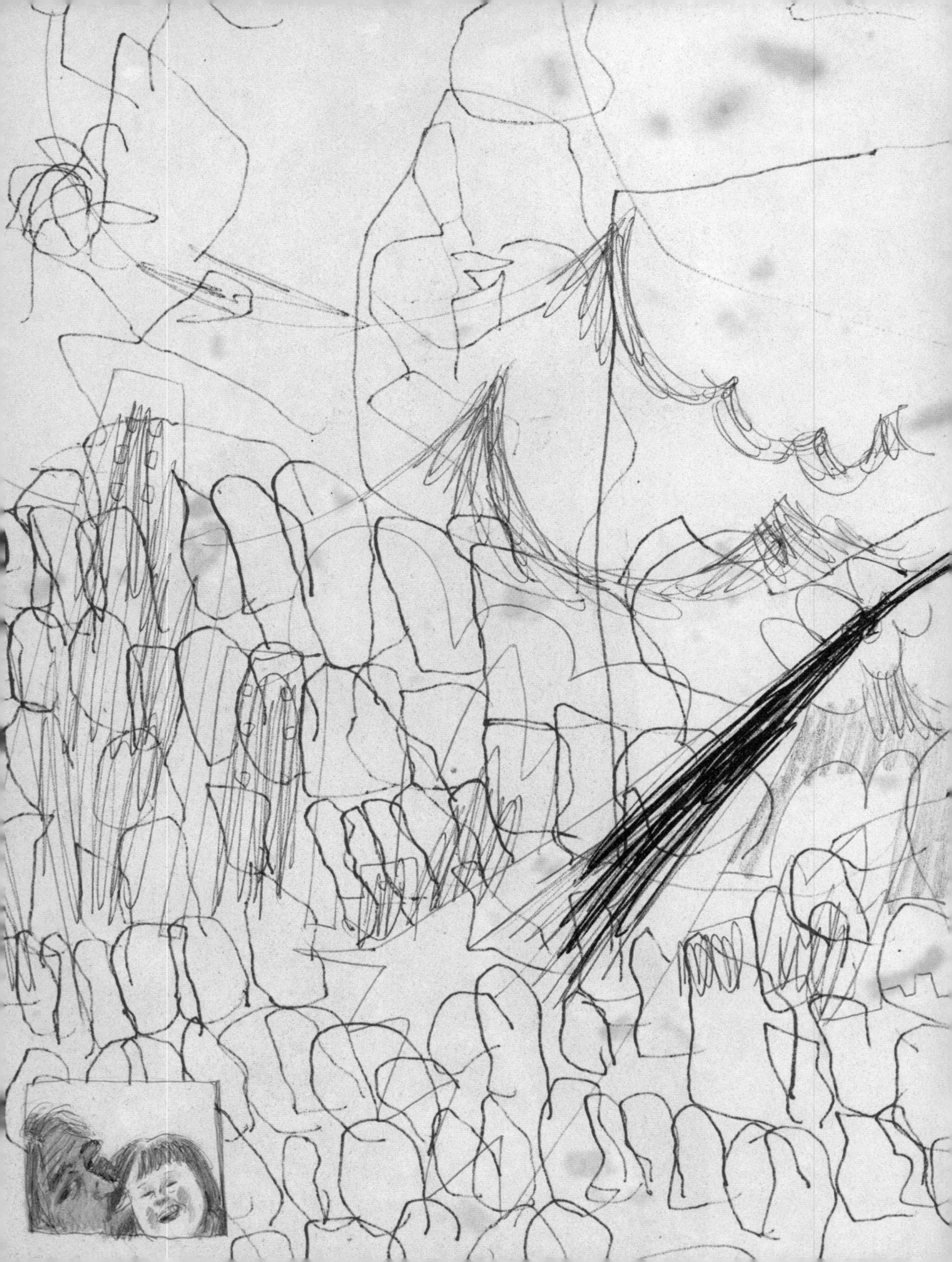

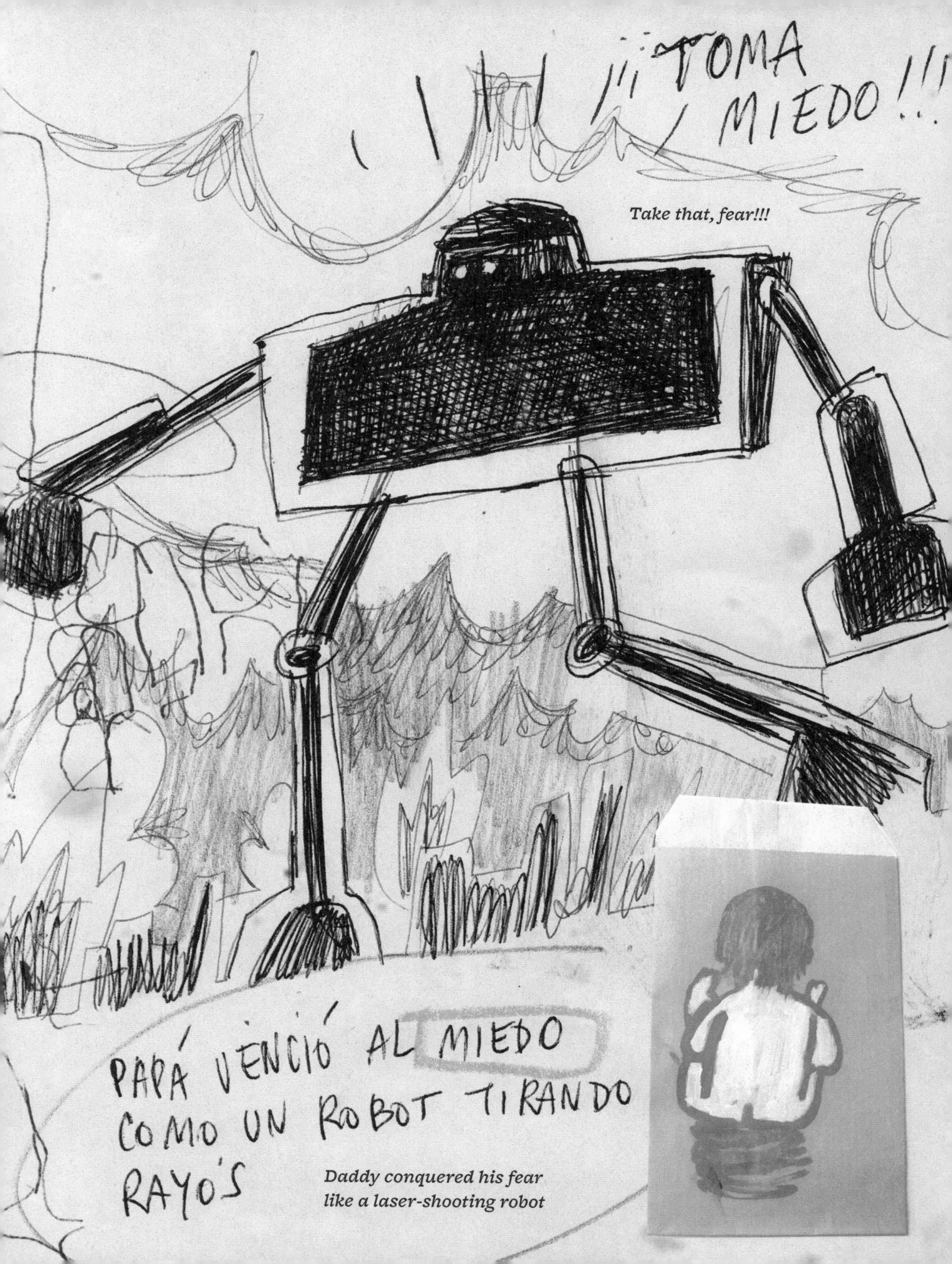
¡¡¡TOMA MIEDO!!!
PAPÁ VENCIÓ AL MIEDO COMO UN ROBOT TIRANDO RAYO'S

Take that, fear!!!

Daddy conquered his fear like a laser-shooting robot

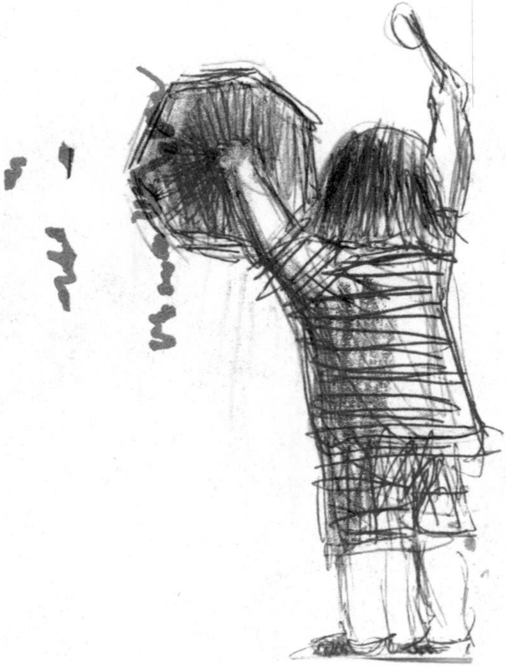

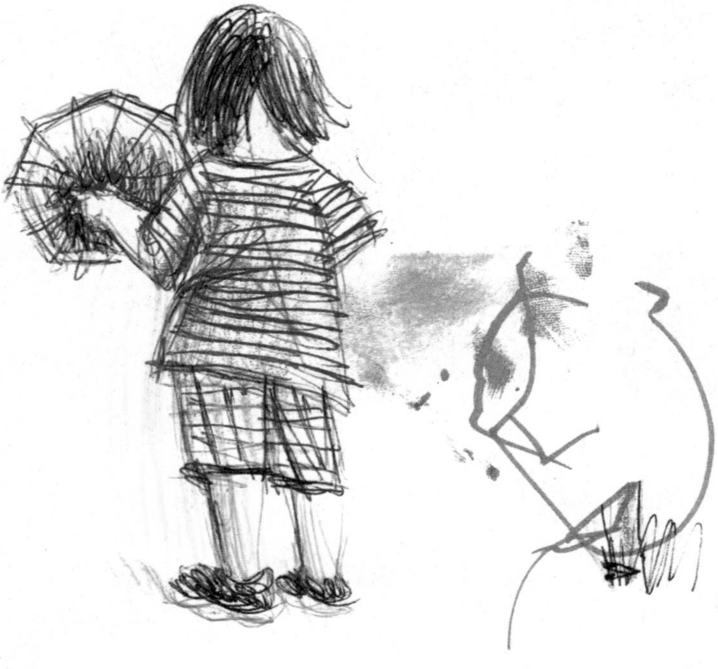

Kids with Down syndrome are an endangered species

"ACCEPTING" IS WIL
RECEIVING WHAT W

LINGLY AND GLADLY
'VE BEEN OFFERED.

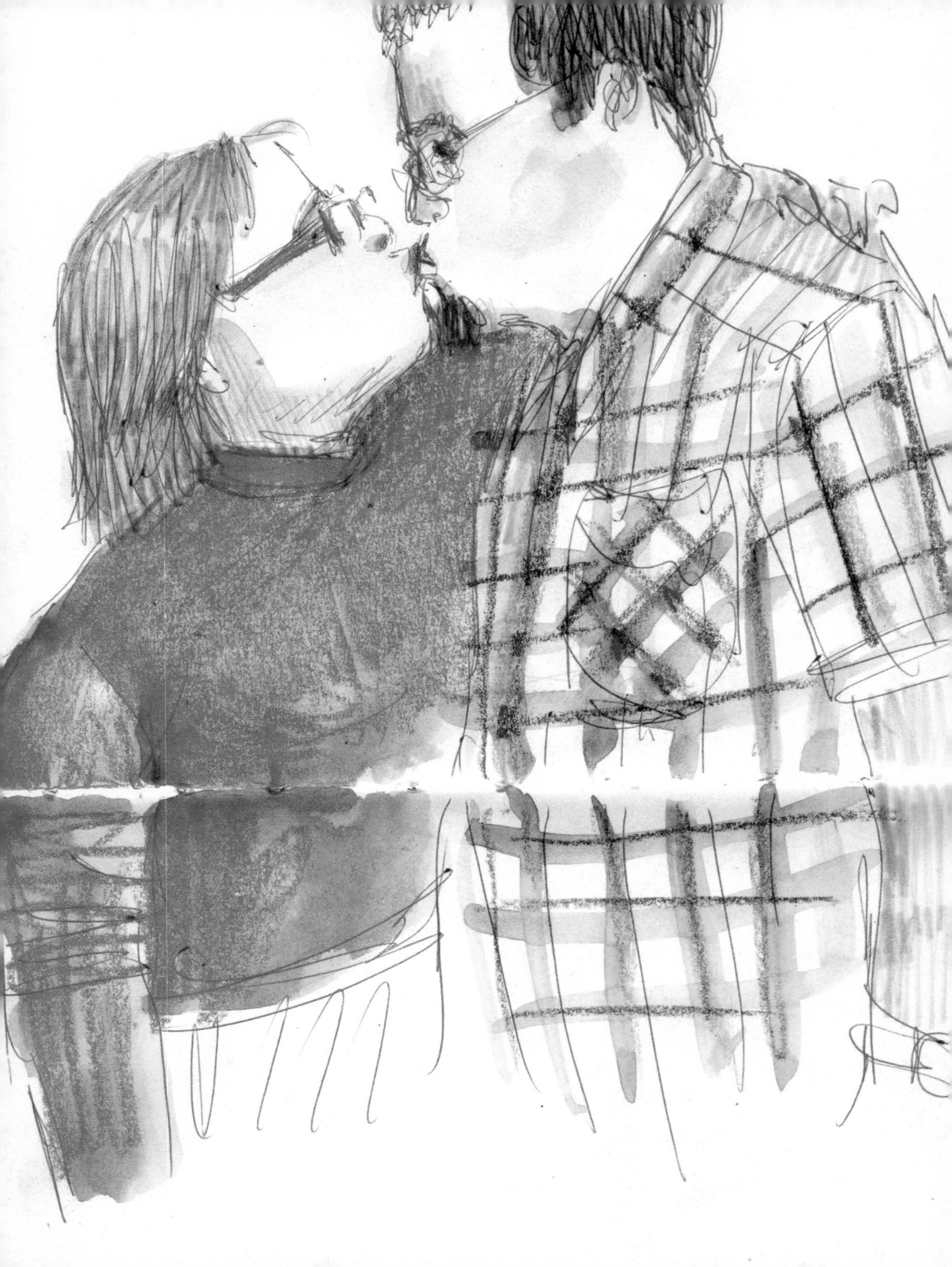

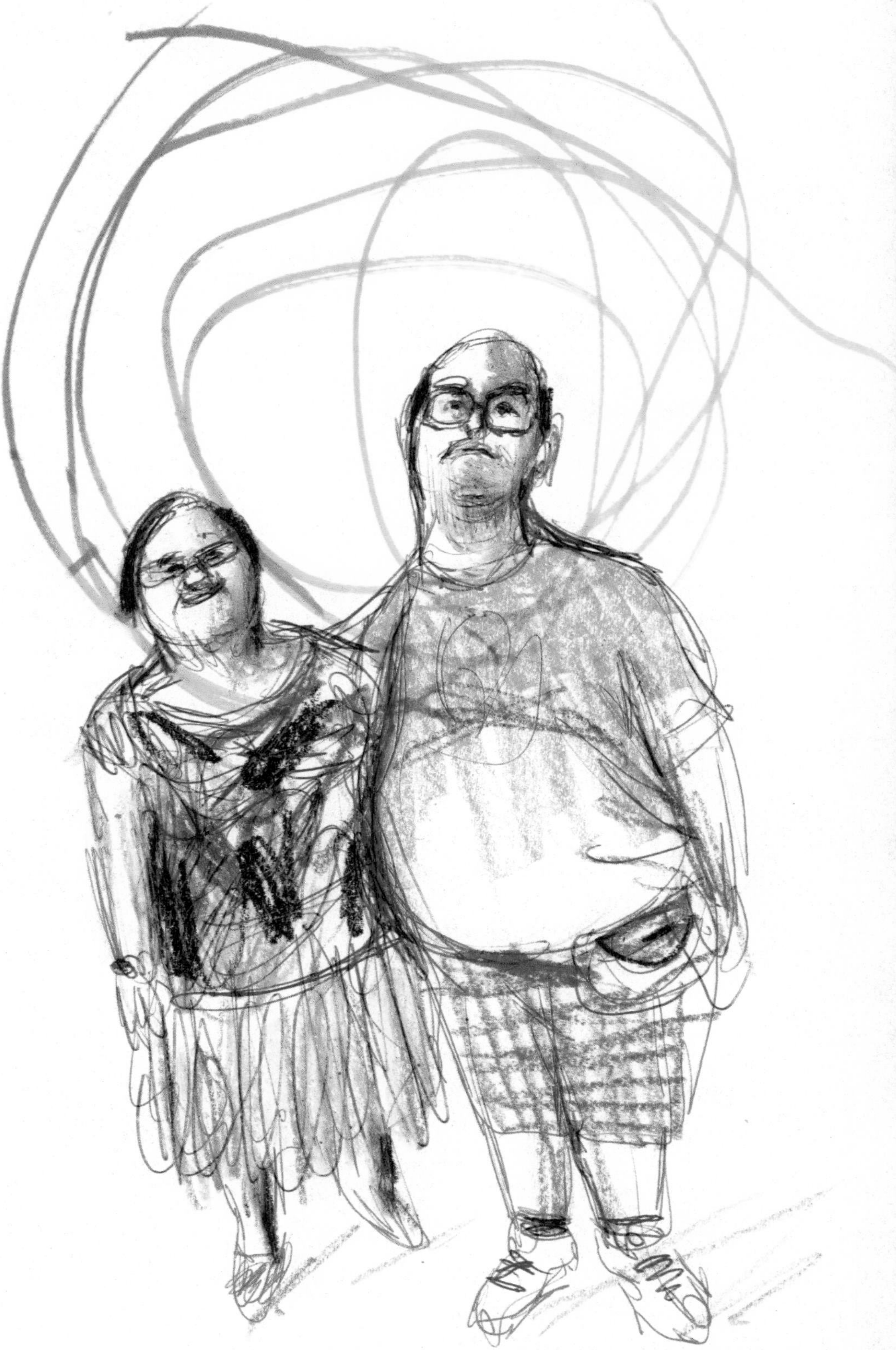

Thank you

Marcelo, you were the first who arrived when Mallko was born, thank you for all your support in those difficult moments.

Niko, thanks for coming to cook and for offering to do the shopping and telling me that these beings are little angels of light.

Yuri. Thanks for helping me take the leap toward acceptance.

Thanks for putting yourself in that place and thanks to all the martians who were there that day.

Thanks, Daniel, for your email to Mallko, for your friendship and trust. And for all your support in making this book.

Thanks, Master Theo. At eight years old, you taught me a great lesson.

Thanks, Anne, for your unshakable faith, and for that bit of sunshine you brought into my life.

Thanks, Adri.

Thanks, Corchito.

Thanks, Tony, for telling me how life on earth was before.

Thanks to my brother Marcos.

Thanks to my dad, you always supported me.

Thanks, Clarita.

Thanks, Barba, for that day you came to drink mate.

Thanks, Ciruelo and Daniela, for taking care of Theo until the storm passed, and for reminding me about when I asked the universe for Mallko and the bearded vultures flew overhead.

Thanks, Juanma, for sending me the stone heart for Mallko the day of his heart check-up.

Thanks to my godparents, thank you, Luis, for that phone call from Patagonia.

Thanks, Juanmeke, the mailman.

Isma Grandullón, thanks for your advice and teachings.

Thanks, Alejandro Magallanes, for awakening the little flame I had snuffed out and helping me to light it again.

Thanks to Jorge Zetner for his invaluable help.

Thanks to Rafael Salmerón always and unconditionally offering his help
with the text.
Thanks to Master Emilio Uberuaga.
Thanks to Georgina, Merce, and all the lovely people at the "Els Xiprers" school.
Thanks to Pablo, Mireia, Pancho, and all the monitors.
Thanks to Jorge Bucay.
Thanks to Miguel Gallardo for calling and offering his help with anything
I needed.
Thanks to Anna Cruanyes for her patience and all the paperwork.
Thanks to Jorge Gonzales for giving me this opportunity to make this book.
Thanks to everyone who offered and offers their help.
Xavi Martí – Lola Barrera – Nuri and Mont from the libraries.
Inge Nows – David – Ana María – Mariona in the name of all the big Mallkos:
Thanks to the people of Argentina, Colombia, Mexico, Belgium, France, Spain.
Elenio, Gustavo Roldan, Daniel Roldan, Diego, Christian Turdera.
Cubillas.
Cesar Lucadamo for the photos. Thank you.
Claudia, café companion.
Seb. Isidro Ferrer. Enrique lara.
Fundación S.D. in Barcelona
Ana Candel and Jose for preparing for the birth, and for being there.
Thanks to Anita Lopez in Madrid.
Henry Flowers – Elena Santolaya.
Thanks, Karen!
Thanks, great spirit!
Thanks, Samuel and the intraterrestrials.
Thanks, Andres Moctezuma.
Thanks, Jeponi Moragas.
Thanks, Nuria Oriol, for the design.
Thanks, Silvia Pérez Ochoa, for taking care of Anne in the hospital,
with your delicious meals.

Thanks to everyone. I'm sure I'm leaving out a
lot of folks, so here I say thanks to all. Thanks.

UNTIL NEXT TIME,
FRIENDS!

MALLKO IS NOW 11
YEARS OLD AND
HE IS VERY HAPPY

THE END

Gusti was born in Buenos Aires on July 13, 1963. He studied at the Fernando Fader Art School. He began working in animation at the Catu Cineanimación Studio. He also worked at the Hanna-Barbera studio, where he made illustrations and animation for television, while also drawing for children's magazines.

In 1985 he moved to Europe: Paris, Madrid, and finally Barcelona, where he still lives. Gusti has illustrated numerous books, several of which have been published in more than twenty languages. He animated the cartoon show *Juanito Jones* with Ricardo Alcántara.

In addition to drawing, Gusti is also passionate about birds, particularly birds of prey. He has volunteered at specialized bird centers, traveling to the Ecuadorian Amazon to study the harpy eagle, and to Patagonia with the Condor Project. With other artists, he also founded the WinDown Association, which aims to foster a more inclusive society.

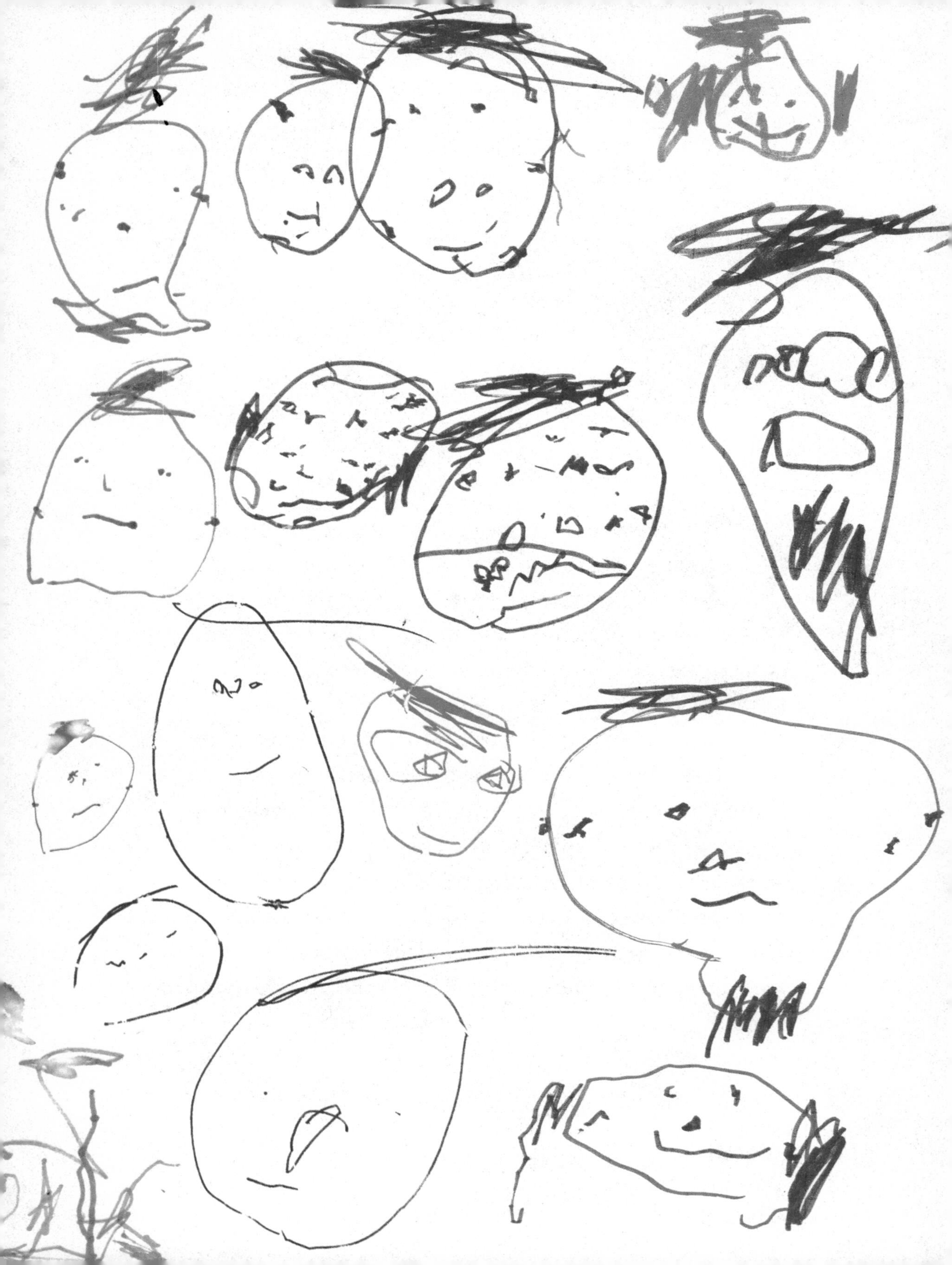